HOMELANDS

WOMEN'S JOURNEYS ACROSS RACE, PLACE, AND TIME

EDITED BY PATRICIA JUSTINE TUMANG AND JENESHA DE RIVERA

FOREWORD BY EDWIDGE DANTICAT

SEAL PRESS

HOMELANDS

Women's Journeys Across Race, Place, and Time

Published by
Seal Press
An Imprint of Avalon Publishing Group, Incorporated
1400 65th Street, Suite 250
Emeryville, CA 94608

9 8 7 6 5 4 3 2 1
Library of Congress Cataloging-in-Publication Data

Homelands : women's journeys across race, place, and time / edited by Patricia Justine Tumang and Jenesha de Rivera.
p. cm.
Includes bibliographical references and index.
ISBN-13: 978-1-58005-188-0 (alk. paper)
ISBN-10: 1-58005-188-X (alk. paper)
1. Women immigrants. 2. Women refugees. 3. Emigration and immigration-Psychological aspects. 4. Migration, Internal-Psychological aspects. 5. Identity (Psychology) 6. Group identity. 7. Home-Psychological aspects. I. Tumang, Patricia Justine. II. Rivera, Jenesha de.

HQ1161.H65 2007
305.48'96914-dc22
2006030701

Cover design and interior design by Domini Dragoone
Printed in the United States of America by Malloy
Distributed by Publishers Group West

In honor of our grandmothers—Carmen Ledesma Recto, Marina Basilio Tumang, Magdalena Alejandrino de Rivera, and Loling Paculba Eltanal—whose spirits and homelands live on in our memories.

Contents

Foreword

EDWIDGE DANTICAT

I always talk to cabdrivers, because my father was one. If they are black and from the Caribbean, I survey their ID cards and mull over their French-sounding names before cautiously asking, "Haitian?"

Mostly there's no need to ask. Haitian cabdrivers often have their radios tuned to Haitian music or political programs, or have a Haitian band playing on cassette or CD, if not a Creole religious program.

Sometimes the driver turns around to have a look at me before continuing the conversation.

"You Haitian, too?" he asks, for mostly they are men.

"Obviously," I reply. *"Ou tou wè sa."*

I let them decide if we should proceed in English or in Creole. They always choose Creole.

Sometimes they're surprised that my Creole is any good.

"How old were you when you came from Haiti?" they ask.

"Twelve," I say.

"How old are you now?"

When I add the two and a half decades that've passed since I was twelve, they're a bit more astonished.

"Did your parents always speak to you in Creole?" they ask.

"Always," I respond.

Sometimes we get into a mutual lament about Haitian youth who stop speaking Creole as soon as they come to the United States, preferring instead to answer their Creole-speaking parents in English. I confess to having plenty of young relatives like that. But it's not their fault, we concede. They're up against strong forces of race, place, and time, a mosaic of cultures other than their own that demand immediate absorption. Maybe they feel they have to forge ahead or be left behind.

These discussions are never over by the time we reach our destination. There's always more to say, other subjects to crack. Perhaps we'll talk longer another time, we say.

When I do speak longer, to other drivers—Haitians and non-Haitians alike—we often slip into politics. Mostly we agree. Coup d'etats are a bad thing. Democratically elected governments should be given a chance to succeed. The United States ought not to impose its iron will on sovereign states for its own interests. Women should have the same rights as men do. The poor always suffer the most—no matter what. Always.

Sometimes we disagree and I become nervous, for suddenly we're on opposite sides of a heated debate, each trying to get in a word edgewise, while my new pal grows more and more irate. Every now and then I back off. "I see your point. That's an interesting way of looking at things. I can see where you're coming from," I recently acquiesced to a Nigerian female cab driver (a truly rare experience).

"Of course you do," she said. "We're not that much different. We all—well most of us—have one heart and two feet."

Sometimes we avoid worldly subjects and talk about things closer to home: weather, traffic, insurance rates, another cabbie murdered the night before, my father.

I tell them that my father too drove a cab for many years, until his death of lung disease last year.

"So I know what this is like," I say.

"No you don't," an aspiring Russian poet once replied. "Only he, your father, knows what it's really like."

Sometimes I attempt to draw my father's experience and theirs closer. I ask how many children they have. "Be careful," I advise. "Keep your partition up. You never know."

One cold winter night, I was on my way home after a late movie when I got into a cab with a driver I quickly realized—by his accent and music choices—was Haitian. He seemed somewhat hesitant to pick me up and even more reluctant to drive me after I told him my address in East Flatbush, Brooklyn. But after looking me over, and observing me blow hot breath into my frozen hands, he decided to take me on one condition: that I pay first. It was the kind of thing my father would never do, no matter how much it might have protected him. On the other end of such a transaction was a person's dignity. With no other cab in sight, I didn't storm off but simply asked, "Why?"

"You might run," he said in a sad deep voice.

"Why would I do that?"

"Leaving our homelands does good things to us, but also very bad things," he cryptically replied.

I paid him up front and made a conscious choice to remain quiet for the rest of the ride. But somehow having the money transaction out of the way had warmed him and made him downright talkative. He told me the story of a woman who kept getting robbed by a masked thief in the elevator of the apartment building where she lived. One day she decided to carry some red paint, which she used to throw in her robber's face. The woman was stunned when the thief removed the mask and revealed that it was in fact her own daughter.

I had heard different versions of that story from my father. A young man had led some school pals to $5,000 his mother was hiding in her mattress, and in a struggle for the money the mother had been shot. A father had killed his only daughter when she and her friends had carried out a break-in at the family's furniture shop. These were the cautionary tales of what our new homeland could turn people into, sworn to be true by every immigrant who recited them and passed them along, as if they had been eyewitnesses, present in the bedroom, in the furniture shop, in the elevator, at the wake. These stories were meant to illustrate a fragment of what we had lost in migrating, but they also illustrated what we had gained: new narratives, in a new space and time, touching, funny, scary, all at once.

Reading the touching, funny, scary, and lyrical essays in *Homelands,* I felt the same sense of sadness and awe I often feel during these so-sought-after conversations with fellow urban nomads, reciters, and ambient voyagers. Whether sowing for lineage or homeward bound, crossing real or imaginary city borders, speeding across bridges that feel like the edge of the world, I realize that both here and there I am always looking for others with whom to share my home beyond exile, the motherland within myself. A timely and moving collection of essays, *Homelands* is a book you'll find yourself reading over and over again. At a time when it's so easy for one to become a refugee even on the soil where one was born (just ask those displaced by hurricane Katrina in 2005), it's both indispensable and comforting to have such a stimulating and thought-provoking gathering of brave and gifted citizens of both the external and internal landscapes that define our fragile grasp on "home."

At times, while reading these marvelous essays, I happily mouthed many of the same words I've found myself saying in all those cabs that remind me so much of my father's. *You may be right. I see your point. That's an interesting way of looking at things. I can see where you're coming from.*

After all, we may be on different journeys, but we all have two feet and a wanderer's heart.

Introduction

You remember the aerial view of the tarmac floating away into a grainy distance, patches of earth so vivid—land that once held you in its vast expanse—appearing minuscule like puzzle pieces on a lost landscape. The scalloped edges of an old photograph, an image of a field "back home" that was taken in a place you've never been to, during a time before you were born. The photo is stamped with the name of a country that no longer exists. Its image is imprinted in your mind along with the sounds of your native language, words that your tongue has been forced to abandon. You recall the fire in your gut the first time someone pointed out your difference and used it as an insult. You remember the rapid fluttering of your heart the first time you met someone whose experience mirrored yours.

The twenty-eight women in this anthology talk to each other about their journeys "home." The essays describe homelands that are rooted in traces of images, odors, sensations, and sounds mingling in harmonious melody and clashing in discordant rupture. Their experiences are simultaneously whole and fragmented, comforting and harrowing. Their homelands are either widely disputed or under threat of erasure. War is branded on their skins, waged on their bodies and mother tongues—the battlefields both internal and external. They keep one foot precariously in the past while the other vacillates in the present, finding neither to be a strong foothold. As they realize that the ground that they stand on is illusive, they become "citizen[s] of the country of longing."[1]

When we began editing this anthology, we were drawn to experiences of longing and the desire to redefine homeland. As first-generation children of Filipino immigrants, we grew up immersed in our parents' myth of return, in the belief that the United States was a temporary home. Far removed from their homeland, our parents recreated the Philippines in our households. Our homes transformed into a country of the past as we lived and breathed in our parents' nostalgia: long-distance phone calls to relatives on static-filled lines, sepia-toned pictures in albums falling apart at the seams, the rich aromas of our families' home-cooked Filipino meals, all of which saturated our American existence. As belief resigned itself to diminished hope, our parents gave in to the reality that they would never return home "for good." The worlds they had created in the United States—with professional careers, American children, and decades of displacement—were permanent reminders of the futility of return.

As we compiled and edited the essays, we entered a process of investigation—of our own complex relationship to our homelands and of the women's in this anthology. The contributors write in English; most had immigrated to or had been born in the United States. Yet for many, the concept of homeland remains an illusive one—like a dream that escapes the grip of consciousness, existing more willingly in the realm of sensation, memory, and imagination. Although "homeland" is much more than the physical place they've acquired through birth, ancestry, or citizenship, many of the contributors longed to name it. Through this investigation, we discovered that the very nature of this longing captured the overall essence of this anthology; essays that examined the nuances of this hunger intrigued us.

This anthology is a testament to the act of reclaiming and reshaping our realities and making sense of the longing that claims our spirits. As women with third world or first world roots; white and of color; queer, straight, femme, butch, or trans; warriors and survivors—of violence, exile, poverty, addiction, abuse, and colonization—the contributors live on the inside as well as the outside of "home," creating new definitions of homeland and reality.

These women conjure a new boundless landscape, one that pieces together the fragmentation of memory. They journey across race, place, and time, leaving one homeland in order to reclaim another. They inhabit multiple homelands—some defined by geography and temporal spheres; cultural and familial inheritances; linguistic legacies; stories and songs of resistance; crossing borders in identity, body, and landscape; spiritual homelands; transience and relocation; displacement and exile; poverty and homelessness. They lose homes, regain them, or reject and replace them wholeheartedly. They reconstruct a new reality from memory's broken remains. They examine this collage and see themselves reflected in a homeland they call their own.

Our vision for *Homelands* is grounded in the belief that writing is a form of resistance and activism, that the personal is political. We ourselves are activists and writers; our desire to merge these two key aspects of our lives inspired and informed our process. According to Gloria Anzaldúa, "Making anthologies is also activism. In the process of creating the composition, the work of art . . . you're creating the culture. You're rewriting the culture, which is very much an activist kind of thing."[2] With mainstream media and those in power misconstruing and diminishing real stories of what is happening in the world, we are, as women, engaged in a war over the nature of reality. Through this anthology, we hope to provide a forum for women's voices and stories so that they can divulge their own truths in a world that distorts them.

In the United States and the rest of the world, the shifting borders of "homeland" have become blurred, and new meanings of home are continually being traversed upon, reconstructed, and reimagined. War, natural disaster, occupation, genocide, militarism, political struggle, and colonization affect these women's relationships to their homelands and impact whether they are able to return home. "Homeland" invokes contradictory feelings and ideas: rootedness and departure, stability and insecurity, reality and imagination. Whether national or international, domestic or foreign, "at home" or "abroad," the idea of homeland has been etched on our psyches.

For our contributors who have immigrated to new lands or who have been exiled to foreign countries, "homeland" often stirs up feelings of nostalgia, sentimentality, and longing, and for some, displacement and utter loss. Contributors who hail from immigrant families harbor dual allegiances. They long for the homeland of their parents' past, while creating new homes for themselves in their adopted countries.

The essays in this collection sketch the concept of "homeland" suggestively, not definitively. As in a photograph, we see the art of narrative as a medium for piecing together the past and placing it in the present. Rather than speak for each essay, we invite you to journey with these women as they reveal their truths. Our hope with this anthology is to do what activism and creativity do best: defy boundaries and borders, allowing memory and imagination to traverse a new geography of homeland.

PATRICIA JUSTINE TUMANG AND JENESHA DE RIVERA
OAKLAND, CALIFORNIA
AUGUST 2006

In Search of the Next Harvest

GUILLERMINA GINA NÚÑEZ

As migrant farmworkers, my family's stays in any given place were intense, temporary, and short-lived. This constant movement and displacement made us search for alternative ways of feeling rooted. Being a migrant farmworker has defined me in so many ways.

My family's seasonal returns to the southern Mexican state of Guerrero, my ancestral homeland located on the Pacific coast of Mexico, created strong family ties and positive childhood experiences. I attended kindergarten, first grade, and other primary grades in Mexican schools, where I developed my math and Spanish literacy skills at an early age. My Mexican classmates coined me the nickname La Chicanita, primarily because I was born in the United States, spoke both Spanish and English, and lived in between nations.

My father came to the United States from Mexico when he was fourteen years old, after having lost his father seven years prior. My mother came in 1970, when she received her green card on Thanksgiving Day. At our house, celebrating Thanksgiving has a whole different meaning, as every year our dinner begins with my mom reciting a prayer: "Thank you God for my green card and for my five children you have blessed me with." My youngest brother, Franco, and I were both born in Salinas, California. I was born on September 11, 1972, and he was born in 1980. In between us, there are my siblings Betty and Thomas, who were born in Phoenix, Arizona, and Juanita, who was born in Camarillo, California.

As a family, we usually traveled throughout the Southwest in search of the next harvest. My parents worked together in an agricultural company harvesting lettuce; my mother wrapped and packed lettuce, while my father worked as a foreman and a field supervisor. I was introduced to agricultural farmwork in my childhood, working alongside my parents during summer and winter school breaks—picking and packing strawberries, onions, cantaloupe, cauliflower, and lettuce.

The processes of migration and settlement were part of my everyday life as we moved from Salinas, California, to Hatch, New Mexico, following the lettuce harvest during the winter seasons. When my parents were out of work in the summers and winters, we moved back to Guerrero, a state well-known in Mexican history for its revolutionary people, its tropical weather, and its infamous Acapulco gold.

I remember traveling with my family in a variety of vehicles, but the one I remember the most is the green Ford truck we had, which we called the *cotorra* (parrot) for its bright green color. We lined the flatbed of the *cotorra* with blankets and small mattresses for us to sleep on. For suitcases we used *cajas de lechuga,* cardboard boxes used to pack lettuce. As a family of seven, we were not able to fit very much into the back of the truck. We only owned what we could carry.

We lived in trailers, motel rooms, apartments, and houses for a couple of months at a time. Finding an affordable place to seasonally rent presented a number of challenges for us. There seemed to be few incentives for renters to lease a place for short intervals to large Mexican families with many small children. Although we were usually fortunate enough to find places in which to live, there were times when we struggled. My parents relied on friends and coworkers to help us find a rental or a family with whom we could stay. I remember one particular cold winter when we were unable to find an apartment to rent. My father's friend and *paisano*[1] let us live out of his garage in Salinas. On bitter-cold nights, the *paisano* or his wife would open the doors to their house, allowing us to sleep on their living room floor—a gesture that is often remembered and much appreciated.

In 1980, my family rented a cramped mobile home. My parents and baby brother slept in the small bedroom, while three of my other siblings and I slept on a sofa-bed. Our cousin Dominga had migrated with us from Guerrero to be our baby sitter. She slept on an army-green fold-up cot right next to us in the living room/kitchen area. Winter nights in Hatch, New Mexico, were unpleasantly cold, especially in the unheated trailer. I recall the nights when my anguished mother covered us with layers upon layers of blankets while we cried ourselves to sleep, shivering in the unforgiving frosty nights. I looked forward to the days when my sisters and I would play house under the sun's warm blanket. We used the triangle-shaped trailer hitch as a small table on which to place our plastic tea cups and saucers, along with all of our favorite miniature toy food items like pizza, eggs, cereal, fruits, and vegetables.

My memories of growing up as a migrant child are filled with pain, laughter, and songs. My blond sister, Betty—also known as La Güerita and named after President Ford's wife—learned the song "On the Road Again" by Willie Nelson. I, on the other hand, learned the lyrics of Ramon Ayala y Sus Bravos del Norte, a well-known *norteño* group; Freddy Fender's "Wasted Days and Wasted Nights"; and Big Pepe's "Hey Baby Que Paso." I also sang along with my mother to religious hymns taught to her in Spanish by her own mother. My siblings and I prodded our mother when we had forgotten certain words or sequences to our favorite ones, and she would joyfully fill in the gaps.

We children took our jobs seriously on the road. My task was to help keep my parents awake while they took turns driving. I usually fulfilled this duty by seeking out a good radio station or by talking their ears off to keep them awake as they drove for days. When my mom was behind the wheel, my job was to pray first, and then help her with directions to avoid getting lost along California's freeways. The rest of the kids would help me keep my parents awake by singing along or by requesting strategic pee breaks at McDonald's.

While on the road, we learned to recognize important landmarks as a way of assessing the time and distance it took from Salinas to Calexico, California. Salinas was as north as we would go, while Calexico, which was located on the U.S.–Mexico border, was as south as we could get before entering Mexico. Being on the road was a way of life for most of my childhood and my teenage years. I always admired my mother's ability to pack our belongings. She used to pack her essential kitchen items, including her mortar, or *molcajete,* to make her grilled *chile* salsas, and her favorite pot for beans. My dad used to pack his essentials, which were a record player and a television. We had all we needed at the time.

As migrants, we faced harsh and discriminatory treatment on various ends. Local residents seemed to resent us for taking what they considered to be their local jobs. School officials and educators were often unwelcoming and unwilling to accommodate my siblings and me in their already-filled classrooms. We were often treated as outsiders and as cultural "others"; some of our schoolmates called us "food tramps" and "wetbacks." We were criticized for being poorly dressed, not speaking mainstream English, and for not fitting in with the already-established social cliques.

Outside of the classroom, my most painful childhood memory is when Anglo children in New Mexico threw rocks at my siblings and me while we stood in line at a bus stop. As they bombarded us with stones, the boys shouted racial epithets and suggested that we go back to where we came from. At the time, I did not fully comprehend these racialized attitudes and hatred-filled behaviors; after all, my siblings and I were "Americans," born in the states of Arizona and California. My shameful memory of this event was not so much my inability to defend myself and my siblings (at the time, we were outnumbered) but it was facing my parents with welts on my face and body, and profound scars in my wounded heart. Having to explain the event to my father was the greatest shame of all. I did not have a rational explanation for showing up at home with bruises and a heart full of sadness. I felt I had dishonored my family by not being strong enough to defend my siblings and myself. He expressed pain, anger, and disappointment at such maltreatment. I got my first lesson from my father about our position as Mexican farmworkers in the United States: "There is no shame in doing what we do for a living; we are the ones who work hard to put food on people's tables all over the world," he said. For proof, my father pulled out a check stub with his wages, tax contributions, and Social Security deductions. He asked me to take his check stub to school to help me prove his case. My father, who was a green card holder like my mother, took pride in his work. I took his paycheck stub to school but never showed it to anyone; I doubted that school-age bullies with rocks at a bus stop would understand this point or would care to see a piece of paper.

On one fortuitous day, my parents received an invitation to attend a meeting in Hatch for parents of migrant children to discuss their rights. During the migrant-education outreach counselor's presentation, one nonfarmworker resident—who had slipped into the meeting—began to make condescending remarks about all of us Mexicans who came into town to take jobs away from locals like her. The counselor gracefully pointed out the various challenges migrants face, which are often taken for granted: lack of housing, weather uncertainties, and the instability of living paycheck to paycheck while trying to raise children. The woman received the glaring look of all of the migrant parents present and shamefully sat down.

That night was a watershed moment for my parents. The counselor shared information about the various programs and laws in effect at the time and strategies that migrant parents could use to advocate on their children's behalf. My father often recalls this transformative moment in their lives with great pride. Soon after, my parents began to challenge school principals and administrators, citing migrant education laws and regulations. After repeatedly being told there was no more space for us in their schools, my parents began to demand that the schools find a place for us in their classrooms.

My family gained a source of pride and entitlement that had not been offered to us before. My parents showed their appreciation to our teachers and administrators by sending us to school with bags of lettuce, cantaloupes, carrots, or anything else that was in harvest at the time. As a child, this was a bit embarrassing, particularly because we had to make several deliveries around school to the principal, the nice secretary who had treated us with respect, and to our teachers. These gifts of fruits and vegetables were, for the most part, quite well received. Our teachers always remembered the five Núñez kids who brought bags of free produce to school. I remember praying and asking God that my parents not go into harvesting watermelons, for these would be too heavy for me to carry.

My family eventually settled to work as seasonal farmworkers in Calexico in the late 1990s. They did, however, remain fairly attached to their homeland in Guerrero, Mexico, and continue to travel across the border several times a year to visit family. My parents attended night classes in English, citizenship, and computer literacy at a local high school. My mother became president of the Migrant Parent Association from 1997 to 1998. In addition to being president, she fundraised and sold food, mainly *tostadas*, *churritos*[2], and sodas at local community events to raise money for migrant education. She became an amazing fundraiser, visiting most of the major businesses and restaurants in Calexico and requesting donations like televisions, microwaves, and gift certificates to raffle off as prizes. She used serious tactics of persuasion, arguing that local businesses should invest in their community's education. She raised thousands of dollars this way. Since settling along the U.S.–Mexico border, my parents continued going to migrant-education meetings, where they eventually became advocates and leaders, traveling throughout California to participate in conferences and workshops to encourage other migrant parents to stand up for their children.

In 2002, I returned to southern New Mexico, the same region where I had lived with my family in 1980, to conduct anthropological fieldwork for my doctoral dissertation. During this time, I conducted household interviews while commuting daily for some ninety miles from Las Cruces to peri-urban border communities known as *colonias*. The commute from the city to the *colonias* was at times physically and mentally draining and increasingly costly due to high fuel prices[3]. I experienced anxiety when I went through the immigration checkpoint on Highway 25. I was fairly unaware of my physical response to this stress until a colleague noticed that I clenched my jaw and became nervous every time we drove by the border-patrol checkpoint. I felt nervous and ashamed while being interrogated and searched by immigration officers.

As a researcher, I was particularly anxious about having to explain my reasons for having to cross the border-patrol checkpoint on a daily basis. I took great care not to carry any documentation with confidential information, and I avoided writing people's addresses to minimize the risk of identification in case my materials were ever scrutinized. I also changed my vehicle's license plates from California to New Mexico to avoid being asked a slew of questions every time I passed through the checkpoint: "Have you crossed the Mexican border lately? Are you carrying anything from Mexico? Where are you headed? What's the purpose of your trip to Hatch? What is a Californian doing in the *colonias* of New Mexico?"

I realized that as an English-speaking U.S. citizen, my reality as a border resident and border crosser was quite different from that of other migrants who could not legally cross and move freely along the border without fearing the threat of detention and deportation. Crossing borders, with or without documents, has been a great cause of stress for me as well as for other migrants and residents who straddle the border.

As I have continued my research on immigrants, borders, and the ways in which people become rooted, I have witnessed the intensified militarization of the border after September 11, 2001. The Department of Homeland Security has relied on sensors, military equipment, night-vision equipment, helicopters, and airplanes to patrol the border. Migrants' journeys have become riskier and deadlier. I have learned that borders have the potential of stripping people of their lives, their dignity, and their value. Yet at the same time, borders—if crossed successfully—can offer the ideals of a better life. As migrants who cross borders, we are required to carry identification and documentation authorizing our entrance, presence, and movements. For us, our value as human beings is devalued when our labor is wanted and appreciated but our presence is not.

My search for a homeland has been a lifelong process. I learned many valuable lessons growing up working in the fields. My father's words ring in my ears: *The people who labor the land feed people throughout the world.* My parents were true organic intellectuals who offered us experiences and exclusive access to what my father calls the *universidad de la vida*—the "university of life."

Throughout my journey, I have grown to live, breath, study, and represent the complexity of a life crossing borders. I have since tried to reconcile the gaps in my memory as I try to recall all the places I have moved to and the people I have met along the way. I was never in one place long enough to call it home. Instead I hold on to many places that, for brief periods of time, held and shaped me along the way. I have reconciled living a life in between two nations, speaking two languages, belonging here and there, somewhere, or perhaps nowhere. I yearn to one day rejoice in the feeling of being rooted, as much as I yearn for the day in which other people in search of a homeland can one day move freely across borders.

The Reciters

AGATE NESAULE

Once upon a time in Latvia, all women knew how to recite. As girls, we memorized lullabies, folk songs, poems, and hymns. Safe in our own beds, warm under goose-down quilts and embroidered linen sheets, we whispered lines to ourselves as we drifted off to sleep. On Christmas Eve, standing in front of trees ablaze with real candles, we swayed back and forth purposefully to emphasize the rhythm of verses we had learned. If we recited correctly and loudly enough, we would be given creamy sweets wrapped in tasseled gold paper instead of bundles of switches reserved for bad children. During the brief white nights of summer, when along with visiting cousins we were allowed to sleep on fragrant hay in barns, we shouted verses we believed were uproariously funny until gentle adult voices silenced us. On marketing days, in front of city shops or village stores, we turned our backs on boys who grinningly teased us. Holding hands, looking pleased with ourselves, reciting in unison, we skipped away.

Es meitiņa kā rozīte

Kā sarkana zemenīte,

Pienu ēdu, pienu dzēru,

Pienā muti nomazgāju.

I am a little girl like a little rose,

Like a small strawberry.

I eat milk, I drink milk,

And I bathe myself in milk.

Our feet, clad in fine white stockings and red shoes with thin straps, moved rhythmically together. Our chants might turn imperceptibly into song. We knew many melodies too, of course, but above all we knew the words.

Women sang everywhere, in kitchens kneading rye bread or slicing apples, in dairies skimming cream or churning butter, in fields raking hay or gathering grain. Alone in parlors lit by kerosene lamps or newly installed electric lights, on dark verandas scented by lilacs, on lonely paths leading through forests, women sang to themselves. Young women walked from one country church to another to look at the new ministers said to be handsome and single, and then, having paid little attention to their sermons, they walked home again, arms linked, laughing and singing. Young men, dressed in dark suits and white shirts, called out to them as they passed in polished wagons pulled by lovingly groomed horses. On St. John's Eve in midsummer, from hill to hill ablaze with bonfires, women and men sang, first in competition, then in harmony. Old women sang together in churches, alone while tending gardens and working at looms.

But always in addition to singing, women recited. On postcards with photos of birches or roses, which women sent for birthdays and names days, they wrote lines they had memorized. They inscribed poems in books given as school prizes, in leather-bound albums presented to newlyweds, on notes accompanying flowers for sick friends. Women gave public speeches less often than men, but like them they quoted the words of Latvian poets on ceremonial and political occasions.

Lines recited spontaneously were even more meaningful. So a woman might quote from a play by major Latvian writer Aspazija to a friend passionately in love; she might murmur a lyric about suffering and loss by the same poet as she comforted her friend later. Women included stanzas from poems in hastily written letters to lovers and husbands away, to mothers welcoming new life, to old people marking the passing of years. That is how it was, once upon a time.

As the independence of Latvia was increasingly threatened by Nazis and Soviets both, lines from poems accompanied flowers laid anxiously at the foot of the Monument to Freedom in the center of Riga. Later, as women prayed to be saved from exile and war, they recited.

The reciting stopped abruptly in 1940, the Year of Terror under Russian occupation, when thousands of Latvians were imprisoned or deported to Siberia. Nazi armies overran Latvia the following year, and Soviet armies took forcible possession again in 1945. For almost half a century, Latvian language was discouraged and Latvian literature neglected. Girls and women who remained in their own country were forced to speak Russian. Those in exile learned other languages. Only 52 percent of the inhabitants of Latvia are now Latvians.

I was six when my family fled Latvia on one of the last ships sailing for Germany. In a camp circled with barbed wire, threatened by Nazi guards barely restraining leashed dogs, we whispered fearfully to each other. Flags with swastikas flew overhead, and nightly bombings continued. The following spring we were forced to watch as occupying Russian soldiers beat a mute boy, executed a man, raped women without children. Dazed and afraid, we remained silent for a long time.

But as hunger turned into starvation, we had to speak. My mother taught me to recite in Russian. She washed my face, pinned an incongruously cheerful wreath of blue bachelor's buttons and red clover above my blond braids, and sent me away from the German village. Holding an empty bowl in my hands, I stood behind a barbed wire fence, watching soldiers drinking, shouting, and stumbling. I waited for the briefest pause and then began, "*Petushok . . . petushok . . .* "

I did not know the meaning of the Russian children's rhymes I had learned by rote. I had to make the soldiers notice me, so I used all my willpower to speak loudly and distinctly. My legs and arms trembled, but my voice did not fail. Usually the soldiers ignored the hungry children behind the fence; they turned away from their comrades and toward us only to vomit or urinate. Or they tried to drive us off with furious gestures.

But sometimes a soldier would hear me and motion to the others to listen. Surprised at my mouthing of Russian words, the soldiers laughed delightedly, as they might at a goose singing or a dog dancing. They flung a chunk of heavy dark rye bread, or sometimes a piece of raw liver, into my bowl.

Walking back to the village, I felt the envy and anger of the German children scorching my back. I tried not to think; I recited instead. Over and over again, I whispered the meaningless sounds. I had to remember them for whatever came next. I set the bowl on the ground in front of my mother, turned away from her, ran to a tree, pressed against it, prayed to grow into it, failed.

Later, in Displaced Persons camps in Germany, I recited in Latvian for the last time. Without books or supplies, Latvians started makeshift schools in every camp. Actors, ministers, writers, historians—all lovers of words—recalled lines they knew and taught them to us. Every week we had to recite—"with appropriate feeling"—a poem in front of the whole class. We learned lines about the white birches, fragrant grasses, and misty blue hills of Latvia. We declaimed defiant speeches of ancient heroes who died defending Latvia against foreign invaders. We chanted hundreds of *dainas,* folk songs about brave girls and proud women and about the healing powers of nature and work. Teachers repeatedly quoted a poem that included the line "The riches of the heart cannot be destroyed." They said it meant that we should study hard, because only our knowledge could never be taken from us. We might lose our family members, our country, and our possessions, but the riches of the heart would remain ours.

Reciting in Latvian ended for me when I left the camps in Germany for the United States. I learned English, won scholarships, completed degrees at universities, taught British poems to American students. I married an American and moved to a small town in the Midwest, away from my mother, away from communities of exiled Latvians. Slowly, through disuse, I forgot most of the Latvian poems I knew.

But life, while harsh, is also miraculous. In 1991, Latvia declared independence from the Soviet Union and was recognized as a sovereign nation. Although the shores of the Baltic Sea are polluted, people now walk more freely on its white sands and pine-bordered paths. They may even find amber there, though they are cautious about picking it up. Some of the lovely translucent yellow pieces are not crystallized pine resin at all, but explosives carelessly disposed of by Soviet military troops, many of whom are still stationed there.

I returned to Latvia in the summer of 1991, after an exile of forty-seven years. I eagerly looked forward to meeting relatives, but of my father's family of six brothers and sisters, only one of my cousins survived. After several painful encounters, I was forced to recognize that our relationships could never be reestablished. Our lives had been too different, our experiences too separate and painful.

Nor could the house where I had lived until I was six give me the connection that I longed for. The large, comfortable country parsonage was now a run-down collective farm, so changed that I passed it three times without recognizing it. Gone were the wide verandas and the silvery thatched roof, gone the apple trees, lilacs, and mock orange, gone the flowerbeds filled with sweet william, irises, and lilies. Even the pond, where storks used to wade, was dry.

Standing alone in the desolate rutted yard, I prayed not to give in to bitterness. If only I could stay open to experience, something else might happen. I had to believe that it would. I did not know yet that a stranger, an old woman reciting, would give me what I needed, and more.

Most people in Latvia have excruciatingly painful stories. They seize a visitor from the outside world by the hand, insist upon attention, prevent departure. They speak about the grim Soviet occupation, of Latvians being subjected to political repression and economic hardship, of being treated as second-class citizens in their own country, of being denied access to education and advancement. Latvians were imprisoned and deported; many died in Siberia; some committed suicide upon returning; others remain physically and psychologically damaged. In spite of the new independence, daily life in Latvia is still unbelievably harsh.

Listening to these recitations, I was rocked by conflicting emotions: sympathy for the people, anger at the devastation of the land, desire to help, guilt that I could never do enough. I wavered between high energy and absolute exhaustion. Desiring connection, I nevertheless found myself longing to be alone.

At an outdoor concert of Latvian folk songs, I allowed my mind to wander from a speaker who said that only in song did the spirit of Latvia still live undamaged. In January 1991, when Soviet Black Berets had killed five unarmed men, among them two prominent young filmmakers, Latvians had not turned to violence, but to singing. Indoors and out, in churches and concert halls, on street corners in Riga and Liepaja, Latvians sang in defiance of Soviet authorities. Journalists had been right in dubbing the independence movement in Latvia the Singing Revolution.

Too depleted to follow the rest of the speech, I watched the choirs arriving instead. Dressed in colorful costumes from various districts of Latvia, young men and old were lining up to sing. Women carried bunches of flowers; girls with wreaths of flowers in their hair walked by with arms linked. The fragrance of pines intensified as massed rain clouds parted for the late-afternoon sun. Finally the singing began.

At first I strained to hear every word of songs I had known once. I tried to remember them; I had to repossess them. But gradually I realized there were too many songs completely unfamiliar to me, songs that had been composed during my long separation from Latvia. Try as I might, I inevitably failed to make out the words. Feeling separate from all the people and the common emotions the songs evoked, I closed my eyes.

When I looked again, my focus had shifted. The choirs had receded into the background, but individual people were now much more distinct. On the steps in front of a women's choir was a seven-year-old girl. She was sitting very still, looking past the audience to the line of birches across an open meadow. Her blue eyes had that clear, almost-otherworldly gaze that one sometimes sees in children at moments when they feel absolutely secure. She made no movement to brush away a strand of blond hair escaping from her braids beneath a small wreath of red clover. Her hands rested lightly in her lap, over a long string of tiny, very dark amber beads. She wore an embroidered white linen blouse and a full red wool skirt, also embroidered. Her long legs and sturdy feet, clad in white thin stockings and highly polished shoes, were planted firmly on the ground.

A woman bent down to whisper to her, another woman brushed away the escaping tendril of her hair, and the little girl stood up. She was ready to sing. Complete in herself, she was also an essential part of the choir. Totally self-possessed, she was cherished and supported by the circle of women around her.

I felt an envy so surprising and so sharp I could hardly breathe. Holding on to myself, rocking silently back and forth, I concentrated on regulating my breathing until the pain began to subside. Shame followed quickly. How could I, a middle-aged, economically secure, politically privileged, well-dressed, and well-fed university professor from America envy this little girl in Latvia? Hadn't I been paying attention as people told me repeatedly of extreme poverty, humiliation, hopelessness? Didn't I know the endless contriving and bribing and patching every mother had to do to send her child out fully clothed in the morning?

I forced myself to imagine the effort this mother had expended finding the string of amber beads, standing in line for a piece of unbleached linen to sew her daughter's blouse, collecting plants to make dye, saving and bartering for the polished black shoes. I could not know every detail, but I was touched nevertheless by the immense devotion and determination that must have gone into raising and clothing this little girl, who now looked as natural as a small berry.

Yet still I envied her. She was exactly where she belonged, in her own country, with people she had known all her life, singing in her own language. She knew all the words, and she could sing together with others. With courage and almost bravado the women were singing now:

Bēda mana liela bēda
Es par bēdu nebēdāju
Liku bēdu zem akmeņa
Pāri gāju dziedādama

I had a great sorrow,
But I didn't dwell on it
I put it under a stone
I stepped over it singing

Perhaps if one were so connected to other people and to the land, one could indeed put sorrow under a stone. But I was sentimentalizing the experience of the girls and women singing. I must remember the harsh lives of all Latvians; I must stop feeling sorry for myself as well.

I tried to imagine the little girl making her way home to a shabby apartment or a run-down collective farm. But I could only see her walking on familiar roads past pine woods and banks of wild strawberries. She was holding her mother's hand and perhaps her aunt's. Tired but satisfied with the events of the day, they were talking softly together. The two women listened attentively as the girl recited a poem she had memorized for school, then lapsed into silence. But soon one of them began to hum; the others joined in. They seemed vulnerable now in the dusk, and I felt a tender protectiveness toward them. I wished fervently for their good fortune, and I regretted my envy once more. But something hard and rough, like a stone shard, remained in my heart.

Just outside the city of Riga lies Latvijas Etnogrāvdabas Muzejs, a large outdoor museum of farm buildings, churches, and mills dating back to the 16th century. Established during the brief period of independence between the two World Wars, the museum has been kept open by Soviet authorities, though it seems sparsely attended, at least on weekdays. Walking on the wooded paths from one cluster of buildings to another, one can almost forget one is in a museum. The effect is of roaming about in the countryside, going from farm to flourishing farm, stopping by the side of a lake, climbing a hill to a Lutheran church.

I was surrounded by blossoming trees, swaying flowers, and ripe berries, several of which I remembered vividly from my childhood but had never seen growing outside of Latvia. Here and there a museum worker dressed as a farm wife encouraged me and the few other visitors to taste the currants, to smell the chamomile, to pluck a bluebell to later press in a book for remembrance.

I accepted everything so generously offered, but my spirits did not lift. For the past two weeks I had heard people speak constantly about the war and its grim aftermath, and I had listened, sympathized, offered help. But not one person had asked me what had happened to my family or me during the war, no one was interested in hearing about the struggle of beginning life in a foreign country, no one believed me when I said not everyone in the United States lives in luxury. Having fought against my own envy, I recognized it in others as they spoke of all Americans as millionaires, without any experience of hunger or fear, totally incapable of imagining hardship. I felt completely depleted; the stone grated my heart.

I closed behind me the wooden gate of an orchard near an 18th-century farmhouse, walked up a flower-bordered path, and entered a dim barn. At first I could see only a shadowy wagon, a few rakes and other implements, some empty bins. Letting my shoulders sag, I leaned against a wall. I wished I could stay in the restful darkness forever.

"Come," a woman's voice called out, "come with me. You look like someone who needs to hear me reciting."

A sturdy, small person, no more than five feet tall, grasped my hand and guided me firmly out into the sunlight, then into the dappled shade under a white birch. She was much older than I had first judged her by her decisive movements. Hundreds of lines marked her round weathered face; dozens of long white hairs grew on her chin; her pale blue eyes were merry and knowing. For a brief moment I was confused; the person before me seemed to be a woman and a man both, and yet neither. But then I saw the gray braids secured at the nape of her neck, the long skirt with its finely embroidered border, the worn gray shawl fastened with a small amber pin. Judged by such externals, she was clearly a woman. But being certain of her gender seemed less important than usual. I felt as if I, though fully awake, had suddenly fallen into a dream.

"Listen," she said, "this is the poem for you."

She let go my hand, stepped onto a slight elevation, closed her eyes, and started reciting. All my doubts about her being a woman vanished: Her voice was melodious and strong, in a word, womanly. She had chosen "Sauciens Tale," ("Call into the Distance,") a long poem of eight elaborate stanzas. I suddenly remembered that I too had memorized it once, when I was ten, in a Displaced Persons camp in Germany. But that had been more than forty years ago, so that now I could only feel the absolute rightness of each line as she spoke it, without being able to produce the next one myself.

"Sauciens Tale" was written by Fricis Bārda for the Latvians who were driven into exile in 1905. Directly addressing a wanderer who has lost his country and everything else, the poet speaks of the pain of separation and the anguish of exile. He urges the wanderer not to forget Latvia and promises a final homecoming. On that distant joyous day of new freedom, trumpets will sound, flags and blossoms will lie in snowdrifts on rooftops, but the wanderer will bring with him the pain of his long years of exile. He will question what he can accomplish in the ashes and ruins of his country; he will be uncertain whether he has the strength to do anything at all. But return he must. He can at least offer to Latvia his heart that has suffered so much.

The professor inside me began to note the formal characteristics of the poem, classifying it as romantic, criticizing it as too nationalistic, filing away words and metaphors I was glad to relearn. But by the second or third stanza none of that mattered.

The old woman had *recognized* me, and she was speaking directly to me about my depletion and alienation. She understood that even though I was now living a comfortable life in the United States, it had been painful for me to separate from family members, to leave home, to experience exile and war. She knew too that returning at the beginning of new independence was more complex than simply joyous.

I felt tears rising to my eyes, then flowing down my face. By the time she finished reciting, I was crying freely. The hard stone in my heart seemed to be dissolving and flowing away, taking with it the pain of exile as well. I was known and totally accepted. She had welcomed me home. I felt connected to every tree and cloud and blade of grass.

She took my hand and waited in silence until I had more or less finished crying.

"Thank you for that," I said when I could finally speak.

"That was good," she patted my hand. "Crying is healing, like some herbs that grow here."

She stepped away from me again, dropped her arms to her sides, lifted her face toward the sky, and recited three brief poems about the beautiful trees, hills, and roadsides of Latvia. These too were poems I had once known well.

The feeling of being in a dream, the sense that the odd and unusual was unsurprising and even fitting, persisted. As if to make certain that I really was awake, I drew myself up straight and rubbed my eyes, but the strangeness did not dissipate.

"This has meant the world to me," I said.

"I know," she nodded.

We stood looking at each other, not quite willing to part yet. And then suddenly I thought of it, a question I could ask, almost a test I could give her. It would bring this significant exchange to a close, and it would certainly return me to the everyday, rational world.

"Tell me," I said, "do you happen to know a poem that contains the line 'the riches of the heart cannot be destroyed'?" For the last three years I had been searching for the poem that teachers quoted to us in Displaced Persons camps. I wanted to include it in a book I was writing, but I was no longer sure I had it right. I had not found the line in a collection by Karlis Skalbe, which I had gone to great trouble to locate. I was not certain now of the author or the title or even whether I was quoting the line accurately.

I had asked every Latvian I knew in the United States about it: my father, old teachers, and women and men more or less my contemporaries who had also spent part of their childhood in camps. Everyone said it sounded familiar, a few volunteered their approval or disapproval of the sentiment expressed, but no one could identify it precisely.

"What were those words again?" the old woman asked.

"The riches of the heart cannot be destroyed."

"Oh, yes," she murmured, "oh yes, that's the last line in a poem 'For Friends' by Karlis Skalbe. But it's a little different. 'The riches of the heart do not rust,' is how it goes."

And of course, I knew it was so as soon as she said it. The riches of the heart were safe. Not only could they not be destroyed by displacement and war as I had been taught, but they could also not perish through disuse.

Es nezinu, kas vakar bija,
Es nezinu, kas rītu būs,
Tik ausīs šalc ka melodija:
Sirds bagātība nesarūs.

I do not know what was yesterday,
I do not know what will be,
I only hear as a melody,
The riches of the heart don't rust.

The past and the present were uncertain, but the riches of the heart were real. She had completed the poem and my return to Latvia for me.

The old woman seemed enchanted. Yet for me and for other exiles, returning to the countries of our childhood, looking for clues to our coming old age, the angle of vision determines magic. For the present, I hope to see the pain of the past as well, without sentimentality.

In the years of independence between the two World Wars, Latvia was indeed full of women reciting in safety and comfort. But nostalgia and envy had blotted out my memory of other reciters.

When she was seven years old, the future poet Aspazija recited to an examining Lutheran minister. Patting her on the head, he sighed regretfully, "It's too bad that you aren't a boy. Great things could come of you, but you're only a girl." My mother, who taught schoolgirls from orphanages to recite, had been told essentially the same thing when she was sent to a teachers' institute instead of a university.

Once, when I was five or six, a thin, almost-emaciated old woman dressed in gray came to the back door of the comfortable country parsonage. Her lips blue with cold, she stood out in the muddy yard, on a low round stump, reciting the Twenty-third Psalm. From the unhurried, matter-of-fact way the housekeeper gave her a bowl of porridge and a *santims,* I could tell that it was not unusual for old women to come begging to supplement their rations at the poorhouse in the next village.

The old woman ate very quickly, handed back the empty bowl to our robust housekeeper, and kissed her hand in gratitude. Then she lifted her face toward the sky and sang "Nearer, My God, to Thee," in a sweet, quavering voice. The housekeeper sighed in exasperation and ladled another serving of porridge, a half a bowl this time. "No more reciting now," she said as she handed the food to the old woman, who looked ashamed.

Once upon a time in Latvia, all women and girls knew how to recite. Reciting united us, hurt and divided us; reciting could heal us. Once upon a time in Latvia, there were so many kinds of reciters.

Journey by Inner Light

MEETA KAUR

It's naptime and my mother's hair becomes a world of my own. Mama unpins her bun and lets her hair fall, rushing down her back. She combs through any tangles with her fingers. Her long, shampooed tresses are thick pieces of rose-smelling silk. Her shiny hair is black pashmina, an endless journey toward the heart of a dark sky. I lie perpendicular to the length of the bed, on top of tangerine and gold embroidered pillows, flexing my feet and wiggling my toes. Mama lies down next to me. I proceed to thread her locks from the crown of her head through my big and second toes. Her hair fans out like a thousand silk threads suspended in air. Nestling both of my feet into the nape of her neck, I doze off warm, happy, and safe. I wake up to my mother combing out the knots. My father is coming home soon. I am only five years old, but somehow I know I will live my life joyfully. Mama is my light. She is home.

Mama teaches me how to take care of my hair during hair-bath days on Saturday mornings. I sit in our white ceramic tub waiting for my shampoo to commence. When the water reaches my waist, I crouch forward and push myself off the front of the tub. I sink under, and under is where I stay. The waves ripple over me as I hold my breath—*one Mississippi, two Mississippi, three Mississippi, four Mississippi.* I release tiny air bubbles with two seconds in between rounds and watch them float to the surface, then hover and pop.

"Meeta, *beti,* please get up so I can wash your hair." My mother places a plastic cream-colored stool next to the tub and squats down with her knees bumping up against the tub's side.

I surface, a humpback whale disrupted from its southern migration. Mama's fingers sink into my scalp as she begins a relaxed massage.

"Close your eyes, *urrahhh,* close your eyes so it will not sting you." Mama piles the strands of hair atop my head and squeezes out more shampoo. She beams as she sculpts my hair into a temple. I tilt my head back for the rinse. The weight of the shampoo washes away, leaving me light as a feather. She towel-dries my hair and draws a line down the middle of my head with a comb. She combs each section of my hair the way she combs her own—carefully, patiently. Mama's slow hands tell me how much respect she gives my body and me. At school, I romp with fluffy, tangle-free hair through recess.

As a child, I never question why all of my family members have long thick hair—we just do. It is a natural extension of who we are. I do not realize until later that hair-bath days only exist in our family household, and that the brothers and fathers in other American families do not have long hair.

My mother silently declares an allegiance to a homeland that is rooted from our heads and connected to our hearts. As a Sikh woman who migrated from India to America, she carries the strength and solace of spirituality in her hair. It is a light that provides a sense of place and home between any borders, on any soil, whether she is in India, America, or any other country. Although I didn't realize it then, my mother has been stoking the same guiding light in me since my childhood—a light that shows me the illuminating life that extends through my thoughts, out of my head, into my hair, and into the world, a light that shows me the path to who I am becoming, a light that sparks with subconscious knowledge and holds a steady glow.

When I am older, in middle school, Mom sends me on solo trips to India during summer breaks. My first trip alone leaves me jet-lagged and anxiously awake in the deep Indian nights. After riding the Shatabdi train from the Bombay airport to Poona, Jeeti Masi and Uncle Ji greet and escort me to their home. Their daughter and my cousin, Baby, is married and has moved away to live with her husband and in-laws in Hyderabad. In her dusty pink-and-bronze room, the night's cool breeze chases the day's humidity out of the room through the half-opened windows. I sit up on the bed not knowing what to do. I slink downstairs and head for the front door and quietly unlock the steel bolt to step outside. I step toward the custard apple tree in the lawn and pick one off. It looks like it has been glazed with green bottle glass. I carry it back upstairs, set it on the wooden nightstand, and wait for sleep to arrive.

The next day, jet lag leaves me drowsy on the velvet maroon sitting room sofa with a set of my cousin's old comic books. They are bent at the corners and have broken spines. They tell the spiritual stories of the ten Sikh Gurus, divine mortals sent as teachers to deliver the wisdom of a new faith, Sikhism. As I read, I travel back in time to the 16th-century Indian subcontinent. Mogul soldiers threaten Hindus to convert to Islam or suffer death. The ninth Sikh Guru, Tegh Bahadur, dons a navy blue turban and a golden robe and has a long silky beard. He states, "All people have a right to practice their own religion."

The Mogul leader sarcastically responds, "If you are so interested in defending these people, are you willing to die for them?"

In the next scene, Guru Tegh Bahadur is beheaded by a Mogul soldier. Another comic book illustrates the story of Mai Bhago, a great Sikh woman warrior who challenged forty deserters of the Sikh army to return to their posts and fight on behalf of Guru Gobind Singh Ji, the tenth Guru, against the Muslims and the hill chiefs to protect the principles of the faith.

As I read the comics, I realize that if there are no people standing at the end of these battles, there will be no principles, because they live within the people. The need to live with dignity and freedom becomes greater than the need to just live. To me, the sacrifices these Gurus made for future generations seem fantastical and out of this world, but in reality the Gurus had compiled scriptures that captured their direct conversations with God, the enlightenment that centered on equality while also drawing from the most progressive Hindu and Muslim tenets to create a just society. On the comic page, the Gurus wear regal turbans that protect their hair. Their long black beards flow freely. They look different from everyone else. I am familiar with the way they look because they remind me of my family, but I also see that they are different. *We* are different.

I spend the next two days reading through all one hundred comic books. I learn that my hair is referred to as *kesh*. My *kesh* represents an outward identity I can choose to preserve as a Sikh woman.

The comic books fill me with information and history. I learn, in preserving this natural uniform, that I commit to the equality between men and women, rich and poor, black and white, Muslim and Christian. *Kesh* is a commitment to a loving state of mind, to self-control, to faith in humanity, and to the protection of individual and communal rights. Through daily meditations; a commitment to just thought, speech, and action; and a faith in the supreme force, a Sikh can reach a state of rapture here on earth. A Sikh can live in utter bliss while serving humanity. What amazes me is the capacity to care enough to protect the rights of people who I disagree with or who are intolerant of me.

I have a hard time developing the discipline it takes to fulfill the destiny that is laid out for me. To me, these spiritual prophets are political ideologues. I dismiss their faith as jargon. I do not see it, cannot feel it, and have no evidence of it existing around me, so I follow my pleasures and passions as a young adolescent American girl who has bought into the illusions of this world: standardized beauty, romantic love, and the power of money. I want the attention of friends. I want the attention of boys. I want to be picture-perfect stepping out of the swimming pool with styled hair. I want to swoon with my classmates over our class pictures, squealing in delight about how cute we look. I want to date Rick Springfield. But all of this is not going to happen with all of this long, frizzy hair. I think to myself, *Maybe if I imitate my classmates' hairstyles—Stephanie's bangs, or Laura's bouncy blond bob, or Mindy's perm—I'll have a chance.*

In my freshman dorm at the University of California at Davis, I am surrounded by young women fawning over their tresses all day and night. Deep conditioners, natural dying, wave relaxers, and mousse are must-have products. Fraternity parties, house parties, and international parties call for one- to two-hour sessions in front of the mirror. But my choices are limited: a ponytail or pigtails, wearing it down with a part in the middle or to the side, a tight or loose bun. Okay, there are choices, but something about my hair feels stale, like old bread. It is ancient, musty, and tired.

In my hair, my mother, aunt, and grandmother nest with their stories, their histories, and their spirits. They sit on my head waiting for me to hatch into a woman who makes a difference in the world, who makes a habit of acting fearless in moments that demand it. The women in my family believe that my hair will purify my thoughts. They believe I can expand my thinking with my hair; all the positive energy in the world will be transmitted to me through my hair. Midnight tresses are rolled up into buns at the napes of my mother's, aunts', and cousins' necks. My grandmother wraps her salt-and-pepper hair into an acorn of a bun, nesting her love for God and her ancestors' heritage into her hair.

But I am convinced that this is not for me. I am convinced that I belong to the world and the world is a better source of authority for me. The distance between my parents and me grows with fewer conversations and an ocean of misunderstanding. I am in America and I want to be American. I decide it is time to push forward with something new—defined by me—something I can call my own.

I step into Select Cut Salons on Fourth and C Streets in downtown Davis. I am convinced that this decision will alter who I am and carve out an entry into my real life, a life waiting to be defined. Inside the salon, peroxide mingles with the receptionist's cigarette smoke.

"Who are you here to see?" The receptionist smashes her cigarette into the ashtray and scans the appointment book. Her sandy blond hair is cut like that of a choirboy who does not own a comb.

"I'm here to see Tiffany for a hairstyle, umm, a haircut," I tell her. *It is no big deal,* I try to convince myself. *Everyone gets haircuts. Relax.*

"Tiffany, your four o'clock is here!"

Tiffany greets and ushers me over to a hot-pink leather chair that competes with the black-and-white checkered floor. Cotton-candy-colored vanity lights line the individual station mirrors. The spritzers, mousse, hair relaxing serums, and alcohol-free finishing-hold sprays confirm that hair care is a commitment that cannot be taken lightly.

Tiffany lifts my thick braid of hair over my head and lets it drop. Her hands are careless, unlike Mama's.

"Wow, what thick and curly hair you have." For Tiffany, my long rope of a braid is just hair, humdrum strands hanging out of my head. "Okay, so do you have any ideas?" she asks.

Her clumsiness makes my heart pound faster. I feel my hands quivering, so I sit on top of them and attempt to look genuinely interested. I scan the top of the mirrors for all the European cuts: pageboys, what looks like a Cleopatra cut, and simple unassuming bobs. It's exciting to think about how

I might change, but something keeps grabbing at me, telling me to leave this place, to just get out of here. But I won't. My head pounds, weighing heavier and heavier as I take in all the pictures. I survey Tiffany's red, curly, turn-up-the-volume hair. It hangs an inch off of her shoulders. I have to answer her, but I don't want my hair to look like hers. "Umm . . . a bob looks nice, or maybe a Cleopatra cut, or . . . I don't know. What's the difference? Just cut it."

Tiffany's eyes widen and her eyebrows bob up and down looking like she is going to skip the *Are you sure?* or *Wanna think about it?*

My heart is thumping, and I see the entire Sikh army falling off their horses as they ride into battle—sliding off cliff edges, pierced by arrows, and losing control of their purpose, their direction. *Just shake it off,* I tell myself, *It is just a head of hair, and everyone gets a haircut.* Well, everyone except for Sikhs, Rastafarians, some Native American tribes—and my *entire* living family. Maybe I'm not a Sikh, or don't have what it takes to be one. I am the weakest link. I'm the soldier falling behind, barely able to carry my backpack, late for daily prayers. I'm the one who cannot get my act together, so what does it matter?

Tiffany's steel blades skim my neck. She struggles to cut off a lifetime of hair in one snip; it will have to be severed off, decapitated. Half of my braid is disembodied from the back of my skull. I close my eyes and wait for it to be over.

"There you go, hon," Tiffany says, holding my thick braid in her hand like a dead animal. "I'll put it in a bag for you so you have a souvenir to remember it by." When Tiffany hands me the bag with my braid, I gingerly set it on the floor. I hear her mumbling something about styling my new hairdo, but my mind is somewhere else.

I really did it. What did I do?

Tiffany uses smaller scissors to "style" my hair. Her glossy lips smack together as she talks, but I can't make out a single word of what she's saying until she's finished with the scissors.

"Okay! A quick blow dry and we are finitzio."

She blow-dries my hair and asks me to do a quick flip of my head. I see myself in the mirror with tussled hair surrounding my face. I had expected something different. I thought it would be different.

Later, I get together with my roommate, Martha. She holds her hands to her mouth when she sees me. She looks like she is going to puke.

"Oh my God! You look so cuuuuuute!" *Cute?* I am empty, cold. I run my fingers across the shaved patch on the back of my neck and wonder about this cycle of growing out my hair, cutting it again, growing it out again. What purpose does this serve? Fashion?

Three weeks after my haircut, I go home to Yuba City to visit my mother. On my way to the house, I pull on my hair at the back of my head trying to tug it to its original length. I ring the doorbell and wait. The lock clicks open and I throw my arms around her. "Mom! Hey!" She throws her hands around me and they search for my head, for my hair. I freeze.

"Meeta!" She whips me back where she can see my face; my hair jostles around near my neck, settling down two inches above my shoulders. Her face crumples and turns red. Her eyes well up. I see the pain denting her face, contorting it into something she is not. She runs toward the kitchen, pleading with my grandmother to enter the prayer room. My mother wipes her face with her *dupatta* and starts her prayers before she even enters the prayer room. She whispers into God's ear. She does not speak to me for four months.

I call my mother on the phone and try to explain to her that it is just hair. My mother swallows her tongue in her attempts to explain that it is *not* just hair. "It is identity. It is your commitment to an honest life, to a compassionate life. It is your character, your credibility. Why would you give up your own credibility?" she asks. I want to cry, swallowing the sobs stuck in my throat. The smell of flowers in my shampooed hair makes me nauseous. I reach for my childhood memories, but they slip away quickly, almost running away from me.

The next few months, I enter into the ritual of growing my hair out, trimming it, cutting it, and growing it out again. I become indecisive about my school major, and my grades falter. I find studying too overwhelming to deal with. I grow silent. I do not know who I am anymore. I drift and float through my sophomore year of college. I develop an identity through a guy I date and transform myself into an accessory for someone else's life.

There is a constant gnawing at my insides for something concrete, something that grounds me. I have no center, so I drift out to sea without direction or guidance. I lose my connection to myself and to the world. I lose my connection to a deeper sense of who I am. I do not realize that I had put that much faith into my *kesh,* into my long wavy hair, the hair I blame for my problems.

Mama accepts me into her house again, but she cannot hide her disappointment. She dismisses me during family conversations. She questions my pride at the dinner table. She tells my younger cousins to follow the example of my cousins in India: "The girls in India know who they are and where they come from." I know my mother doesn't mean India when she says this to my cousins. She doesn't pledge an allegiance to the geography of India or even America, for that matter, but to the spiritual homeland of Sikhism. She stamps my passport: DEPORTED. I am exiled from my family's homeland. I am a foreigner in my family's home. The border between my mother and me expands. She sets up a front line to protect the sanctity of her life against the impiety of mine. I hold on to my illusions, declare my mother narrow in her thinking. We never talk about it–the hair, the *kesh,* the identity I abandoned.

A few years after graduation, I join Narika, a South Asian women's hotline that supports survivors of domestic violence. The hotline serves women from India, Bangladesh, Sri Lanka, and Pakistan. There are quite a few counselors who know Hindi, Urdu, and Punjabi and communicate with the women on the hotline in their native languages. I stick with English because it is essentially the language I understand best.

I attend two counseling training sessions in the summer and prepare to wo-man the hotline. We receive a directory of domestic violence resources ranging from legal help to emergency room phone numbers. Shoba, our counselor, suggests we prepare a hot cup of tea to keep at our side during our shift. She tells us that we will receive a range of calls from women who may hang up, content with having heard a soothing voice on the other end of the line, to professionals asking for the names of good divorce attorneys.

It's a Tuesday night, and I'm naively excited about my first hotline shift. I dial into the hotline and pick up one voice mail. I call the woman back. I listen to her pauses and hesitations when she speaks. I let her know it is okay to talk about what's happened to her, that it is okay to speak her truth. She tells me he has hit her. We rest in the silence between us after she speaks. In this moment, I am humbled by my own history of Sikh women charging into battle, leading communities to fight oppression, and try desperately to pass on this historic courage, this timeless fearlessness through my lips into this woman's ears—down to her heart.

Eleven voice mails, three cases, and some court appearances later, the world has turned inside out for me and the distortion of it all hurts my eyes; these women's stories leak onto my pillow night after night. The counselor-training sessions ring true. Violence transcends class, education, and race. Even though these same realities exist within Sikh communities in America and abroad, the scriptures state that mothers, wives, sisters, and daughters deserve the highest respect from their families and the society around them. Anyone who dares to harm them is violating sacred law. I begin to question the world I am living in. I recall how quiet most of the Sikh girls were at school, how much they held in. I remember my mother demanding that my father respect her as an equal partner in those moments he lost sight of her right to make decisions in our household. I remember my own ability to dismiss myself because I had the ability to shrink, become invisible, smothering my own light because I am scared of where it could take me.

I walk down streets imagining that any man passing by is preparing to go home and beat up his wife. I lose two to three nights of sleep during any given week. On weekends, I'm in a deep slumber coma, not waking up for the sunlight, lunch, or even early-evening tea. The sleep pushes the days full of hotline calls into a semidistant past, but the women's voices continue to scream in my head. I help one woman secure a restraining order against her husband who consistently molests his youngest daughter. On the morning of her court date on the way to the courtroom, she shields me with her hands when she sees her husband. She turns to me and says, "I will not leave you alone with him." She sees her daughter in me. I put my arm around her shoulder and let her know that I will not leave her alone with him either.

Colleagues and friends see me absorbing these women's lives and making their pain my own. The daily hotline calls push me into daily meditation and prayer. I practice rising early in the morning with the sun. I brush my teeth, bathe, and then have a cup of tea. I recall my mother's and grandmother's practice of sitting down to pray, to clear their minds of any disturbances, to reach a solution or relief from a situation. I return to my bedroom, sit cross-legged on my bed, and cover my head with a *dupatta*. I reach for my Nitnem bound in red velvet. The small book holds Sikh prayers in Gurmukhi on the right side of the page and gives English translations on the left side. In the concentration of these prayers, I ask for peace of mind and strength, a calming of my nerves that will sketch a decent mind-size portrait of a sane world. I ask for guidance—grounded, firm guidance.

The meditation becomes a daily practice I cannot live without. Little by little, I chase fear out of my body to make room for more light. Three months of heavy meditation help me create a healthy detachment from the women without sacrificing my compassion for them. The prayers center me. I realize that all the little hells created on this earth are what the Sikh Gurus fought against. I realize there can be no peace or rest if members in a society suffer or are denied their basic rights.

My hair has grown three inches longer. The meditation increases and with it my hair expands in length. I focus on the strength of my mother's hair and the strength and safety she gave me as a child, the comfort I find in my spiritual homeland.

I feel a crack in the older self that I mummified when I cut my hair into that Cleopatra bob three years ago in college. The new growth of my hair is the outgrowth of my new mind. I see the world for what it is and realize that faith and my contributions toward realizing the vision of a socially just society are what I have to hold on to. I protect my mind's thoughts with my long wavy hair, warding off the severity of the world, nurturing my ideas and visions for my bright future. I realize all will not be resolved overnight, but I see a spark of light flicker from the steady glow of childhood. The thick plaster of the bandages breaks off, and I return to the original homeland of myself, with the gift of *kesh*.

My hair becomes witness to all the love and atrocities in the world. My hair holds the strength, pain, and love of these women on the hotline who I will never forget, cannot forget. I realize that I, too, am on a battlefield similar to the ones I saw in the comic books, even though the landscape is different, and I'm not holding a sword. The guiding light I inherit from the women in my family finds a way to penetrate me at my core and transform me from the inside out. I am duty-bound to the world around me according to the *kesh* I reclaim. I rise daily to my original locks, which are now younger than me. My hair has grown back out to its former length, and I no longer question preserving it until I die. I am on the path to becoming the woman my mother and grandmother prayed I would be.

Oburoni No More

KIM FOOTE

"Passport, please."

I hand over the blue book with the gold eagle on the cover. The Ghanaian customs official behind the counter doesn't smile as he flips to an empty page in my passport. He raises his eyebrow with an air of importance and stamps hard enough to set off a miniature earthquake. A red seal shows my official exit date: July 2003. As the customs official writes around it, I reflect on my yearlong stay in Ghana.

When I arrived in September 2002 as a Fulbright Fellow, I had housing difficulties and made slow progress with my research, in addition to feeling as if I'd dropped in from the next planet. The end couldn't have come sooner but now that it's finally here, I don't want to go. I'm escaping from the cultural nuances that began to annoy me, but I'm also sad to leave the Ghanaian friends who've become like family to me. At the same time, I worry that I've become a burden to them. I assume they grew tired of consoling me every time I felt out of place; I was the unwelcome African American in a place I used to romanticize as home. I imagined them thinking: *I have so many seri-*

ous problems, and here she comes again, fussing over this minor one! Sometimes, I was aware that they didn't want to be seen with me. At the market or on a road trip, their attempts to bargain would become complicated because of my presence. The vendors, assuming I was the stereotypically rich American, always raised their starting bid.

The customs official stops scribbling in my passport and looks up. He's smiling. "So, madam, will you miss our country?"

I bite my lip.

"Madam?"

"You're gonna make me cry," I reply.

"Sorry, eh." He pushes my passport back to me. "But you will go and come, yes?"

I do want to return to Ghana for many reasons, but mostly because of my friends. If not for their support through taxing crosscultural experiences, I would have left long before my fellowship ended. I don't know when or if I'll see these friends again. For me, the plane fare is too expensive. For them, acquiring a visa to the United States is next to impossible. In addition to paying a fee, most Ghanaians must enter a lottery to get a visa. Even if they win, an American has to write a letter to the U.S. Embassy and send a bank account statement proving that he or she is willing and able to sponsor them.

My eyes start to sting. I mumble a reply to the customs official and drag my weighty suitcase into the airport waiting room. A large TV broadcasts a popular Ghanaian soap on GTV, but, for the first time, it doesn't make me laugh.

As soon as I take a seat, I notice a man standing near me. He has that dark, cherrywood complexion that Ghanaians describe as "red." His Nike T-shirt is neatly tucked into black slacks, and sunglasses are perched atop his bald head.

"Are you an Ewe?" he asks me.

I'm speechless. Ghanaians have rarely mistaken me for one of them.

The man is shocked to learn that I'm American. His mistaken assumption about my ethnicity is an affirmation that comes too late.

Some of my ancestors originated in Africa, but I don't know where. They came to the U.S. long ago as slaves. Slave-ship records identified human cargo as items, not as people with names and places of origin. While I was living in Ghana, I felt the yearnings of a foster child, as once described to me by a man who'd been adopted. He said he always looked into the faces of older people and wondered: *Could they be my birth parents? Could they be my blood?* As I scrutinized Ghanaians' faces for a sense of familiarity, they returned my gaze and called me *oburoni*—stranger.

In the United States, my visible African ancestry—no matter how mixed—made me a hyphenated citizen. For a long time, I dreamed of going to Africa because I thought my blackness would blend in. I was crushed when I discovered that in Ghana I could never be black enough. For one, it was obvious that I looked nothing like them. They called my skin red, as is the case of the man in the Nike T-shirt, though mine was much lighter, more like cinnamon. A Ghanaian with my complexion typically has a white parent; my skin tone comes from very distant European and Native American ancestors. In Ghana, it didn't matter that I learned local languages, ate local foods, and adopted other aspects of local culture. To Ghanaians, "black" is a color. For me, it's a culture, the foundation of my existence.

The man in the Nike T-shirt tells me his name is Kofi and asks to sit next to me. I just want a peaceful, quiet moment where I can digest my last days in Ghana before boarding the plane to return to the United States. I don't want to talk to anyone, let alone deal with another flirty Ghanaian man.

After I reluctantly oblige, Kofi asks, "So, how long have you stayed in Ghana?"

"About a year."

"Ah! Then you are a Ghanaian now. Ghana is your home."

Ghanaians started making that statement after I'd passed the six-month mark, but still his comment throws me off. Maybe it's because I'll soon be stuck in a space between two countries, neither of which has quite welcomed me. The last place I felt truly comfortable was in the predominantly African American town of East Orange, New Jersey, where I was born. I haven't lived there in fifteen years. Since then I've relocated to several different places and have had plenty of time to think about what home means to me. After this year in Ghana, where I was never anonymous, I've concluded that home is a place where no one gives me a second glance.

The airport intercom announces that my KLM flight is ready for boarding. As I drag my suitcase to the gate, reality hits the pit of my stomach: When I reach my layover in Amsterdam and continue on to Newark International Airport, I'll be a racial minority for the first time in a year. I want to flee from Ghana's strict definition of blackness, which often made me feel like a lone red pistachio in a cup of coffee beans, but am I ready for the whiteness of Europe and America?

It makes me wonder if I'd accept Ghana's citizenship offer if it ever came to fruition. Over the past few years, Ghanaian politicians have talked about giving automatic dual Ghanaian-U.S. citizenship to African Americans descended from slaves. It's a great gesture on the surface to offer us a home, but I'm afraid of the realities of a multitude of African Americans bum-rushing Ghana. Some of them might arrive with a romanticized impression of Africa, as I did, and grow embittered and frustrated when they realize that it's an imperfect place with imperfect people. I also suspect that Ghana's motive behind the proposal isn't purely sentimental; the influx of American dollars would greatly benefit the country's economy. I worry that African Americans with shrewd business minds and little desire to connect with Ghanaians will try to take over, do things *their* way, and exploit Ghanaians in the process. They might become the new oppressors.

Plenty of slave descendants from the Americas are able to settle in Ghana with good intentions and call it home, but I've come to understand that they've faced challenges and made necessary sacrifices. For one, they don't usually arrive alone, as I did. They can therefore hibernate together away from Ghanaians who misunderstand them or label them foreigners on the street. Because I didn't intend to set up a permanent residence in Africa, I believe my level of persistence and tolerance was lower than theirs. During my year in Ghana, I wondered how much of my personality I'd have to alter or suppress in order to feel accepted. Even though I curbed my bawdy and sassy ways, dressed conservatively, used Ghanaian mannerisms, and even picked up the lilt of Ghanaian English, it still wasn't enough for Ghanaians to fully embrace me.

Some Ghanaians and African Americans have declared that we should mingle our blood to create a strong, unified nation. Yet, I'm an unmarried woman who doesn't want to be pressured into marriage before the tender age of thirty. I also wouldn't want to marry someone whose family shuns me because I'm a woman who hates to cook. If I were to marry a Ghanaian from a matrilineal society, I'd worry about the fate of my descendants. Traditional inheritance laws are determined by the mother's bloodline, so my descendants might not be able to inherit because of my foreign blood.

I've begun to realize that no matter where I choose to settle, life will be a struggle. Ghana, with its easygoing "it will happen when it happens" pace, might be a respite from the uptight, time-consumed, capitalistic culture of the United States, but Africa isn't perfect either. I've witnessed how much damage European colonialism has caused in less than one hundred years. In Ghana, for example, I often found that I was more "African" than the Africans. Since most of the women get perms and see straight hair as a mark of beauty, my unpermed hair caused much confusion. I preferred outfits tailored from colorful, locally made batik cloth, whereas many Ghanaians wanted ready-to-wear American and European imports. I wanted to investigate indigenous spirituality, which most Ghanaians no longer practice extensively because of their longtime devotion to Christianity or Islam.

Though I don't foresee rooting myself in Ghana any time soon, I'm not returning to the country of my birth with open arms. After all, it's a place where some historians have debased and erased my black ancestors' contributions, where whites have forced their culture and standards upon African Americans. Still, I feel that the United States has something to offer me. There are luxuries and conveniences I've had trouble living without, such as American supermarkets. After seeing that people in other countries can't even get bare essentials, it disturbs me that in the United States, whole aisles are filled with endless assortments of candy, soft drinks, and pet toys; yet, I sure won't miss the chaotic open-air markets in Ghana and having to bargain for everything. I miss sidewalks, toilets that flush, mosquitoes and flies that don't cause disease or death, clean drinking water, schedules and maps, fixed prices, and water that runs hot from the tap—all of which I took for granted while living in the United States.

I'm also craving the diversity of American people—the proliferation of ethnicities, accents, skin tones, hair textures. I especially yearn to be around African Americans, who embody not just one but a multitude of African nations. Our Ebonics is so different in rhythm from British-influenced West African pidgin. I miss hearing the way we laugh, the many ways we dance, from subtle and gentle to booty shaking, which Ghanaians eschew as "waist dancing." I miss seeing folks with locks and other unpermed styles and having no one ask me why I don't straighten my hair. African Americans have forged an American culture and existence distinct from anything African (or European, for that matter). I'm no longer ashamed to recognize that and validate it.

Back on American soil, I'm having trouble breathing, and it's not just because my carry-on suitcase is overweight. As I lug it down a long hallway at Newark International Airport, passengers from my plane rush all around me, heading into the customs room. Most of them are white, and they make me nervous. In Ghana, I got sick of Ghanaians staring at me, but I never felt physically threatened by them, as I have around some white people, especially after seeing Civil Rights documentaries that showed them terrorizing and murdering blacks without fear of punishment. Though I was born long after the Civil Rights era, I grew up with reminders of the violence lurking behind strained white smiles. Black lynchings and church bombings still occurred, and the Ku Klux Klan even had a website to recruit members for their campaign of hatred. In Ghana, I never felt like people doubted my intelligence, humanity, or right to live just because I had less melanin than they did.

After having lived one year in a black nation, I'm afraid of how I'll react to white people, rather than vice versa. When an African American friend of mine flew to the States after three months in Ghana, her first horror story took place at the airport. The flight attendant let several white passengers aboard the plane but blocked my friend, demanding to see her passport. My friend had on a Senegalese outfit and wore her hair in braided knots. Believing it to be racism, my friend shoved past. When the flight attendant threatened to get a security guard, my friend told her, "Take your racist shit and shove it, lady." She admitted that prior to spending so much time surrounded by black people in Ghana, she wouldn't have said something like that aloud.

I don't like confrontations, and I don't like getting worked up over someone else's biases. Like my friend, I've also gotten more brazen in the absence of white people. I'm wearing an African-style dress made from shiny indigo-colored fabric with a matching head wrap. I anticipate going teeth-to-teeth with a white customs official about my citizenship status.

"Yuh dress is pretty."

I jerk my head sideways to locate where the distinctly Long Island accent is coming from. A short, orange-haired white woman in shorts, a T-shirt, and sneakers is pulling a suitcase beside me. After living so long among women dressed in elegant skirts, dresses, and heels, her clothes are a strange sight.

"Where're you coming from?" she asks me.

"Gh . . . Africa," I find myself quickly saying, even though it sounds odd. Before college, when I truly learned to appreciate my African heritage, I had reduced the continent's numerous countries to that one word. Over the past year, I've rarely spoken that word. I once took it to mean an insignificant speck on the globe, but I've come to know Africa as an immense land with distinct, diverse, and valid groups of people.

"Oh, wow. Africa," the woman says. "My husband and I just returned from visiting aw son in China. He's doing Peace Corps there. Were you on Peace Corps?"

The hallway's air-conditioning is on full blast, but I'm sweating. I wish this woman would go away. "No, I didn't do Peace Corps."

A white-haired man approaches, waving two U.S. passports. He stops next to her and doesn't greet me. Grimacing, he scans my outfit. I narrow my eyes and return his stare until he takes his wife's arm and practically drags her away. She looks over her shoulder, calling to me: "Take care, hon!"

This woman's husband may just lack social skills, but my instinct tells me otherwise. The United States has trained me to sniff out racism. Many Ghanaians I met couldn't relate to this type of sensitivity. Despite a century of British rule, the majority of them haven't had direct contact with whites. One of my Ghanaian friends once pointed out that African Americans are defensive, to which I immediately (and heatedly!) responded, "What do you mean! How can you say that?" When I calmed down, I realized I'd never seen my own defensiveness because it was so ingrained in "my culture."

When further comparing myself with Ghanaians, I noticed that we African Americans have a hard edge to us—we can be distrusting, blunt, and demanding because we've needed these skills to survive in a hostile, racist society. It makes me reflect on a comment made by a white American nurse at the U.S. Embassy in Ghana. When I told her that I was researching the transatlantic slave trade, she commented, "You know, seeing how hard it is here in Africa, I always wonder: If people back then had a choice, would they have preferred to stay or leave?"

Stay or leave? Maybe I should have asked her: Would they have wanted to lose their family, land, home, children/husband/wife, and freedom, and risk their very lives? Would they have wanted someone to force them to work, to beat and rape them, marginalize and dehumanize them?

I've felt compelled to examine the nurse's question critically because she wasn't the first to pose it. In *Out of America,* African American journalist Keith B. Richburg expresses gratitude that the transatlantic slave trade occurred. While covering a few war-torn African countries, he concluded that his ancestors were better off leaving, even if they had to do so as slaves.

Some of us in the diaspora *are* faring better than our African kin today. My non-American black friends who live in the States constantly stress to me that despite my country's shortcomings, poor blacks in America have many more opportunities to gain economic and political power.

But is it really fair to weigh the present situation of Africans and their diasporic kin on the same scale? Keith B. Richburg and the embassy nurse can easily make their comments because history has shaped their lives positively. I doubt they would have the same view if they were African American, homeless, poor, in jail, on welfare, struggling and hustling just to make it through the day.

Instead of asking if the enslaved would have chosen to remain in Africa, I have more fundamental questions: What if European men had decided not to export human beings from that continent as slaves? What if Africa hadn't been so severely depopulated? What if European men hadn't ruthlessly divided land and kin and subjected them to colonial rule and hegemony? What if the inventors, writers, artists, activists, musicians, architects, intellectuals, mathematicians, scientists, doctors, and entrepreneurs of the resulting diaspora could have remained in Africa and thrived?

Africa would have still seen warfare, inequality, political corruption, and poverty, but probably no more than what any society has experienced throughout history. Yet, African ethnic groups split by European-imposed borders wouldn't need passports to visit each other. There wouldn't even be a Liberia or a Sierra Leone for journalists like Richburg to talk about.

I finally reach the doorway leading to the customs room at Newark International Airport. My breathing becomes even more difficult when I see the confusion of bodies scrambling every which way. I try to distract myself by focusing on my future in the States, on what will happen in three weeks when I relocate to Chicago for graduate school. The thought doesn't sustain me, because I immediately think about how I don't have any friends there and have never visited.

The wave of people behind me pushes me through the doorway. Inside the huge customs room, two snaking lines lead to several customs booths. At first glance, I don't know which line to join. The faces in both are brown, white, and yellow. They're of Asian, African, European, and mixed ancestries, like me. After seeing in black for the past year, I'm sharply reminded that the world isn't projected in black-and-white, but in *Technicolor.* The States, with its fusion of immigrant cultures, is no exception. If not for the sign indicating U.S. AND NATURALIZED CITIZENS, I wouldn't know to join the people in the right-hand line.

I keep glancing between the lines, awestruck at the similarities. I feel myself relaxing among these myriad tongues and colors and shapes. Back in Ghana, all of us in the line would be called strangers. If dropped into a white American suburb, we'd be outcasts. We're all different, and for the first time in a year I feel at home. I'm reminded of high school in Belleville, New Jersey, where everyone I befriended had been born outside the U.S. They practiced Islam, Buddhism, Christianity, and Hinduism; ate foods I'd never seen before; and spoke languages besides English, but I bonded with them. Unlike my African American peers who thought I was snooty, or my white American peers who despised me for being smart, my immigrant friends accepted me for who I was. We respected each other, despite our seemingly strange ways.

I thought I would find that widespread acceptance in Africa because of my skin color and because I have roots there. Long ago, men created a fake science called race, which put Africans and me into the same boat: "black." I've come to understand that it's a label of force, not of choice. It also has different meanings around the globe. Whether in Ghana or predominantly white America, I am self-conscious about my skin color, hair texture, and accent. In either country, I've felt most comfortable among my friends, who are members of many races. Here in this line of multinational, multiethnic American residents at Newark airport, I blend in. I belong.

To my relief and pleasant surprise, the U.S. customs officer who stamps my passport isn't the disdainful white American I was expecting. He has a milky cocoa complexion. He wears his hair in zigzagging corn-rows, chews gum, and speaks a Caribbean patois. He smiles at me as he hands over my passport.

"Welcome back home, miss."

¡Venceremos! Words in Red Paint

ANANDA ESTEVA

SI TE VAS PARA CHILE

When we go back to Chile . . . became a refrain from a song my mom kept singing over and over throughout my childhood. *When we go back, baby.* Her eyes would light up, then drift to some secret place. *When we go baaack.* Her voice embodied a singsong quality, and the word *back* stretched out over time—too much time.

We left Chile when I was two years old. During our first few years in San Francisco, the prospect of returning to Chile felt alive, hot, and breathing. The wind wisping through my hair along San Francisco's Baker Beach would sing, *"Si vas para Chile, Chile, Chileeeeh, te ruego viajero, le digas a ella que de amor me muero."* (If you go to Chile, I beg of you traveler, tell her I am dying of love.)

We never planned on staying in the United States, so we brought few possessions, but the songs traveled with us like an auditory shadow, harmonizing with our words, the wind, and with even the sigh of our lungs. My mother had been a singer in Chile and my father an artist; our community was rich with music and stories shared.

Months before the coup d'etat that would force artists into silence, into exile, or into the ground, a death threat was delivered to the door of our little house in Chile. We had few neighbors so there was no mistaking that we were the intended recipients. Was it a bluff? Who could have known? My parents decided we'd visit Northern California with the intention of returning once the right wing uprising was squelched. My parents didn't share this information with me directly, but I observed its effects in so many ways.

I remember we had almost no furniture in those early days in San Francisco, and I didn't have any toys other than a plastic phone and the plush Ben Davis monkey that sucked his own thumb. The furnace was my friend. I used to lie on my belly, staring at his blue flames and conjuring secret landscapes. The fire showed me snow-covered mountains, water slamming against coastal cliffs, and everything else I believed Chile to be.

We clung to black-and-white photographs of our house in the fishing town of El Tabo. Those pictures colored the majority of our blank apartment walls; we lived through photos, promises, and songs. I remember being three years old, lying on orange-and-green-striped army floor mats with my parents, drinking warm milk with cinnamon and sugar, imagining myself in Chile. I saw the cove where my parents baptized me by dunking my head in the Pacific. *I am in shades of gray, my mouth open wide. Wet boulders below me glisten in low angles of light. Creatures grip sleek surfaces of rock while my mother's thick hands grip my shoulders and hips. The light bounces on the water below, making shimmying patterns in the otherwise-still photograph.* I saw our home, overlooking the ocean, in Chile. The inside of our house looked like something out of Renaissance Venice. Papi had made furniture out of sheet metal, finely shaped and embossed in intricate patterns. He enameled the furniture with designs resembling tidal pools bursting with life. I believed the furniture he had made marked the day of my baptism, the day when my parents chose not to seek a priest's stamp and seal and instead asked the ocean's spirit to protect me. By doing so, my parents united me with Chile's wild, icy ocean—the one that takes lives on a whim. I carried that connection to Chile all the way to San Francisco, feeling the *va y ven* of Chile's tides pulling me while gazing at the photos of my baby body, of the water dancing below, and of our furniture finely crafted like an homage to Neptune.

Chile felt close when we went to Amilcar and Carmen's house for lunch in San Francisco's Mission District, a community with a spattering of exiled Latinos and Spanish-speaking Latinophiles sharing idealistic talk, smokes, music, and food. I recall black beans simmering and tamales steaming in big pots. Our friend El Argentino would play guitar and sing folk songs, his fingers dancing over the strings like pixies. Less experienced in guitar, my mom played backup and sang, harmonizing in haunting minor keys.

In Chile, she sang in a folkloric trio dedicated to preserving songs from villages, some hundreds of years old. We lost contact with her group once in the United States. She sent letters, but received no reply. Playing with El Argentino at parties filled up a small fraction of the hole within her. One of my favorite songs, "Río Paraná," an Uruguayan litoral, spoke to me with its lyrics: *"No matter where you wander, you find yourself back at the shores of the Río Paraná."* As my mom's group strummed that waterlike rhythm, my mind floated with them. I heard warm mud squishing between my toes and frogs singing in time. Would I ever see Río Paraná in life? My Papi would always say, "This phase in government will be over soon. . . . We'll go back."

In those early days, we still hadn't heard about the disappeared, *Los Desaparecidos*. A few years later, as my parents became active at La Peña Cultural Center, created for Chilean émigrés in Berkeley, the news of *Los Desaparecidos* came not through the wind but through letters sent by other people's loved ones in exile and was shared with the community at large. Years later, we would learn of the mass burials in Llonquén and in the northern deserts near Arica. *Los Desaparecidos* became lost in a vague limbo of passive voice, casting no blame, casting no shadow.

The fresco mural painted on the front of La Peña portrays a proletarian Chile: people huddled together in protest, chanting, with mountains in the background, and animals, including a dove, painted in the pattern of the Chilean flag. At the top, overhead, Victor Jara, with his giant severed hands, plays the guitar. Jara was a singer-songwriter who honored workers' struggles. The military cut off his hands when he refused to stop playing his guitar, but on La Peña's wall, they play and will play until the fresco crumbles away.

Fleshy and pulsating with streams of color, Jara's hands scared me. So often I dreamed of detached hands in the window of our bedroom, where Papi, Mami, and I slept together on the floor. I'd will myself to wake up, but there they were, hands slowly waving at me. I'd pull down the brown paper curtain, but even then I could see their shadows behind the thin film. My parents snored like trains, their bodies stiff and weighted down. I was Chilean enough to know not to wake them but American enough to lie there wishing I could.

By the time I turned five, we came to believe our names were recorded on a list and we could not go back until the government changed. My mom freaked out and told me to sign fake names on petitions demanding the investigation of those who had disappeared. For the first time, my parents started to admit that if we had stayed in Chile, we would have had trouble. Around that time, I found out we had received death threats because of my mom's artistic friends and her singing. We heard the stories of women getting red-hot wires shoved through the most tender sections of skin, their breasts cut up like one would carve initials in a tree. Although I was too young to hear such things, since my parents took me to work, on errands, or to parties, their circles became mine and so did their stories. *What was happening to our friends?* We didn't know. We heard about communities of musicians and artists forced underground either figuratively or literally—by keeping quiet, by hiding, by escaping.

We talked less and less of returning to Chile as time passed. My mom stopped playing guitar, but sometimes at night she sang to me a cappella. Even now, I consider those my fondest memories of her: playing guitar, singing South American folk songs. The lines in her face would relax, and her features would blossom. Now, when I look at her face full of lines, I see how the past we thought we had escaped still managed to carve its way into her.

The more we accepted living in the United States, the unhappier we all became. Papi raged over nothing. Mom cried over nothing and drank for nothing. I became quiet, bottled in my own world. We were American. We lived in cozy subsidized housing, every unit a clone of another. It was as if our whole block was covered in brown shag carpet and yellow linoleum. We were comfy, having acquired furniture, toys, a color TV, books, clothes, and junk. Chile, once a guest at our home, became more like a spirit-plate left as an offering for a dead relative, like a faded memory of who we once were.

On my fifteenth birthday, Papi promised once again that we would return to Chile. I stared at him in disbelief, though he did keep his promise. We did go back—Papi and I—for one month in 1987 when I was fifteen. My father tried to prepare me for our journey, explaining what I couldn't say and do, how I needed to act in order to be safe. I imbibed his words like a good drink. I felt them swirl around my innards and join the consciousness of my body. I would run when I needed to run and hold my tongue if I had to. I intended to survive. As much as I practiced these evasive tactics, nothing could prepare me for the reality of living in such a militarized place.

When we arrived at the Santiago Arturo Merino Benitez Airport, military men in green uniforms shuffled me, Papi, and fifty other passengers into a large gray room. "Whatever you do," Papi said, "let me do the talking. Don't answer any questions unless I say it's okay." The men lined us up in two rows. They escorted the first pair of passengers through steel doors and into another room while the rest of us waited; the next pair went through the steel doors, and then the next. We stood in the middle of this long double-line of passengers with ice-cold expressions. It reminded me of the Virginia Reel dance but without the music, skipping, or smiles. *Grab your partner, do-si-do.* A steel-framed doorway replaced the arched bridge, usually formed by the dancers' interlocked arms. Instead of dancing under the bridge and coming back to position, the people at the airport never came back 'round.

As I watched the people file morbidly through, a couple in front of us walked under the doorway in slow motion. I saw a crowd of men in dark clothing waiting for them, carrying cameras with oversize flashes. I watched the woman's spine stiffen and her partner put his arm on her shoulder. The lights flashed all around them and swallowed them like the alien glow in the movie *Close Encounters of the Third Kind.* Then the couple disappeared into the crowd. "Papi, are those people famous?" I asked. "No," he said, holding my hand tight, "they'll be taking our picture, too. Nani, don't look at them when they take your picture, but don't look down either . . . and don't say anything. Okay?" I held my breath, clutching his hand with mine. I trusted he could keep me safe. After a long, hushed conversation I only half understood, the men let us pass.

That evening, when I lay down on a stiff, nearly wooden mattress, I heard myself sigh long and loud but my body never fully uncoiled. I felt as tense as that darn mattress. I wondered if this place where I was conceived would ever feel womblike to me. Could I snuggle up to Chile as I did with that lofty feather pillow, the only tender thing I found my first day in Chile?

A BIRD CALLS ON AHUMADA

On our second evening in Chile, Papi took me to Calle Ahumada in the center of old Santiago, where palatial buildings stand proud like rock cliffs along the shores of pedestrian rivers. At the feet of these cliffs you can see shops, restaurants, banks, and cafés. At the crown you can find business offices, lawyers, and secret havens for changing money—if you know the right people.

As we walked along the gray cobblestone road, my eyes ping-ponged, following the flowing masses of people; brown- and black-haired heads swirled around me at eye level. I felt stunned. I could actually *see* in a crowd for once. In California, I was stuck staring at gold neck chains or shoulder pads. If these weren't my people, at least they were my size! I looked around and realized I could almost . . . fit in. Back home, we were one of two Latino families in a black neighborhood flanked by whites.

"Papi," I said, "there must be no racism here. Everybody looks the same!" I thought I knew about racism from having been raised in the projects, from having watched the television miniseries *Roots,* my best friend Angie breaking down each scene and connecting past and present.

"Ah," he replied. "Look more carefully. There may not be racism as we know it, but there is classism, though the poorest people tend to have darker skin, especially in the villages. Look at that woman over there!"

A woman with sun-smoked skin, the color of rich cinnamon, stood over to the right. Her blond wooly hair stuck out on both sides of her head like triangular clouds. Her calico dress could have been from any era. Her body was shaped like a wire model—a tool some artists use for drawing—except for the large hump between her shoulders. In the near distance I heard a harmonica playing a folky tune—sounding so *familiar.* The woman stood transfixed, focused on something we couldn't see, her face tied up in knots. I assumed the fabric of her mind spread as thin as her clothing. But as we drew nearer, we saw what she was looking at: a blind fellow playing a *charango,* and tied to that *charango* was a stick, like a popsicle stick, and tied to that stick was another stick, and tied to that stick, another and another, climbing like a crooked stairwell until the last stick attached to a harmonica. I wondered how long it took him to scrounge for and fasten each of those sticks so he could play the guitar and the harmonica at the same time. He played like a Chilean Bob Dylan, intertwining strings, harmonica, and voice. He suctioned the harmonica with his lips and switched between pipe and song so seamlessly.

That woman, who looked like she had survived decades of natural disasters, been tumbled by tidal waves, dragged through muddy river bottoms, scooped up by tornados, and always missed the Red Cross relief van . . . *that* woman stepped forward and plopped a large coin into his tin can and walked off smiling. Well, if *she* could donate, then so could *we.* I would have felt embarrassed *not* to give him money. But men strode by in pressed suits and silk ties without a second glance. Shouts of walking salesmen entered our ears along with countless conversations. The experience of the musician and the humpbacked woman was, for me, one of those rare honest moments, though it was soon eroded by swarms of people ambling here and there like dust storms. They could not see the honor that the musician aimed to express.

Music was a way of gaining dignity. The pensions, food subsidies, affordable housing, and healthcare Chileans were accustomed to have been stripped since the dictatorship. Being blind didn't afford the musician any favors. Most likely he lived in a *población,* a shanty made of cardboard and other found materials. His music may have been his only income, the only thing that separated him from beggars. I didn't know it at the time, but by playing music, especially nestled alongside government buildings, he risked receiving negative attention from police or military men. Depending on their orders or whims, he may have risked his life.

The Chile of 1987 was not the same Chile of my memories, nor the one I had imagined. It was as if we had been traveling at the speed of light in outer space and returned to a country brutally aged by the everyday realities of oppression. This oppression lived, breathed, and stalked people until it managed to plunge inside them, invisible, seeping out of their pores like booze. It swept into view when I saw a human body bobbing down the Mapocho River. I could trace its path in the furrowed brows and worry lines of passersby. I remember seeing a wall spray-painted in fierce red, *¡Venceremos!* (We will win!), chipped and pockmarked from rounds of bullets like teeth marks from this hungry creature—this oppression that ate away at people's lives.

Nightmares haunted me during those four weeks in Chile. I felt something dark, gray, and gaseous twisting itself into the cracks of my body. I woke up unusually cold. I befriended the kerosene heater. The nauseating odor was worth the heat it emitted for its ability to temporarily relieve me of the thing that twisted and gnawed at me. Even Papi couldn't protect me from those feelings. I had to face them raw and vulnerable.

As Papi and I walked along Calle Ahumada, I heard a sound like a heartbeat down the road. As we wandered, the beat grew louder and stronger. Papi pulled my hand until we came across a *conjunto,* a four-piece band that plays "traditional" Andean music laced with songs of struggle, *of taking down the fences, of hands that work the land owning the land, of the garment workers and miners.* We joined the small crowd of spectators. On the left, a tall drum took over my heart's beating. The drum is called *la tumba,* the tomb. *It is this rhythm that weaves our world, that holds us together, yet gives us space to be,* I thought. That drum could swallow me whole. I scanned the other musicians to see a guitar, mandolin, and *zampoñas. Zampoñas* sound like wind through the mountains way above the trees. *It is this wind-spirit that gives us our voices.* I closed my eyes. The instruments and singing bled in and out of each other like sky and clouds moving fast.

Papi led me farther down the road. We found another *conjunto,* this one with a woman singer, a *charango,* a guitar, a *quena* (a type of flute), and drummer playing an over-the-shoulder drum called the *bombo.* The drumbeats danced, more fast-paced than the *tumba.* The drummer used the side of his drumstick to hit the metal rim around the head to make the *ba-bada-ba* beat of the Chilean *cueca.* The guitar followed the beat-path of the drum. The singer's voice heated up the night air with her warm honey notes. A crowd gathered, and I noticed a group of chess players lined up along the side of the road. A lady sold wallets under a lamppost. A man sold linens and stood nearby listening too.

The high pitch of the *quena* rose above the other instruments. The *quena,* like a vocalist, carries the melody of traditional Andean music. As I listened I could make out her words. *The quena sings like a bird telling spriteful stories of her flight above the trees. She tells of the Precordillera and the world of stone and sand of the Atacama. She tells of the* vicuña *and the llama and of the* caimán *over to the east. She sings about the condor and the time he beat the Spanish bull, scratched his back and made him run to death. She tells of oceans turned silver with the bounty of small fish to the west and of water spirits to the south who cry like wolves through curled dead trees. She tells of fine flavors of streams seeping out of rocks below Machu Picchu. This is the best water in the world! She tells of how* la flauta andina *fell in love with the African drums, giving birth to the cumbia, who would fly across the earth making grandchildren in Mexico, their bloodline never to die.* And as the *quena* bird-flute sang her melody, I felt as if I were joining her flight, seeing what she was seeing and had seen for more than one thousand years. I felt whole, united with the songs of my ancestors. I wanted that feeling to last forever. But suddenly, she cawed out a warning, *"Look out, predators coming! Look out! Look out! At your tail they fly!"*

I tried to follow the *quena* bird-flute but she was gone, her song cut short. My consciousness crashed to the stone-paved ground. Back to reality, I saw the street musicians tuck the *quena* and *charango* under coats. The woman selling leather wallets covered the *bombo* and scurried to the left. The linen man engulfed the guitar with his sheet and walked away, whistling a windy tune through his chapped lips. Even the chess players stuffed their games into inconspicuous bags. Musicians, street sellers, chess strategiers, and listeners swirled around each other, a final dance before they disappeared. Only Papi and I still stood there bewildered. *What was that? Did the crowd swallow the concert?* Then I saw the military police approach. The pair on patrol strolled right between us as if we didn't exist, looked around, and walked off. The bird sounds I heard must have been a person whistling, warning the musicians: *They are coming. Take cover.*

I recall when Victor Jara gave his last concert and his life in the stadium in Santiago, when military men came and cut off his hands. They laughed and called out, *"Play your guitar now!"* Jara opened his throat and sang despite the pain and terror of his lost hands, and his life, which was soon to follow, when he sang, *"You can take my hands but you can't take my song!"* With those words they shot him dead. In front of thousands they murdered him, an act intended to weave a mantle of fear in all who heard the story. In 1987, playing traditional music in Chile was considered subversive. All in the name of progress, they tried to mute Jara's voice and kill his song like the ancient trees bulldozed in Chiloé, where six-thousand-year-old trees once flourished. I witnessed his song live on that night in 1987 as the musicians risked their lives to play. I heard his cry in the *quena* flute of the Andes. The *quena* tells stories, of the *Pachamama, la madre tierra*. I heard his song take the form of a warning: *Look out. They are coming. Take cover!* And I heard his song shape itself into a promise; *I will help you hide, my brother, so you can play another day.*

By then, my mother had stopped playing for nearly ten years. She had once been part of a musical movement that sang of rivers, of mountains, of miners, of hands that worked and owned the land. If we had stayed in Chile, I wonder if my mother would have kept playing in protest. Would she have had the guts to play? Would she have had the hands?

PISCO SOUR

One day, I was on my way to the Mercado Central, the main shopping complex for folks with not a whole lot of money to spend. I walked across La Alameda Avenida Bernardo O'Higgins, named in honor of the famous liberator of Chile from Spain. Along that wide multilane corridor, a canvas-covered vehicle stopped right in front of me, blocking my way. Young men in the back manned a bazooka. I couldn't go back because more trucks rolled up behind me. A young man tilted the cannon's projectile away from the sky and pointed it at me. In response to the expression of horror on my face, he looked me in the eye and grinned, deranged, like a man after too many sleepless nights. To him I was one more conquered bitch, one more notch, one more clumsy, drunken story after a night of drinking too many Pisco Sours.

Pisco Sour is the national drink of Chile, and I'm sure he felt *he* represented the nation. Yes, he would go all the way to prove his loyalty. He, a dark-skinned man in a country trying to be European where class lines and color lines intersect. He was young, with some education but not enough to make him question the orders given by lighter-skinned men with more status and more protections. I could tell by the look in his eyes, he was ready to breathe life into his orders and execute them. His eyes told me that if there were an alley nearby, I would be there, pinned under him, his buddies 'round the corner to back him up, pretending not to look. Oh what stories they'd tell that night over shots of Pisco. I was on his turf, and he knew it. That much he could claim. And this country I was taught to think of as home for fifteen years, what did it mean at that moment—standing between his cannon and a wall? I had nothing. This Chile, this home I hoped would shelter me, only let in cold night air and wicked winds to rattle me around, to rip out my roots. Now I knew what Papi had always said was right. I was a gypsy, a person with no home, destined to wander.

But as I stood there between the vast black hole of his cannon and the stone wall behind me, I recalled the wall with the word *¡Venceremos!* spray-painted in red. Rounds of bullets were forced into that wall again and again, like teeth into flesh, creating pockmarks surrounding *¡Venceremos!* They could have painted over that word, but its existence among bullet holes made a stronger message: *You can try but you can never win!* I'm thinking somebody died for that word, just as Victor Jara died for his song.

"*We will win! We will win!*" I knew that somewhere inside of me I had to *be* that word *¡Venceremos!* I had to breathe life into it just as the man on the other end of the bazooka had to breathe life into his orders to inflict terror. I had to be red, strong, with an exclamation point at my side. I had to get out of this walking proud, not crawling. I had to win! The military underestimated the power of that word, the word that shakes the bullet holes from its ledger, as a freed man shakes the shackles from his ankles and wrists. *¡Venceremos! ¡Sí! ¡Sí!* I sang these words under my breath, praying that they'd give me strength, breathe a life into me. . . . *¡Venceremos!* Embodying red words, I slipped out of the bazooka man's crosshairs and into the street beyond. Yes, one day Chile will be home to me again!

Filipino Secrets and American Dreams

PATRICIA JUSTINE TUMANG

I'm anxious about the trip. At sixteen, I lack patience and dread flying. I take out my CoverGirl compact from my bag and dab my sweaty nose. It's March 1995, and I'm standing beside my parents at Los Angeles International Airport as we check in for our flight to the Philippines. I put my compact away and pull the handle of my hefty luggage, following my parents to the airline counter. Dad lifts the first of our three suitcases onto the scale, while Mom hands our passports and itinerary to the ticket agent, whose red curly hair frames her pallid face. The agent pauses. She gazes at her computer screen, and then at Mom, repeating this motion several times.

Mom looks haggard, the dark circles under her eyes an indication that she'd been crying the night before. Her dark brown eyes appear dismal, bruised. *Wow,* I think, *Lola Carmen is really dying.* As I consider this possibility, my petite frame shrinks. I absentmindedly rattle my silver hoop earrings in an attempt to shake away my thoughts: *My grandmother is dying.* I desperately crave a tall glass of Long Island Ice Tea, a tequila shot, a cigarette, some weed—*anything* to help me cope. *What if she's dead when we get to Manila?*

The sounds of the airport bring me back to reality. All around me, people are jabbering and jostling their suitcases to the counter.

The ticket agent clears her throat and gives Mom back our passports. "Coach seats, is that right?" she asks.

Dad stands silently beside Mom, brushing his hands against his dark denim jeans. Flight announcements echo around us.

"Yes, we're all coach," Mom replies. The ticket agent starts typing in her computer. She looks up, her green eyes widening.

"There are only two round-trip tickets?"

"Uh-huh," Mom agrees, her voice soft and low.

I tug at Mom's sleeve. She looks at me, her right eyebrow raised, and gives me that *Patricia, let me handle this* look. I keep my arms to my side. I trust that she will correct the mistake.

"But there are three passengers? Two round-trip tickets and one going one-way to the Philippines. That right?" The ticket agent asks, biting her lip.

Mom puts her arms over the counter, hovering a few inches from the woman's face. "Yes," Mom whispers, talking sideways from her mouth. Mom is acting strange. The ticket agent looks irritated. I glance at Dad, who's nearby, obsessively filling out and tying address tags to our luggage.

I tug at Mom's sleeve again. "Why is there a one-way ticket?" I quietly inquire.

She shushes me, putting her index finger over her mouth. "Secret," she whispers, winking at me, enthusiasm coating her voice. As the ticket agent types away, Mom pulls me close, whispering under her breath. "Because we're going to get a good price from a relative," she informs me, "who works at a travel agency in Manila, that's why."

Something doesn't seem right, but I shrug it off. *Perhaps it has something to do with Lola Carmen's cancer.* My thoughts drift back to my sick grandmother.

"Here are your tickets, Mrs. Tumang; have a nice flight." The agent hands the tickets over, and Mom slips them into her black leather purse. My parents and I gather our things and leave the counter. Dad seems sad. There's something unsettling about the way my father looks at me, as if he is saying goodbye.

We walk toward the gates, together, as a family. My parents haven't told me the secret yet: that this trip isn't really about Lola Carmen's cancer; that they plan to leave me in the Philippines because they're afraid of what I've become in the States; that I won't return in time for school; that a year will pass before I return through these gates again; that when I do, Tagalog will be enveloping my once-English-speaking tongue; that my arms will be browner, my skin smeared with the salty scent of Manila Bay; that the girl they left behind will become a young woman, carrying a suitcase of tears and a huge secret of her own.

In my family, secrets—like seeds in the wind—scatter in different directions: over miles of sea, across land, through spans of decades. From one generation to the next, they grow and proliferate. I was born and raised in the United States, but the secrets of my family in the Philippines haunt me. Tito Jackie, Mom's first cousin, who died of a sudden heart attack in his midforties, had suffered silently from alcoholism—*but we don't talk about it.* Lolo Mike, my maternal grandfather's brother, battled alcoholism his entire life, up until his death in 2005—*we don't talk about that either.* Before he immigrated to the U.S. in the 1980s, Dad's father owned a gambling enterprise in San Fernando, Pampanga, the province where Dad's family originates—*but that's all just a fragment of the past.* Lola Carmen's daily mah-jongg games in Manila—*nothing but a hobby.* Tito Nestor, Dad's gay first cousin, died of HIV/AIDS complications in Pampanga in the mid-'90s—*but he really died of tuberculosis, poor thing.*

I am eleven when I have my first secret to keep. I steal a pair of earrings from a store in the Glendale Galleria, ten minutes away from where we live in Burbank, California. I slip the dangling silver hoops into the front pocket of my hoodie. I walk out of the store, giddy, energized, and elated. I crave this "high" feeling, slipping by unnoticed and committing an illegal act without repercussions. But by the time I turn fourteen, the stakes aren't high enough.

In Burbank, I secretly dabble in recreational drugs and drinking. Most of my friends are gangsters. I hang out with the "wrong" crowd: a brood of roughhousing Filipino American guys who are at least five years older than I am; who conceal butterfly knives in their socks; sport tattoos all over their muscular, burly bodies; pick fights with anyone who invades their territory. They abuse their girlfriends, take all kinds of drugs, and consume hard liquor like it's water. I run away from home a few times and hang out in L.A. neighborhoods where a slew of bullets explode like firecrackers on the streets. When I turn sixteen, I wear my regular hoochie getup: burgundy lipstick, a black halter top that constricts my breathing, and a skimpy skirt short enough to make Mom scream. By the time I'm a sophomore in high school, most of my girlfriends have had at least one abortion. We lose our virginity at fourteen, some of us at twelve. Secrets fuel my teenage existence.

But this is all I know of home. Like me, my friends and most of the kids in my school are children of Filipino immigrants. Something has brought us all together in Los Angeles, in this lifestyle of destruction, violence, and addiction. How far back must I trace a secret to find the source of its shame? How many homes must I search for before I can find what is missing in mine?

For as long as I can remember, Dad has come home angry from repressing his rage at the world for being treated like an immigrant. He takes out his fears, his frustrations, his agony, his loneliness, his unrelenting depression on Mom and me. Although he ultimately reaches a point of financial success, he is never happy enough. This is the immigrant mentality: If you do not own a BMW and a house with a white picket fence, then you are a *failure*. Dad buries this vicious belief until something happens at work—a white boss beats him down, another white coworker gets a raise—and then Mom and I experience his pain—his failed "American Dreams"—on our bodies, in our psyches, in our hearts, scars both visible and invisible, scars that leave permanent, damaging stains.

I get kicked out of my first high school at age sixteen. I transfer to another one, but don't stay there long. My parents aren't home much. They work long hours, and when they come home, they're emotionally absent. We have a routine: Mom comes home after work to cook and clean the house. By the time the dishes are washed, the table cleaned, she plops on her bed, exhausted. Dad comes home late, beat down by his job and his unforgiving self-deprecation. Nothing can "feed" his hollowness. Years later he'd confess to me that his life is tinged with regret—for what he wanted in America but couldn't have. Despite the violence he inflicted in our home for most of my childhood and teenage years, I now embrace Dad with compassion. I can see clearly how life in America, while giving us new opportunities as immigrants, had crushed my father's hopes. Dad had high expectations of himself and of me, his only child, and when neither was fulfilled, our home, as we knew it, fell apart.

I start to run away from home fairly regularly, but I don't stay away long. I am unable to communicate with my parents about the depth of my grief, how the simultaneous violence and absence at home leave me wounded and feeling unsafe. No one tries to understand me. In my parents' eyes, I have failed them. In my eyes, they have failed me.

By the time we land at Ninoy Aquino International Airport, I've been awake for nearly fifteen hours. My body shifts in my cramped seat, awake with anticipation. When we disembark, the Manila heat stings our faces. The city's polluted odor nauseates me. Mom holds my hand as we walk toward the customs line and the baggage claim beyond. Dad's mood elevates as he peers through the floor-to-ceiling windows along the corridor. "Hey, Pat, look at that sign," he says, pointing outside, "*Mabuhay.* Do you know what that means? Welcome home." I glimpse the neatly trimmed hedges that border the letters made of white flowers. *Mabuhay.* I don't feel at home. Already I miss my soft blue-checkered comforter, my homecoming pictures and stuffed animals on the shelf above my bed, my circle of friends in the States.

Lola Carmen's driver picks us up from the airport, and we arrive at her Taft Avenue house without much traffic. When Lola greets us at the door, I cling to her body in a desperate embrace, my suitcase still at my feet. When I see Lola, my fears are assuaged. She is bubbly, warm, and robust. Her beige skin has a healthy glow. She walks with a steady gait, fingers still clutching onto her rosary. Her dyed brunette hair is styled into a bouffant, her thin lips are coated in orange-red lipstick, and she wears her finest linen pantsuit. She doesn't look sick at all. At sixty-nine, she still possesses the charm and elegance that made her a province beauty in her twenties. A string of delicate, shiny pearls dangles below her breastbone, the site of her recent excavation. The mastectomy of the prior year has left half her chest hollow. Her billowing silk blouse hides the knotted scars that remain.

We enter the house, and Mom's brothers and their families greet us with kisses. One of my *titos* approaches me in the *sala* (den) and gives me a big hug. "So Lola's sick again, huh?" I ask him, sadness in my heart. My uncle looks at me quizzically. "What do you mean? Lola's been fine! Your parents know that! She's in remission. The mastectomy removed all of Lola's cancer." A knowing feeling resurfaces, and I sense that something terrible is about to happen. *Why did my parents lie to me?*

I feel afraid to confront my parents. Ironically, their secret makes me feel safe, that by not being exposed to the truth, I will be able to prolong a semblance of naivete, despite my intuition telling me that my world will soon break open at the seams. I desperately want to believe that my parents could do me no wrong, despite evidence to the contrary.

I sit on what I want to say for eight days. After more than a week of endless visits with relatives and hushed conversations, I find myself in the car with my parents. When we arrive at Makati Medical Hospital, I am bewildered and suddenly scared. I know we're not here to find out about Lola's prognosis, but I can't imagine why we're here.

Finally, Mom confesses that she wants me to take a pregnancy test. "We were so worried about you when you ran away. We just want to be sure." I had run away a week before we'd boarded our flight to Manila, but I hadn't suspected that it was the final straw for my parents, that my running away was what had initiated this trip. I don't know if I'm more pissed off that Mom thinks I had slept around when I ran away, or that they lied about Lola's cancer coming back, or that they don't believe me when I tell them I've gotten my period since we've been in Manila.

Inside the hospital, Dad paces the length of the hallway, and Mom sits quietly in the chair next to mine. I'm nervous. I've never taken a pregnancy test before. "How long are we supposed to wait?" I ask.

Mom's eyes silence me. I see tears well up in the corners. She faces me directly and shudders.

"What's wrong, Mom?" I ask. "Are you sick? Is that really why we're here?" My heartbeat is steadily rising. Mom starts crying into her hands. "Mom?" I tug at her sleeve. She is oblivious. Dad runs back toward us from the other end of the hallway when he sees Mom crying. He puts his hand on her shoulder.

"What's wrong?" I ask both of them again. "Why isn't anyone telling me anything?" I want to scream inside the small, claustrophobic hallway. I want to shatter the eerie silence.

Mom pulls out a handkerchief and wipes her eyes. She sighs. Her eyes are red. Dad's brows furrow. "Your mother and I . . . " Dad begins. "We . . . we . . . "

Dad, who is normally proud of his unaccented English, appears to lose his ability to speak. I hear voices at the end of the hallway, doctors making their rounds. I smell Band-Aids and chemicals and different kinds of perfume. I smell flowers and body odor and air freshener. I smell my parents' fear, an invisible, pervasive stench.

Mom's face is near mine, and I can see that she is crying and smiling at the same time. I know this expression well. She smiles when she's upset but I can never tell what lies beneath the facade. There is never just sadness. There is never just happiness. It's always a combination of both, as if each were trying to one-up the other for time on the stage.

"We're leaving you behind," Dad finally manages to say, his voice low and languid. His cheeks are ruddy and pockmarked under the fluorescent lights. "We don't know what to do with you. We worry about your safety. We don't know when you'll come back. You'll stay here for as long as it takes. When we leave for the States in four days, you'll remain here with Lola."

During the year that I live in the Philippines, I make new friends, go to a Catholic all-girls' school, adapt to Philippine weather, and embrace Filipino culture as my own. I take on a different skin as a Filipina living in the Philippines, as someone who has learned in a year how to *bola* with my elders, how to make *tsismis* and *tsika*, and how to drink San Miguel beers till my eyes see hazy through a film of drunken stupor. I learn how to speak Tagalog fluently. I take over Mom's childhood bedroom in Lola Carmen's house in Malate, which is now imprinted with my endless array of beauty products and photos of me and my new *barkada* (group of friends) taped to the bathroom mirror. The house that Mom grew up in now feels like home, and this strange country that I'd only seen in whirlwind visits from the States during Pasko (Christmas), I've made my own.

I have forged an identity here—despite my Americanness. I've been accepted by my homeland's people; I've made new friends; I've gotten closer to my relatives. I smoke cigarettes and drink beer with my *titos*—unheard of for a *dalaga* (young woman), but since I'm a *balikbayan* with a rebellious streak, I get an automatic "in." That's Filipino culture, my family's culture, my *barkada's* culture: Drink your worries away. My *titos* are musicians; I see them play at their gigs, a beer in one hand, a guitar pick in another. Tito Ed buys me a beer. So does Tito Martin. Then another, and another. When the gig is over, I'm sloshed, tripping over my platform heels, my uncles ushering me home to Malate.

I lay awake at night, nauseous and drugged. I skip school often. I lie to Lola Carmen about my whereabouts. I manipulate my way in and out of sticky situations. In trying to recall my memories of the U.S., I feel like I'm conjuring up a past life, long gone. My parents are thousands of miles away, and I am unable to articulate the rage I feel at being abandoned by them. Instead of expressing it outwardly, I turn inward, taking every given opportunity to punish my body. As I form a closer relationship to my parents' homeland, I develop a drug and alcohol habit, which is unlike my occasional drinking and recreational drug use in the States. It's every day; it's my livelihood; it's the only way I know how to survive in my new home.

I also witness Lola Carmen's slow disintegration over the course of the year. One day she has an appetite; another day she doesn't. Mom mails bulky packages of Ensure supplements from the States. Lola adjusts to a liquid diet. The Lola who has always been a voluptuous woman, with thick *brazos* and wide hips, is shrinking. Lola Carmen, the one person who has stood by me as I struggled to regain myself in the Philippines, is slowly dying before my eyes. In anticipating her death, I experience the loss of an emotional home that is rooted in Lola's presence.

One night I come home drunk at 5:30 AM. In my bathroom, I'm puking in the toilet some time before Lola barges in. By the time she finds me, I've fallen asleep with my head on the toilet seat. She's ready to leave for her six o'clock mass at Malate Church. Her voice rings in my ears, "Patricia, *naga ano ka?"* ("What are you doing?") I open my eyes. Saliva drips down my chin, the putrid aroma of bile clinging to my breath. Lola shakes me, telling me to get up and go to sleep.

"La . . . la . . . sing ako, Lola," ("I'm drunk") I tell her.

"Sabad sa imo! Indi ako kaaguanta!" ("You're disobedient! I'm fed up!") she yells in Ilonggo and walks out, slamming the door behind her. I hate what I force Lola Carmen to endure during this time. She is disintegrating and so am I. I want to be the good *apo* (grandchild), but my addiction to *shabu* (methamphetamines) and alcohol clouds my judgment and ability to be present to myself and to the world. My time in the Philippines, while bringing me closer to Lola Carmen and to reclaiming my identity as a Filipina, is also a journey to a homeland of addiction.

In the Philippines, I meet other Filipino Americans who had been sent back under circumstances similar to my own. We are all displaced, all far away from home. In our collective "homelessness," we find home in each other, in our newfound survival tactics: the drugs, the drinking, the partying. There are many moments when I risk my personal safety to get "high." I get thrown in a decrepit jailhouse with some of my new girlfriends in Quiapo, a poor Manila ghetto, because our drug dealer's neighbor had tipped off the police. In that lonely, dirty jail cell, I am frisked and humiliated. I am afraid that the male cops will kidnap or sexually assault us. Instead, they confiscate our drugs, and one of my friends tells me that they're most likely using them to get high themselves—a common irony. The Philippine police regularly conduct drug raids, not to abide by the law—the cops are corrupted by the government and a poor economy anyway—but to quench their own addictions in a country that is so devastated by poverty, violence, and colonization.

Without realizing it, I do not know who I am if I'm not high or drunk; I don't want to face myself because I feel so out of control. My parents' decision to send me away confirms this: I am too much too handle. I internalize Mom's emotional duality of sadness and happiness. Like Mom, I can't distinguish between the two. When I'm "high" I feel so happy; my problems seem to vanish the more I binge. When I come down from my high, I crash hard, my sadness devouring me in its brutal completeness. Either way, I feel "homeless." But my feelings of elation when I'm high are only temporary. Once they wear off, I'm stuck knowing that I can never feel completely happy in one place—that I have no homeland to speak of. Not in the Philippines. Not in the States.

When I return to the U.S. at my parents' request more than a year after they left me, I carefully guard the secret of my addiction.

Back in my parents' home, I feel disoriented once again. It's too late in the semester to start school. I soon find a new *barkada,* a group of Asian American addicts whose primary purpose in life is to get high. My friends give me drugs, and I sink deeper into my drug habit. During this time, my parents are clueless. And though I keep it well hidden, I recognize that my addiction has become my identity.

More than a decade has passed since then, a decade during which I've tried to re-create new homes outside of secrets. Having grown up entrenched in deceit, I sometimes stumble in my path toward recovery, toward making myself whole again. When I returned to the Philippines in November 2003, I returned to my homeland with a different perspective. In my seven-year absence, Lola Carmen passed away, having finally lost her battle with cancer. I couldn't afford the plane ticket to attend her funeral.

In 2003, I am back in the Philippines without my parents. I am able to take stock of all the changes happening inside and outside of my body. The stinging heat of Manila still packs the same intensity as it hits my face. The sights and sounds of Malate, once so familiar, have altered since I was last there. I return at twenty-four, not only as a sober adult, but with a new identity, and a new secret: I am a lesbian. Instead of confronting my addiction-induced haze in Malate bars, I see Adriatico Circle, the nightlife epicenter of Malate, for its thriving gay and lesbian culture. Malate has evolved into a gay mecca in my absence. The sight of drag queens singing karaoke at a Malate nightclub overwhelms me. Just as Manila has changed, so have I. My once portable home of addiction, in which I had felt both blindly comfortable and completely out of control, was a home I was finally able to abandon on my own terms. Marching down Roxas Boulevard, the panoramic waters of Manila Bay glistening to my right, I am thrust into a new sense of home—as a Filipina American lesbian participating in an LGBT pride parade in Malate.

I visit Lola's grave at the family plot in Parañaque. I had buried my tears when Mom called to tell me that Lola Carmen died a year earlier. Now, grief consumes me as soon as I enter the cemetery. *Now that Lola is gone, the Taft Avenue house sold, what do I have left to connect me to this country?* At Lola's grave, I light incense and say a prayer. I behold the cold marble monument that bears my Lola's name and say goodbye to her. In the bleak morning of that dreary day, Manila's sky withholds its potency, the sun hidden behind gray clouds. I resist the urge to flee, to bury my pain deeper into my body like I've done so many times before. The tears trickle out slowly, until I can't hold them back any longer. "Lola," I say, "I miss you." The marble stares back at me, impenetrable. I cry harder, releasing all my secrets. I tell Lola Carmen all my truths, what I can scrape together from a lifetime of deception. "I'm home, Lola," I shout out loud. At that moment, the sun peeks out from the clouds. The heat comes back with incredible force. I can't help but believe that this manifestation is Lola's presence. I hear the wind whisper, the birds chirp above. I watch the sky turn cerulean blue. I feel the sun's warmth permeate my skin—a deep, lingering feeling of peace and connection to my homeland, my body, my grandmother, my identity, my painful past—a chain of secrets finally broken.

Journeys to Jerusalem

LISA SUHAIR MAJAJ

For almost forty years I have been going to Jerusalem. Although I grew up in Amman, my earliest memories tap into the hills and stones of Jerusalem and splinter in its rocky soil. This is true even though my coherent recollections of Jerusalem began later, after I turned seven, when the eastern part of the city fell under Israeli occupation. At what point does experience turn into memory? Traces register at the deepest layers of consciousness, and we are heir to things we cannot always name.

Before 1967, my older sister recalls, we could drive from Amman to Jerusalem for lunch and back in a single day, untrammeled by checkpoints and borders. (Now, when Palestinians cannot even go the short distance from Ramallah to Birzeit—much less from Amman to Jerusalem—without being forcibly reminded of their occupied status through multiple checkpoints, ditches dug across the roads, and the steadily encroaching separation wall, this is wondrous to contemplate.) This earlier time of unhindered Palestinian access to Jerusalem exists, for me, before the onset of clear memory, residing instead in a shadowy realm of impression that is almost mythical. After all, despite the long legacy of United Nations resolutions, Palestinian claims to justice appear to have taken on the characteristics of a fairytale: a story of wish fulfillment told at night to credulous children, but dismissed by the powers of the world in the light of day.

I have no explicit recollection of those early family visits to Jerusalem: the drive down into the richly fertile Jordan valley past fields of banana and tomato, and then up again toward the dun-colored Palestinian hills that formed the bass note for Jerusalem's symphonic walls. But subtle impressions of light and shade, the smell of freshly turned earth, the springtime syncopation of poppies and wild mustard by the roadside, the off-white facades of stone buildings rising on the eastern approach to the city whose chipped facets held light like an internal glow must have made their way into my subconscious, emerging later as a sensation of mysterious familiarity till it seemed I had always been traveling this route. Mingled sights and sounds and smells of the city itself must similarly have registered on my earliest awareness: the majestic vista of the Dome of the Rock, its golden hemisphere casting a glow over the city; the worn bulwark of the Old City walls, eloquent with antiquity; the streets filled with snarls of cars, people, and sometimes donkeys; blaring horns, drivers shouting at each other, vendors calling out their wares; and the proliferation of odors as car exhaust and perspiration collided with the distinct aromas of *za'atar* and freshly roasted coffee.

In contrast, my relatives' house off Saladin Street, near Herod's Gate, provided for us an oasis of calm: The cacophony of the street would fall away as we passed through the tiled corridor leading to the internal garden fragrant with lemon and jasmine, and then to the house itself, where we were welcomed with kisses and exclamations. For me, the child of an American mother and a Palestinian father, the embracing welcome offered by my Jerusalem relatives was a comfort: proof that one could be different and yet still belong. I might be *Americaniyeh;* my brown hair and hazel eyes might set me off from my black-haired, black-eyed cousins, whose fluency in English,

German, and Arabic put my monolingualism to shame. But with family, we were all *beit Majaj,* of the house of Majaj. And when my aunt called us to lunch, to a table groaning with *kusa mahshi* and *wara' dawali* and *baba ghanouj,* there was no distinction made among the cousins: We were simply "the children," expected to behave properly and eat well.

Within the context of Israeli occupation, moreover, we were all, U.S. passports or no U.S. passports, Palestinian. As a child I did not fully understand the words "occupation" and "military rule." But I could see how my father's face froze to an impassive mask when we approached Israeli officials at the bridge crossing between Jordan and the West Bank, how soldiers gave orders and we were forced to obey. Although we made the crossing along with other foreign-passport holders, our documents processed in air-conditioned buildings instead of in the sweltering (or, in winter, freezing) tin-roofed areas where West Bank Palestinians spent long hours waiting to be cleared for passage, we were invariably treated differently: called to one side, searched and questioned while tourists moved through unhampered. Most unsettling, from my child's perspective, was seeing my father, at home the epitome of power, drained of his authority by these gun-toting Israelis rifling through our documents. As we waited for transportation to take us into the occupied West Bank, I stared out at the Israeli flag blazoned onto the Palestinian hillside like a tattoo on raw flesh and wondered what Palestinians had done to deserve this treatment.

When we finally reached Jerusalem and the haven of my aunt's house, these humiliations seemed, in some way, like badges of honor. The more harassed we were on our journey to Jerusalem, the greater was our sense of being Palestinian. Even my American mother participated in this sense of communal belonging, as if by marrying a Palestinian she had married not only into a family, but into a national experience. This was hammered home years later, when she checked into an Israeli hospital, seeking a diagnosis for the mysterious and debilitating skin problems that later proved to be manifestations of cancer. The Israeli nurses, who knew she was married to a Palestinian, did not change her blood-stained sheets; after she had asked for fresh linens for days, they finally tossed the clean sheets on the floor and told her to make the bed herself. When she died at the age of fifty-one, after years of futile searching for a cure, the memory of such indignities lacerated me.

Even at an early age, I could see that to be Palestinian meant being part of something larger than the immediate family and its expectations. It meant being connected to a land, a people, and a history, all of which were symbolized by a single city: Jerusalem. If Palestine was the homeland whose echoes reverberated through our lives no matter where we lived or how we sought to distance ourselves, Jerusalem was the emotional center of this homeland. Despite the fact that I grew up feeling in many ways distinctly American, on some level I too wanted to be included in this national definition.

As such experiences poured, wave by wave, over my consciousness, they laid down traces, so that even before I could recall specific trips to Jerusalem, this homeland had become part of my mental landscape. Going there seemed a bit like visiting a grandparent: something natural and inevitable, a right as well as an obligation. Jerusalem–and through Jerusalem, Palestine–lived in me the way a grandparent's genes live on in the body of a child: a mysterious habitation linking generations. No matter how much time passed between my visits, Jerusalem echoed through my consciousness, and with each arrival I was transfixed by that deep chord of familiarity: summer heat beating on stone, the drumming of winter rain.

Since childhood I have been testing my voice against this echo. And for forty years I have been making this journey to Jerusalem–the way a musician rehearses a melody, the way a swimmer goes to the sea.

In my childhood recollections, Allenby Bridge, then Jordan's only portal to Palestine, was a simple wooden structure across a murky channel of water that seemed wholly unworthy of its mythical reputation. Was this muddy stream really the famous River Jordan, the place of Jesus' baptism, the river celebrated in literature and song? Even on winter crossings, when the water moved more swiftly and rushes laced the surface like camouflage, the river seemed disconcertingly unimpressive. Gazing down at it as we rattled across the bridge in the bus designated for that purpose (or, on occasion, walked across, suitcases in tow), I marveled at the importance of this seemingly insignificant body of water. And I marveled, too, at the fact that this stream was all that separated Jordan and Israel: Would these muddy banks really hold enemy tanks at bay?

I knew that "crossing the Jordan," whether in American culture or biblical stories, was supposed to signify a passage from slavery to freedom. After all, I attended an American school until I was a teenager, and my best friends were missionary kids. But in the local Palestinian context that I also inhabited, the Jordan River stood, instead, as the demarcation line between dual oppressions: exile and occupation. On the eastern bank of the river, Palestinians lived in forced separation from their homeland, often in desperately poor refugee camps. On the western bank of the river, Palestinians lived under Israeli military rule, often again in refugee camps forgotten by the world. Although my family lived comfortably in a middle-class neighborhood of Amman, I was aware of these alternate universes where refugee children with dirty faces and hungry eyes begged for food. And I knew, too, that being middle class did not exempt my father from the experience of exile: Like Palestinians everywhere, his future was held hostage, his identity denied. Between these two banks flowed the river itself, spanned by the insubstantial web of wood named after General Allenby, the commander who led British troops into Palestine in 1917, starting, one might say, the whole Palestinian tragedy.

Crossing the Allenby Bridge to the West Bank on our journeys to Jerusalem provided a hands-on education in the realities of Palestinian identity.

After the 1967 war, Palestinians who had fled the war were denied the right to return to their homes. Many of these were refugees for the second time, having first been made homeless by the establishment of the state of Israel in 1948. For them, the flight across the Jordan River in search of safety proved a life sentence of exile. Unlike them, we were able, by virtue of the U.S. passports we possessed (my father through marriage to my American mother, my sister and I through birth), to make that journey across the Jordan River in the opposite direction, toward Jerusalem. But we still could not escape the ramifications of being Palestinian. We crossed the river on transit visas, our stay limited, the parameters of our journey beyond our control. Although we might be detained at the bridge three hours instead of seven or twelve, we were not usually subjected to strip-searching, did not have to send our shoes to be x-rayed, and were generally spared the humiliations that were the lot of most Palestinians. Yet we knew that to the Israelis who controlled our access to my father's homeland, we were still Palestinian, still a threat.

For me, one of the particular hardships of the crossing was that we could not carry anything printed or handwritten across the bridge. Carrying published material, even a novel, meant long delays while we waited for clearance from the censor. I noticed, however, that these restrictions did not seem to apply to foreign tourists: I would watch jealously as northern European travelers sat casually reading books while they waited their turn.

Handwritten documents were even more problematic. Once we were delayed at the bridge for hours because my sister had a letter from a pen pal in her purse; we had to wait while the censor examined every word of that adolescent note for incriminating evidence. After that, I became paranoid about having anything printed in my possession. Even discovering a stray candy wrapper in my pocket with Arabic writing on it would send me into a frenzy of anxiety. And heaven forbid we carry names, telephone numbers, or addresses: These would trigger special attention and would leave us worried over what trouble we might have inadvertently caused the persons so named, since one never knew how information would be used. For this reason we never mentioned our relatives' names at the bridge, and we told the authorities that we would be staying at a local hotel.

Once, when I was a teenager—it might have been 1975—we planned to cross the bridge in company with British friends. At the bridge, an Israeli soldier looked up our names on a computer and then motioned my father into a cubicle. I could hear my father's angry voice and the insistent voice of the soldier. Then my father stormed out of the cubicle and told my mother that we were going back to Jordan. The official wanted to strip-search my father, something our American passports usually spared us from. My mother was in a quandary: If we turned back, we would be abandoning the guests we had promised to accompany. Finally, the Israeli soldiers told my father he would only be required to take off his shirt and loosen his pants, and my father, urged by my mother, grudgingly agreed. We passed through border control without further incident, but as we seated ourselves in the Arab car that would take us to Jerusalem, I could still see the set of my father's jaw.

Years later, in the early 1990s, I found myself standing in a cubicle at the bridge with my sister, my pants around my ankles, my jaw so tightly clenched that my teeth ached. A female Israeli solider had ordered me to unclothe. My sister, who had only been required to take off her shoes, raised her eyebrows and shook her head at me. But I was too upset to heed her silent warning. "Why do I have to take off my pants but she doesn't have to take off her skirt?" I demanded. "If you're worried about security, why don't you check us both?" Without looking up, the Israeli woman shrugged. "She can hide something in her shoes; you can hide something in your pants." I looked at my sister, whose open sandals revealed most of her feet, but whose long skirt, unlike my tight Capri pants, could have hidden all manner of things. The point, evidently, was not security but harassment. I had appeared angrier than my sister during our initial questioning, and I was being punished for it. I had a sudden vision of my father in perhaps that same cubicle, stripped to the waist while a bored young Israeli man wrote on a clipboard. Ten or fifteen years had passed, but the humiliation was the same.

In 1997 I traveled to Jerusalem through Tel Aviv for the first time. The terms of my United States Information Service speaking tour contract required me to fly the Israeli airline El Al, and as I entered the waiting lounge in New York, my stomach clenched with nervousness. But no one in the predominantly Orthodox Jewish crowd seemed to notice that I was Palestinian.

On the plane, the woman next to me was eager to talk. She told me that she had made *aliya* (moved to Israel) a year before and was still bringing her things over. In fact, she said, she had managed to sneak an extra suitcase onto this flight. "What do you mean?" I asked. She responded, clearly pleased with herself, "I went up to a man with only one piece of luggage and asked him if he would carry a suitcase for me." I was horrified. "But how could he take something from a stranger?" I asked. "Oh," she replied, "I knew he was religious, and I am too. We both knew it would be fine." I stared at her. For a moment I thought of telling her that I had agreed to carry a suitcase for a Muslim I did not know, just to see her reaction. But the image of armed marshals escorting me off the plane made me refrain.

In Tel Aviv I made my way out of the airport and avoided looking at the posters lining the walls: I didn't want to see Jaffa, my grandmother's hometown, billed as an Israeli tourist spot. The landscape on the drive from Tel Aviv to Jerusalem, a road I had not traveled before, seemed utterly familiar. When I arrived at my aunt's house in crowded East Jerusalem, little seemed to have changed. The parlor was cool and dark, as always. I drank lemonade flavored with rose water, tasting like years slipped from memory, and listened to news about life under occupation. Conflicts were erupting over Jabal Abu-Ghnaim, a green area in the West Bank taken over for a settlement against the protests of Palestinians as well as Israeli ecologists. That night I slept in the guest room, a room cluttered with books and photos. A picture of my dead mother looked down at me from the shelf above the television set; her face smiled me to sleep each night I was there.

A few days later, on Easter Sunday, I stood with my cousin on the Mount of Olives in the predawn, looking out over Jerusalem. We could see the yellow lights of Road Number One, a swathe of highway built over the ruins of many demolished Palestinian homes. Nearby, another set of yellow lights marked a settlement bypass road. Behind us, a hymn rang out from the assembled congregation. At that exact moment, the call to prayer resonated from one mosque, then another mosque. The sounds of worship, Christian and Muslim, wove together on the cold air without conflict.

Later, I sat in a parlor, waiting for a car that would take me to Amman, listening to two relatives and a neighbor share memories: the massacre of Deir Yassin, when survivors were paraded in trucks through the streets of Jerusalem and my father and uncle threw jackets up to women in the trucks to cover themselves; the 1967 war, when a neighbor fled with his family on a road specified by the Israelis as a safe route but returned soon after, alone, his entire family burned by napalm; 1948, how a family fled from Lydda on a road they were told led to safety but that led instead into the desert, a road on which many died. The tellers' eyes were sunk in their faces, their voices quick and low, as if relating something they didn't want to remember but couldn't let go of, as if history could be exorcised through narration.

When the driver who was to take me to the Allenby Bridge finally arrived, he told me that the West Bank roads had been closed down. A Palestinian student had been killed at a checkpoint; there were tanks outside every town. We drove through back roads of the West Bank, passing by settlement after settlement, stone facades claiming the hillsides aggressively, occupying the slopes above Palestinian villages whose contours, in contrast, blended in to the landscape. When we arrived at the bridge, my passport was processed at a high window that made me feel small. My last view of the occupied West Bank was of an Israeli flag leaning out over the muddy water of the Jordan River, planted on the last possible span of earth. Above us, even the sky seemed captive.

The first time I entered Israel through Haifa was not by choice. It was June 1982, and I was a senior at the American University of Beirut. A few days before exam period, the Israeli army began their brutal invasion of Lebanon. I fled the city, squeezed onto an open truck full of sweaty, jostling bodies. Then I fled the country, crowding into an open cargo boat filled with university students.

As dusk fell, our boat pulled away from the shore. Although the Israeli forces controlling the Lebanese harbor had granted our boat clearance, after an hour out of port we were apprehended by an Israeli gunboat. A spotlight moved slowly over the boat, pinning us to the night. Then Israeli soldiers came on board and took four students off our boat. Three were taken to the Israeli gunboat for interrogation; one, we later learned, was placed in a small rowboat with a soldier and rowed about in the dark in absolute silence with a gun held to his head, apparently to terrorize him. The rest of us stood on the open deck of our boat for hours, dizzy with exhaustion, clutching our passports and waiting—for the students to be returned, for further orders, for news of our fate. When dawn came we realized that our course had been changed: Our boat was heading toward Israel.

At the port of Haifa I gazed, stunned, at the coastal view I had never imagined I would see: red shingled roofs, a backdrop of brown earth. Soldiers brought bread and tomatoes on board in wooden crates while television cameras rolled. We must have made good headlines: *Israeli army feeds hungry refugees.* But as soon as the reporters left, the interrogations began. After some time, the American citizens on board were taken to the U.S.

consulate in Haifa. There we were offered the choice to return to our homes via Israel. For me, home was in Amman: I could have gone to my relatives in Jerusalem and then crossed the Allenby Bridge. I thought about the option all night. But when morning came the land seemed like a closed fist: I could not bring myself to enter.

Sixteen years later I came once more to Haifa from the sea. This time I was traveling from Cyprus to Jerusalem with my Greek Cypriot husband and our one-year-old daughter. Unable to find plane reservations to Jordan or Tel Aviv, we had decided to travel instead by boat. We journeyed all night, the boat's engine a steady roar beneath our sleep, and as dawn broke we found ourselves approaching Haifa. As we disembarked, memory washed over me like the ship's wake: light beating the coast, the land submissive beneath its weight. Inside the immigration hall, a female Israeli official chatted with my husband and smiled at my infant daughter. Then a burly Israeli man looked over her shoulder at my immigration form with its space for "father's name." He said something in Hebrew, and, within seconds, my passport had been stamped—ensuring that I would have to get a new passport if I wanted to travel to some Arab countries—and I was hustled to one side for interrogation. Who was I? What was my relationship to my traveling companions? Were they really my husband, my daughter? What was the purpose of my visit? Whom did I plan to see? To speak to? Where did I plan to go? Did I have family in Israel? Did I intend to visit them? I wonder: *Do they think we travel so far and will not see our families? That we will wander like strangers in our grandparents' land?* Their questions were relentless. When my child wailed, the interrogator merely raised her voice above the cries.

By the time I emerged from the immigration hall, I was furious. Despite our quantities of luggage, I insisted we take a local bus instead of a taxi to the depot where we planned to catch a bus to Jerusalem: I didn't want to spend any more money in Israel than I had to.

The bus from Haifa to Jerusalem wove through city streets melodious in morning light, past landscape so painfully familiar that I wanted to cry out in recognition. My grandmother's hometown, Jaffa, was called by its Canaanite founders Yafi, which means "beautiful." Haifa lived in my mind as its sister. Yet history had made me an outsider to the land.

The bus was half-filled with soldiers, men and women, who cradled their guns casually, commandingly, their smooth faces a reminder of how youth is sabotaged in defense of the state. I held my daughter close, whispering in her ear. It was her second journey to Jerusalem. The first time, I had carried her deep inside my body, secure from the probing eyes of the security officers who wanted to know what I carried with me, whom I planned to speak to, where I intended to go. In my oversize coat, I did not look pregnant, and so she slipped across the border without being noticed: a small victory I knotted deep within me, a talisman against the humiliations of interrogation. A few days later, at a concert in Birzeit, my father's hometown, I felt her move for the first time. A female vocalist was singing lines of poetry by Mahmoud Darwish—something about longing and freedom. She hit a high note and held it; the child stirred violently with me.

As we traveled inland, the scenery shifted from brown earth to cultivated fields, orchards, houses. The sun moved higher in the sky; olive trees leaned toward each other like old men trading stories. The road curved toward Jerusalem through wooded hills that made deep swells in the land's body: a lover's terrain. Eventually my daughter grew restless, her uneasiness a reflection of my own growing ambivalence. I had only once before approached Jerusalem from the west, and the discord between the land's Arab past and its Israeli present strummed through my body.

Then Jerusalem broke upon our view like a wave cresting: stone and light on the ridge, buildings overtaking the land. The scene was as resonant as sunlight, the city rising from the hills like the stone it was made of, integral to earth, inseparable from it. I felt a surge of mingled emotion: ache of familiarity, the painful atonality of alienation. As we wound through West

Jerusalem neighborhoods, past stone houses that looked like those of my relatives, I saw that West Jerusalem was a splintered mirror image, part familiar, part strange. The city shone from every surface, as if breathing from within, indignities of entry and exclusion temporarily replaced by the constancy of stone, by light cascading down the hills, illuminating gray-green of pine and palm. But West Jerusalem was a closed world; we passed through as transients only, till the bus spat us out onto a summer sidewalk near the Green Line—into history, into the present.

Jerusalem is a mosaic. Our personal stories, images, and recollections are chips of stone enmeshed in the grain of history: the Damascus Gate at sunset, an Israeli soldier atop the Old City walls, a street crowded with traffic leading to a quiet interior garden. We come to the city bearing private histories, private sorrows, and find ourselves in the heart of a public space that is, like history itself, ancient and tormented.

Yet despite its historical and mythological aura, Jerusalem is not just a metaphor; it's a city. It has trash on the streets, graffiti on the walls, pollution and traffic jams, death and taxes. And for Palestinians, Jerusalem signifies land confiscations, home demolitions, ID revocations, the shrinking circle of occupation. While Jewish Jerusalem steadily expands into the eastern part of the city and the surrounding West Bank, Palestinian Jerusalem contracts to an ever-smaller space. This shrinkage, paralleled by the ever-more constricted conditions of daily life, is consolidated by the Israeli separation wall that has already relocated vast swathes of Palestinian land within illegal Israeli-defined boundaries and cut large numbers of Palestinians off not only from Jerusalem, but also from their orchards, their wells, their hospitals, their schools—from the basic necessities of life. Meanwhile, in East Jerusalem normal life becomes more difficult by the day. It is almost impossible for Palestinians to get permits for new construction; newlyweds are often forced to live with their families. The policy of confiscating Jerusalem residence permits from Palestinians for any and all reasons, thereby reducing the number of Palestinians in Jerusalem, has led to the steady diminishment of the community. Similarly, a legal ban enacted in 2006 forbidding Palestinians from living in Israel with an Israeli spouse seeks to further curtail the Palestinian presence within Jerusalem and Israel more broadly, while Palestinians holding foreign passports are increasingly denied reentry. Such policies consolidate the sensation of a tightening noose around Arab Jerusalem.

Going to Jerusalem is like entering a wound. We go to Jerusalem like bleeding medics, helpless against the injustices of the world. We go to Jerusalem like refugees from history, bearing nothing but our children, the future gripped between our teeth. We go to Jerusalem because the city lives inside us like the stone of a fruit. We go because we have voices, although the world does not have ears. We go because above Jerusalem's ancient walls the sky still rises, leavened with light.

Different Blood:
A Journey to Myanmar

WENDY MARIE THOMPSON

Had I been sneaky I could have torn out the yellowing page in the St. Theresa's Catholic Church directory on Father Neri's wooden desk while he took a telephone call in the back. On the opened page was the information I had come all the way from California to Myanmar to see: a record that confirmed that my mother had existed and actually lived a life here in a city previously known as Rangoon, when Myanmar was still called Burma. But I did not want to embarrass my boyfriend David's local Kayin[1] relatives who had accompanied me on this outing, so I behaved and waited for Father Neri to return.

In the 1950s, a Chinese Father had neatly inscribed my mother's Chinese name next to her newly Catholicized one. Father Neri was ethnic Kaya and did not handle the Chinese names well. He copied only the Catholicized names on the piece of paper before stamping it with the church seal and handing it to me.

In random order:

My grandfather's name was Paul.

My grandmother's name was Martina.

My mother's name was Maria Carmela.

This was their lives in English, as transplanted Chinese and as Catholics. They had been part of a small minority of Burmese Chinese brought together by a Chinese Catholic priest in a predominately Buddhist country full of pagodas.

Despite my grandfather's insistence on maintaining a Chinese household in Burma, my mother ended up in the States, where she found home in Chinatowns, Chinese churches, Mandarin soap opera television programs, ancestor worship, and celebrations where pork barbeque thick with sweet sauce and sautéed noodles were served. For my mother, Burma was only the house she once lived in, now standing empty since the tenants had long ago moved out.

My mother still speaks Burmese, although with a Chinese variation. And upon becoming a naturalized American in 1979, my mother picked up English with an immigrant accent. Her American life followed a rough trajectory: After settling with her mother and siblings in California, my mother met my African American father while she was an ESL high school student working part-time at the main public library in San Francisco. Soon after, she was run out by her family when they learned of the relationship. To them, my mother being with a black man was possibly the worst thing that could have happened to their Chinese family name and lineage.

I was born soon after in an American home where there was nothing specific in our food, television, language, customs, or celebrations to indicate the presence of Burmeseness. But in the houses of my aunts and uncles, there were artifacts that marked them as more than just hardworking, suburban Chinese Americans: a painting of Burmese women in traditional costume, a miniature replica of the harplike *saung gauk,* and *mohinga,* a soupy Burmese noodle dish. Framed photographs of their lives in Burma were absent, and there seemed to be no strong nostalgia for the life left there.

As a girl, I connected everything in my life to my mother, and therefore to Chinese culture. Given that it was her hands that prepared the meals in our immediate household—actually a mimicry of what my Southern African American grandmother would do in the kitchen with ham hocks and collard greens—I came to believe that even the Southern black cultural objects around me were also Chinese.

Race, culture, and home became polarized. Because we did not travel much as a family, we grew up isolated, my two sisters and I feeling much more at home when our mother spoke Mandarin (having long ago been forced to give up her spoken Burmese in order to reclaim her Chinese heritage). Our mother wrapped us in an affection that we did not sense from our African American father, who did little to offer an explanation of or defense against those who teased us about our hair texture, which did not match the wrapped rice food we brought to school.

Since his boyhood, my father had harbored an intense shame because of his race, his alcoholic father, and the poverty he grew up in. His family struggled to find their footing in the shipyard worker housing of Marin City, California. They left Louisiana for a place in the Golden State during World War II, which saw the largest continual migration of blacks from the South. My Chinese mother eventually learned how to make cornbread and red beans.

But much like my father, and because the table had already been set by my mother's family, I grew up to internalize feelings of embarrassment and inadequacy toward my working-class parents and my mixed race. I hardly ever felt at home in my own skin except for a few captured moments when I was myself: unprovoked, boundless, and free when out in nature or in quiet places with books. I adopted my father's frustrated anger, his defensiveness and cut downs, his feelings of defeat brought on from racism, from working dead-end jobs. We felt the brunt of this when my father came home angry after being put down day in and day out. The reasons for my father's aggression were never conveyed to me. My parents kept the contexts buried, believing that by shielding me, I would not be as traumatized as my father had been by racism and the stigma of blackness; that somehow I would naively be able to walk away dark-skinned, yet unscathed. Things only became complicated when I later found out that my parents were wrong, that—like my father—I too would be wounded by racism, the few times I was called a nigger and did not know how to fight back.

I grew up feeling that my birth, color, and race were terrible sources of shame. With this internalized, I strove to be more Chinese, to seek out a homeland that carried the face of only my mother. I arrived in her place of birth more than thirty years later, speaking only English with a regional Bay Area dialect, the face in my passport photo revealing my identity as an African Chinese American citizen.

I had wanted to see Burma, a place where my mother had still been in full form, at her best before moving to the United States and having a coarse and risky life. When independence came in Myanmar, the Chinese became like scabs on the skin, always an itch, a reminder of colonial power and privilege. My mother remembered hiding under her bed with her brothers and sisters while Burmese police would raid the household. In no time, the Chinese began to flee. But what I wanted to see was the wild and untamed place that my mother knew before the scab was picked, before the Chinese flowed like blood into larger streams in Canada and the United States. But what I found in Myanmar was an entire beat-down and scarred nation, a place where a bribe could buy you a bus ride, a checkpoint crossing, an entry or exit.

I knew that my mother had left Burma in 1965, when she was nine years old. In her absence, my maternal grandfather died, her siblings and mother were displaced, military rule was declared, and Burma changed its name to Myanmar. Three of my grandfather's children, including my mother, left Myanmar when they were young, while six siblings stayed behind. My grandfather could not afford to send them all; only my mother and two of her brothers were sent to Taiwan to "learn how to be Chinese." They had already begun to come undone in my grandfather's eyes, eating with their fingers, running barefoot in the street, speaking the local language. He saw these as an affront to being Chinese, his children assimilating into the local Burmese culture at the cost of becoming disconnected from their heritage.

My mother and her siblings did not attend Chinese school in Burma; it was assumed that they would receive a more thorough education–both in language and culture–when my mother and her two siblings moved to Taiwan. While there, under the watch of extended relatives, my mother was physically punished for speaking Burmese with her brothers. She was encouraged to speak Mandarin and told to forget all things Burmese.

In an earlier era, my mother's Burma once boasted numerous Chinese schools and colonial houses lived in by overseas Chinese merchant families with Burmese housekeepers. This was before the British were expelled in 1948 and the government changed hands. Burma had once been considered a safe Southeast Asian asylum for a people in constant relocation because it provided the freedom to trade, open up Chinese schools, erect temples and homes. In the 1960s there was severe political rioting and harassment against Chinese merchants and cultural institutions under the assertion that pro-communist demonstrators were bringing pro-Chinese propaganda.

Many felt that local Chinese merchants were creating a petit bourgeoisie class that oppressed the native Burmese. My maternal grandfather's occupation in the jade trade and the political instability in Burma forced my mother's family to flee to the States and assume a constant life of transience. My mother reunited with the rest of her family in California in 1974, after spending eight years in Taiwan.

Even now I do not know what to call it: Burma or Myanmar. When it had meaning to my mother, it was still Burma. Now the name is something else, curving over the flat text of the tongue, a foreign word that falls without the exotic pretext.

On the afternoon of January 2, 2006, my boyfriend, David, and I took our first ride in the back of a pickup truck after landing at Yangon International Airport in what is now Myanmar. I had no way of articulating what Burma would look like thirty years after my mother's leaving. And even though she described it to me as a young woman, I could not picture such a wildly different place: seeing an exalted Hindu cow at an Indian temple, eating sweet breads bought at the night market, watching a sweeping *longyi* sticking to the backs of bare legs during the monsoon season.

What I saw upon arriving could not be captured in its entirety by camera. A photograph would leave out so much of how foreign this world felt to me. Women wore *thanaka* makeup powder swathed across their faces, and barefoot Buddhist monks walked among armed soldiers at militarized posts. The beauty of lush banana palms, old crumbling buildings from the British colonial period, and narrow crooked streets with pedestrians spilling over into the way of traffic blended with the pace of women balancing baskets carefully on their heads. I tried looking beyond the surface, but I could not see my mother's face here.

I spent half an hour trying to locate my mother's house in Rangoon with the assistance of David's local relatives. And when we thought we had found it—a three-story occupied building painted light blue—I was too afraid to ring the bell and ask the neighbors if they could remember. You are related to *whom?* I did not look like them, these people who are all a color gradient of dust: brown, gray, tan, and taupe.

I was invited for lunch at David's aunt's house in a compound located down the street from St. Theresa's Catholic Church in Ahlone Township. The neighborhood consisted of Christian churches, sparse shading trees, and makeshift houses with wood slats for walls built on stilts above dirt ditches. There were no clear demarcations for yards, and the neighbors kept an assortment of things around their property: stray dogs, ducks, chickens, a one-eyed pig tied inside of a wooden wheelbarrow. David's relatives lived among the sounds of people speaking Kayin, Burmese radio programs blaring from small transistor radios, the washing and rinsing of metal cooking tubs. I was invited to take water from the barrel in the yard and wash my feet and arms, which had been bitten by mosquitoes. The swelling spots on my brown skin marking—like proof—the fact that I was not from here: I had different blood.

I wanted to make a good impression in Myanmar. I felt that I should live up to my own claim to this place, as peculiar as it was to me. I was not just some random American tourist. I was born to a Burmese Chinese mother, whose own citizenship of this place once made her native. Didn't that maternal proximity, those roots, matter? But I was traveling abroad with the face of my African American father, and I could be nothing other than foreigner to the native Burmese.

David's relatives never asked where my father was from. Perhaps they thought nothing of it, but surely they must have noticed that I was one of the few people in recent history to be black and traveling through Myanmar. Even the Burmese Indians—who were significantly darker-skinned than me—examined my face when I went by. It was a strangeness that I learned to accustom myself to.

This was not like the wild staring I received as a mixed-race adolescent back in the States, where Americans of various ethnic backgrounds took their liberties to touch and examine my hair; I became defensive and they wondered why I took offense. But in Burma, the assessment was somewhat different and more forgivable, as I was also encountering the strangeness of the country and its people. So when the priest who had first inscribed my mother's name for me at St. Theresa's Catholic Church told me that I looked like a "Negro," I only flinched a little at the connotation, figuring that it is simply the result of the British colonial period, when Burmese people experienced black people through caricatures in novels or early period films.

As much as I wanted to pass as Burmese, I had a difficult time doing so and eventually began to entertain myself with it. While in Mandalay, I became frustrated that my once-spoken Chinese had become eclipsed by my English. I was humiliated and angry that speculating military personnel in green flak jackets and dark-hued *longyis* kept insisting that, as a foreigner, I had to pay $3 above the regular admission price to enter the museums. I knew I could have bribed them, that all they were looking for were a few more American dollars to float in their busted economy. But I was not the ugly American tourist. I was not some white, upper-class woman, and I did not want to be treated as such. And so I put on my own show, throwing around a few words in my pidgin Chinese—anything other than English.

I remember first learning what I thought being American meant: living with money, speaking English, and embodying a kind of suburban middle-class whiteness. How was I American when I grew up with none of these? Still, I had grown up and traveled this far. Not being able to converse in Burmese was yet more proof, along with my ambiguously raced face, that I was not native. This knowledge was reiterated over and over through the curious stares from people on the bus, in the street, in the shops, at tourist attractions. In Bangkok, no one questioned my ethnic origin or color, and tourists had twice mistaken me for a Thai street vendor.

Still, as the face is foremost visible before language, it became the constant reminder of how alien I was, how far the Burmese Chinese lineage of my mother had delineated and changed, even on a hilltop temple made entirely of mirror shards, the neon colored turbans of ethnic Shan pilgrims reflecting in the cool morning sun.

The realization came gradually and was undeniable: This place was not home. Not in this land of a thousand pagodas, where monks diligently practiced compassionate, spiritual acts. Not here, where the night was ushered in under a wide black sky collected with stars, watching over a landscape scattered with military checkpoints and internal borders. There was no motherland for me here.

Myanmar had only been a temporary home to my mother, once. Had I any sense, I would have chosen China as my initial destination for a homecoming, following the Chinese patrilineal roots of the father (or in my case, maternal grandfather) and making a pilgrimage to his ancestral village. Yet my return to Burma was a journey to a place of rootlessness and to the possibility of belonging temporarily in one place, only to pack up and belong somewhere else.

Before leaving the country, I went to the night market in Yangon to buy pretty silk-stitched fabrics, which I hoped to wear back in the States. I also found wooden miniature Burmese dolls for David's mother, each painted in the traditional garb of the major ethnic groups of Burma: the Chin, the Mon, the Shan, the Kaya, the Rakai, the Kayin, the Burman, the Naga. I visited several temples and pagodas where Burmese girls sold Buddhist religious artifacts—wooden pieces of effigies, clay faces of antique statuettes—that I did not buy since they were always priced too high.

When I returned home, I was unable to describe Myanmar, the place that my mother has refused to visit after all these years. *Too dirty, too uncivilized,* she would claim when I begged her to take me back. And in the same way, I was at a loss over what to tell people who, in asking, were waiting to hear about a tropical Southeast Asia with elephant rides and white sandy beaches. How could I explain a country where I could not wash the dust from my hands, where the sound of Nina Simone's voice from a transistor radio in an open-air teashop in Mandalay reminded me of a connection to my father many time zones away? Her voice a harrowing testimony to my blackness—as unexplainable as it was to Burmese people—that would always follow me, both in face and in history.

When I tell my mother the stories about driving past Sule Pagoda, watching an otter stand up like a man on his own two feet at the Yangon zoo, nursing a sweet *falooda* at a soda shop, and wrapping over and over a draped *longyi* around my waist before stepping barefoot onto wet tiles at a pagoda, she is amused, moved to scrape from memory what fragments she can remember, those colorful nine years as a young girl in Burma.

Dakota Homecoming

DIANE WILSON

The motel clock on my bedside table read 4:10 AM, too early to get up and too late to hope for more sleep. I lay still with my eyes closed, trying to recall the dream that woke me and left a feeling of anxious violence lingering in its wake. I threw back the covers, then pushed open the drapes so that I could at least see the prairie night sky and a few stars beyond the casino's bright lights.

My overnight bag sat on the luggage stand, neatly packed and ready for an early departure. I had left my notebooks on the table, along with a few reference books, to packed quickly in the morning. My books detailed the history of the Lower Sioux Reservation, where I was staying at the Jackpot Junction Casino in Morton, Minnesota, about three hours southwest of Minneapolis. Before falling asleep I reread the chapter on the 1862 Dakota War, a bloody conflict between Dakota Indians and white settlers that had been fought in this area. The images haunted my dreams.

Later that morning, just before sunrise, I would meet my younger brother Dave in the motel lobby. I wondered how many other rooms were filled with people like us who had come to be part of the first-ever Dakota

Commemorative March. This event was planned to honor the Dakota people who were forced to walk 150 miles from the Lower Sioux Reservation to a prison camp at Fort Snelling after the 1862 War. We would begin the march shortly after dawn, walking more than twenty miles each day, regardless of weather, arriving at Fort Snelling the following week. The march would follow roughly the same route as the original, commemorating the 140th anniversary of a painful history that had never before been publicly acknowledged.

Eleven years of retracing our family history led me to the 1862 War, a long journey that began even earlier with my mother, Lucille Dion Wilson. She was enrolled on the Rosebud Reservation in South Dakota, where she grew up. Between the ages of ten and sixteen, she attended the Holy Rosary Mission School, a boarding school on the Pine Ridge Reservation. After moving to Minneapolis, she eloped with Chuck Wilson, a tall Swede from central Minnesota, and raised five children in a white suburb. When I was growing up, she told me that she was done with "all that"—referring to her Indian heritage. "We were poor," she said, "I'm glad to be out of it." With a stubborn lift of her chin, she refused to say more. Her reluctance to speak about her past seemed impenetrable.

At that time, I had no idea why boarding schools existed, nor did I have any sense of the history that surrounded the reservation system. Reading the word "assimilation" in my history book at school inspired the same yawn-inducing, this-is-dry-as-dirt reaction that I felt reading about history in general; it seemed nothing more than a list of names, dates, and places to be memorized for a test. Manifest Destiny, Lewis and Clark, and the 1862 Dakota War meant nothing to me. I believed that those events had all happened a long time ago to other people and had no relevance to my life.

My mother, on the other hand, was a mystery. All of us kids kept asking questions, trying to squeeze out whatever information we could get any time we were alone with her. Her life, her unimaginable life, dangled before us like a long thread reaching into the past, the single unraveled edge of something that was much larger than we could even begin to guess.

In my thirties, I began to retrace my family's history across South Dakota and Nebraska, where I gathered facts, anecdotes, and sepia-tinted photographs of relatives faded to ghostlike images. The struggle to understand the gap between my mother's past and my life, and the leap she made from Pine Ridge to Golden Valley, led me to the 1862 War and the Lower Sioux Reservation. What began as a simple question about my mother evolved into a search to understand my culture, identity, and family legacy.

At 5:00 AM I turned on the lamp and began to pack. On the desk lay the flyer that had come in the mail a month earlier, offering its scant details about the march. On the cover was a line drawing from the June 1863 issue of *Harper's New Monthly Magazine* that showed men and women from New Ulm attacking Dakota captives riding through town in a wagon. A shower of sticks and rocks fell on the Indians, while white women in long dresses stood poised to hurl more, their faces focused in rage upon their victims.

I was surprised that so much attention would be given to the march, an event that was little more than a footnote in history books. Most of the accounts focused on the six-week war that exploded in August 1862 on the Lower Sioux Reservation as a result of the frustrations of failed treaties. Hundreds of white settlers were killed; their farms were destroyed. When the war was over, much of the white population of Minnesota demanded that the Dakota people be forcibly removed from the state, regardless of which side they had supported during the war. The march was usually mentioned briefly as a four-mile train of about 1,700 Dakota—mostly women, children, and elders who were forced to walk under military guard through towns filled with outraged settlers to a prison camp near the Mississippi River at Fort Snelling.

I had stumbled into this history two years earlier while searching for information about my great-great-grandmother, Rosalie Marpiya Mase, or

Iron Cloud, a full-blood Dakota. After years of chasing my family's story, the trail finally led me to Rosalie, who lived directly across the Minnesota River from the government-run Lower Agency on the Lower Sioux Reservation, an assortment of buildings that included a school, sawmill, and stone warehouse. No one in my family knew much about Rosalie or her involvement in the war. When the fighting started, she and her French Canadian husband, Louis LaCroix, took refuge at Fort Ridgely with white settlers. Rosalie and her seven mixed-blood children were among the few Dakota who were not forced to march to Fort Snelling; they remained behind in Minnesota after the war.

Rosalie was the reason I had come to be part of the march. Although she was spared the traumatic experience of the march, she was involved in the violent war that preceded it. My theory was that Rosalie's separation from her community was as harsh, in some ways, as the experience of the people who were imprisoned at Fort Snelling. Her survival had also come at a terrible cost. The legacy of Rosalie's separation was then passed from one generation to the next as the pain and trauma slowly drove a deep wedge in my family's Dakota identity.

What I did not know in those early-morning hours was whether the Dakota people whose families had lost everything, sometimes even their own lives, would accept my family's tenuous connection to the march. The 1862 Dakota War had inspired a deep hatred between whites and Indians, feelings that sometimes still lie just beneath the surface. My brother is dark like our mother, but I look like a middle-aged, middle-class, green-eyed *wasichu*.

My comfort came from those notebooks and history books still stacked on my table. Within this collection of facts and theories lay my connection to the past, and my only protection against the forces that had drawn me here.

At sunrise on November 7, the sky was bright and cloudless, the air still sharp and cold, and the sun had not yet melted a thin layer of frost that covered the grass. After stopping once to get directions to the community building, Dave and I walked into a windowless basement and paused near the door, getting a feel for the room and the people who had already gathered there.

The center of the basement was crowded with a long table filled with metal trays of food donated by the casino—bacon, sausage, eggs, sweet rolls, orange juice, and coffee. About two dozen people were scattered at tables. Almost immediately, one of the march organizers, Angela Cavender Wilson, greeted us with a warm handshake. She and her three children had flown in a few days earlier from Arizona, where she teaches American Indian history at Arizona State University. She waved a hand at the food table, urging us to eat. We would leave following a short prayer ceremony after breakfast.

Angela's father, Chris Mato Nunpa, then came to shake hands with us. He taught Indigenous Nations and Dakota Studies at Southwest Minnesota State University in Marshall, not far from Morton. He had taken on the job of organizing the logistical side of the march, finding places for the marchers to sleep each night and asking for donations of food from various tribes and organizations. He said later, with his quick laugh, that his Indian name ought to be changed to Worry-Wart.

"Who are you here with?" he asked.

"Ourselves," was my reply.

This brought a laugh from Chris. "I mean, do you have Dakota relatives at the Lower Sioux?" He was trying to understand our connection to the march.

"Our great-great-grandmother lived across the river from the Lower Agency when the 1862 War broke out," I said. I didn't explain that she was not part of the march. Chris nodded his head, pleased to hear that another Dakota family had returned to the area for this event. He introduced us to several other people at one of the tables and then greeted new arrivals.

After breakfast we gathered outside in a large circle, about forty or so people who ranged in age from five to eighty-five. The sun was beginning to warm the air, but my breath still formed a cold cloud as I waited, arms folded against my body for warmth. One of the men slowly walked around the circle carrying a bowl of burning sage as Chris Mato Nunpa welcomed us. He reminded us how our ancestors had left the Lower Sioux Reservation 140 years earlier, when almost the entire nation of Dakota people was imprisoned or removed from Minnesota following the end of the Dakota War.

"On November 7, 1862, a four-mile train of mostly women and children was forced to march to the concentration camps at Fort Snelling. Many of our people died on this trip," he said. "The townspeople from Henderson, New Ulm, and Sleepy Eye threw bricks and stones as they passed by, and one woman even threw boiling water. Some people ask why we need to remember this, why we can't just let it go. The march has never been acknowledged for the tragic event that it was. It's been covered up and forgotten. It's time for the Dakota people to remember their ancestors, to grieve for their family who were part of this march. This used to be Dakota land. It was all taken away from us. When you allow these things to be covered up, that's part of colonization."

Chris would later explain that colonization meant that not only had Europeans stolen ancestral lands and sought to dismantle Indian culture, but that Indians themselves had absorbed these attitudes over time. If historic trauma occurs that is never resolved, never acknowledged or forgiven, then the act of closing one's eyes to it is a form of collusion with the colonizer. Even if the event occurred 140 years earlier.

Up until this point, no one had explained our family's experience as part of a broad historical process: Christianity, boarding schools, land allotment, and blood quantum were all persuasive tools in assimilating families like ours. My first reaction was one of relief that our family experience was shared by many others—followed quickly by a return of the simmering anger

I now carry as a result of my research into Dakota history. I was beginning to understand how abstract concepts like assimilation or colonization can raise a feeling of rage when applied to my own family.

After a closing prayer spoken in Dakota,[1] we formed a loose group that moved slowly down the long driveway leading to the road. The group was led by Leo Omani and his "red pony," a vehicle of mature years that Leo and his nephew had driven from their reservation in Saskatchewan, Canada.

We walked along the shoulder of the highway behind an eagle staff of thirty-eight feathers that commemorated the thirty-eight warriors hanged at Mankato after the 1862 War. After a mile, the "red pony" stopped and Leo climbed out carrying a three-foot wood stake with a red prayer tie near the top and the names of two of the original marchers written on each side in Dakota. Leo asked one of the elders to translate the names. After we listened to the names, he began searching the ravine for something to pound the stake into the ground.

"Aha," Leo cried, holding a large rock above his head. "A Canadian hammer!" He nailed the stake swiftly into the ground. One by one, each of the marchers placed a pinch of tobacco around the stake, pausing a moment in silent prayer.

The march had begun.

Each day we walked at least twenty miles, following approximately the same route as the original marchers. After a long day of walking, we hobbled into a church or school gymnasium, sat wearily at the tables, and ate supper. Shoes were immediately loosened. When it came time to fill plates with food, many people moved to the table on slow, stiff legs and sore feet. After dinner, marchers offered their stories about their families' experience in the original march or during the war.

One evening, Angela explained that the march was conceived as a way to understand how the social problems that Indian communities struggle with—alcoholism, depression, suicide, abuse—are a consequence of colonization. "We need to come to terms with the violence that was perpetrated against us because I think many of us today carry a great deal of what we might call historical grief[2], that pain that hasn't been reconciled for all of the injustices perpetrated against us."

Sleeping mats were unrolled on the floor for those who stayed, and each night we fell quickly into deep, exhausted slumber. Each morning began with breakfast, prayers, and sometimes a pipe ceremony, and then the group returned to the last wood stake that had been placed the night before.

We walked through the towns of Sleepy Eye, New Ulm, and Mankato, names made infamous by townspeople who channeled their own grief into murderous rage. But this march was peaceful, and we passed through these towns without incident. The route became more difficult as the long caravan of marchers began walking on the shoulders of increasingly busy highways.

After the first warm day of marching, when the afternoon sun still felt like late summer, the weather soon reverted to fall. By the fourth day, arriving in Henderson after long hours buffeted by the high winds that swirled behind each passing truck, the group marched silently for the last hour into a bitter, cold sleet.

On the morning of the seventh and last day of the March, I woke at 5:00 AM, my hip aching so much that it hurt to stand. I had been dreaming of the eagle staff moving steadily down the road ahead of the group, my legs following behind with strong, sure steps. I drank my coffee, burned sage and prayed for strength for the marchers, swallowed four ibuprofen, and drove through the predawn morning to the Little Six Casino in Prior Lake.

The group had grown larger with each passing day as more marchers arrived from the Santee Reservation in Nebraska, the Sisseton Reservation in South Dakota, and reservations across Canada, where Dakota people had fled in 1862 rather than risk hanging or imprisonment. This march was their homecoming, the return of the Dakota so many generations later to our ancestral land.

After breakfast, we regrouped at mile marker 92 on Highway 13, where the previous day's march had ended. The woman who offered the morning prayer wept as she spoke. Already the mood of the group had begun to shift, feeling the weight of six days of remembering, of sharing stories with other descendents, combined with the sense that we were about to end this long, exhausting journey. The march was approaching what had been the prison camp at Fort Snelling, where many more of the original marchers had died of disease.

We walked along the shoulder of the highway with red prayer ties braided in the women's hair, tied to the antennas of a long line of cars and vans, and wound around the arms of the men who carried the eagle staff at the head of our procession. The wind was strong and cold that morning, rising up to meet our group with its own challenge.

Many of the marchers who came to walk for a few hours or a single day ended up returning again and again, compelled by a force that none of us could name. My brother walked with a broken toe on six of the seven days. He had made a name for himself on the first day when he carried the eagle staff at such a brisk pace that the other marchers had to walk fast to keep up with him. Later he would say what all of us had felt—that we were filled with an energy that made walking twenty miles seem, if not easy, then very attainable.

Sometimes when we stopped to place a stake, it broke and had to be mended with one of the red ties. Leo said that this was a symbol for the march itself: The relationship of Dakota people to their ancestral land that had been broken by the original march was being mended. When marchers recognized the names of relatives who had been part of the original march, they stood near the stake, wiping away tears.

That afternoon, when we stopped again to place yet another stake at one of the mile markers, Leo said, "This one is easy to understand; no translation is needed; it is not an Indian name." When it was my turn to say a prayer and place tobacco at the base of the stake, I read the names: Narcisse and Louise Frenier, my grandmother Jenny's great-uncle and another relative. I felt an electric shock of recognition travel down the length of my arms, all thoughts of prayer momentarily suspended. These names belonged to my family.

In that single moment, all the years of research that I had done about my family, about the 1862 War and the removal of the Dakota people—all of the reading, writing, interviews, reimagined stories, and even the walking and the hearing of names of the original marchers—came together in a single, overwhelming feeling of grief. Where I had felt compassion for the other marchers and a strong interest in the history, suddenly it became personal. It was *my* family who had been abused as they passed through the towns of New Ulm, Henderson, and Mankato. It had been *my* relatives who were hit by bricks, stones, and scalding water, who had been spat on, taunted, and hated. I was stunned by this realization, watching as each one in the group took turns offering tobacco and prayers to my relatives, to my family. I stood there and wept.

An hour later I was walking next to Clifford Canku, a spiritual leader from Sisseton. We exchanged stories about our relatives and what had drawn us to be part of this march. He asked, "Has it made an impact on you?" I told him how I had just read my relatives' names a few miles back and had felt, for the first time, a powerful sense of grief for the original marchers, that in mourning for my own family, I had felt the march become personal for me as well as for the Dakota people. Clifford told me that we are all part of the collective unconscious, and the people's connection to it is growing stronger, partly because of events like the march. When people come back to their heritage, he explained, when they learn their language, when they march to reconcile a part of history that has never been acknowledged, then they are slowly putting together the pieces of their lives, like a puzzle.

By midafternoon, when we had marched almost fourteen miles, we turned onto Highway 13. At one of the last mile markers before we reached the Mendota Bridge and crossed to Fort Snelling, Leo stood in front of the group and announced that it was time for the men who had led the march with the eagle staffs to step aside.

"This march is to acknowledge the women and children and elders who made this journey, and they need to go ahead of the men. They are the givers of life," he said. "The men will walk beside them and behind them."

As the men moved in silence along both sides of our small band of women, a palpable wave of grief settled in. The history that we had recreated began to blur the distinction between past and present, and my sense that we were not alone on this journey grew even stronger. I was near the back of the group of women and children, and I could see how we had been transformed by Leo's words. Angela, the woman who was the heart of the march and the only person to walk the entire 150 miles, became the lightning rod for the dark feelings that washed over us. She was the first to begin weeping with deep, shuddering sobs, her head bowed while she continued to walk with her arms wrapped tightly around two of her children. One woman waved an eagle feather around her head, while others patted her gently on her back.

Clifford filled a tiny bowl with sage and moved through the group, stopping briefly to allow each woman to wave the smoke into her face, hair, and breath. It became difficult to continue walking as my limbs grew heavy and weak, and I was filled with an absolute sense of despair that deepened the closer we came to the bridge that led us to the prison camp below. The pain in my hip had returned, and my entire right arm and shoulder ached as if I had been carrying something I could not set down—a baby perhaps, or the weight of an elder leaning on my arm.

As we continued to walk, it was as if the pavement beneath the women's feet began to fade and disappear, the rigid layer of tar and gravel slowly giving in to the prairie beneath. With each step we moved further back into the past, until long-stemmed grasses from the original prairie bent beneath the hems of the women's long skirts. We began to move in our own private landscape, all of us marching together in the same dream. The wind traded the fumes of truck exhaust and fast food grease for the rich scent of leaves decaying on moist earth, crushed by the slow rolling of wagon wheels. The fields had been turned under for fall, a thick layer of pungent manure spread across the black soil, its neatly furrowed rows a testament to the white farmers who now owned it, who subdued it with their plows and horses. Even the land had lost its freedom, lost its wild mane of prairie.

Now our small group of marchers moved slowly in a long line that covered most of the bridge as we crossed to our final destination. Women walked in silence, heads bowed, weeping quietly. What a sense of hopelessness we all felt as we moved forward: grief, uncertainty about the future. We had to pause once when one of the young girls, who had been walking with her arms wrapped around her mother, simply stopped, weeping, unable to go on. Again, the other women came to her and wrapped a red scarf around her head, shielding her face from the view of the river, wrapping a blanket around her shoulders. As we approached the far end of the bridge, we could hear the ululations of some women who had reached the camp ahead of us. At that same moment, the sun broke through the clouds, brightening the bridge with the first rays we had seen all day, warming the hills above the river with a soft golden glow.

As we moved slowly downhill, we heard a solitary male voice welcome us with a traditional song, a poignant end to an exhausting journey. The singer was Art Owen, son of Amos Owen from Prairie Island, and he told us later that when he saw the group crossing the bridge he got choked up, and felt tears on his face. "When you were crossing the bridge," he told the marchers, "I could see blue lights surrounding the group. Those were spirits traveling with you."

After a ceremony dedicating a commemorate plaque to the original marchers, there was an honor dance for the current marchers and a feast. Afterward, we were asked to gather for a closing ceremony.

When we were all seated in a large circle, Art talked about the emotion of the day and the importance of the march in healing and reconciling the past. He told us about his own experience on other marches–how beer bottles had been thrown at marchers, how people had yelled out swear words and racial epithets. He said that as long as you're in prayer, nothing can stop you. Each step you take on a march should be for a relative. When something gets in your way, you don't go around it, you go through it, otherwise it might become an obstacle next time. He explained that the presence of the spirits on the bridge meant that the healing had begun. The march we had just completed was a symbol of the indomitable strength of the Dakota people and our determination to survive. At the end of the evening, I was more exhausted than I have ever felt in my life–physically, emotionally, spiritually. As a witness to my family's experience, and that of our people, I finally understood that our daily lives are only the tip of a mountain that rises above hundreds of years of generations whose experience–acknowledged or not–has everything to do with the people we have become. We are the sum of those who have come before us: good, bad, wise, and indifferent. We build our lives on top of that mountain.

Homeward Bound: The Journey of a Transgendered Korean Adoptee

PAULINE PARK

Homeland has been for me the elusive destination of a lifelong journey, a search for my identity as a transgendered woman and as a Korean adoptee.

I was born in Korea in 1960 and was adopted, along with my twin brother, at the age of eight months. Northwest Orient Airlines brought us from Seoul to Tokyo, and from there to Anchorage, and then to Chicago. Our new parents—the only parents I would ever know—picked us up at O'Hare Airport. In a photo taken at the airport the very moment when our adoptive parents first held us in their arms, the shock of seeing two seriously underweight babies registered on their faces. Our adoptive parents took us back with them to Milwaukee, Wisconsin, to the house with white aluminum siding that would be my home for the next seventeen years until I left for college and moved to different cities in the U.S. and Europe, each move presenting new opportunities for me to explore my relationship to home, my identity, public and private spaces, and the world of my dreams where I could express myself freely.

My father was Norwegian American but we grew up largely with our

German American mother's extended family and, above all, my maternal grandmother, who lived with us until my senior year in high school. Grandma's first language was German, and she would sometimes read to me from her German Bible as I tried to make sense of the elaborate traditional Gothic script. I connected with her most powerfully through music, playing the piano for her as she lay on the sofa listening intently. My grandmother was happiest when I played from the Lutheran hymnal, many of whose hymns were from Reformation Germany. For us, music provided the opportunity to reinforce a bond that was spiritual as well as cultural.

While I honored my mother's German heritage and my father's Norwegian background, I felt compelled to try to connect to the land of my birth, the "homeland" I never knew. I had a small, flexible, loose-leaf binder in a deep burgundy color that I would write in when I was a child. I remember writing my birth name on its cover, frustrated that I could write my Korean name only in the Roman alphabet because I did not know Hangul (the Korean alphabet). Without any opportunity to learn Korean, and with none of the infrastructure of Korean culture camps like those currently available to young Korean adoptees, I had no direct way of connecting to my birth culture. And so I connected to it through books. In our local branch library, there was one book in particular that resonated with me, *The Land and People of Korea,* but no matter how many books I found about Korea, none of them offered an answer to the elusive question: Where was my *real* homeland?

It's true that I had known no homeland other than the United States, but to strangers I was Asian, and therefore a foreigner. My Asian features automatically defined my status as the other, the outsider. Because others challenged my Americanness, I came to doubt my own sense of belonging. I belonged neither here nor there.

When I went out in public with my family, the striking physical differences between my adoptive parents and my brother and me made it impossible for others not to notice. "Whose children are they?" complete strangers would often ask. But that was life in my all-white neighborhood on the south side of Milwaukee in the 1960s and '70s.

My brother and I were the only nonwhite children in our elementary school. We were harassed often enough by white kids both inside and outside of school. The constant hurling of the words "Chink" and "Jap" made me feel ambivalent about my adoptive country, and also made it nearly impossible for me to think of myself as American.

Through my struggle with feeling like the other, I also struggled with another aspect of my identity. I knew that I didn't belong in my own body since I was in kindergarten. When I asked my mother to buy me a pair of stretch pants with stirrups, which was what many of the girls in school were wearing, her shocked response ("But those are for girls!") made me realize that I had crossed an invisible gender boundary that I hadn't been aware of. My mother and society assigned me to the category "boy" without consulting with me. I realized that neither the public space of school nor the more private space of home was a safe environment in which to explore my gender identity, so I buried it very deep inside me. Despite my parents' religious dogmatism on matters of sex and gender, my brother and I enjoyed the freedom to pursue whatever interests we wanted: We read, watched TV, and practiced piano and violin as we wished.

The piano played a central role in our family life, along with the making of live music, which included the frequent playing of Lutheran hymns. Music provided a refuge for me. At home and at school, it allowed me to connect with others and express the truest sense of myself that I had at that time. For our seventh birthday, our parents offered my brother and me a choice of a family vacation or a piano; without hesitation, we chose the piano. One of my fondest childhood memories is playing the Bremen spinet in the living room while my mother and grandmother listened.

Despite a modest family income, our parents paid for our private piano lessons. Later, my brother and I began violin lessons at our public school, and I would eventually take organ lessons well into high school. My brother and I delighted our parents and our grandmother, filling the house with music and exploring our own adopted heritage through the music of Bach and others.

When our father died just before we turned twelve, the household that had provided the only security I knew became insecure. The loss of my father's modest income plunged the family into poverty, and we remained dependent on Social Security and veterans' benefits throughout our adolescence. Losing the house, the only home we ever knew, was a very real possibility. I worried that we would be forced to live with one of my aunts, all of whom were bossy and domineering.

My fears intensified when our aging grandmother, by that point in her late eighties, was in declining health. Our mother's three sisters decided that she needed to be moved to the eldest sister's house. Losing my grandmother was a huge blow to me, even though it meant I would get my own bedroom after more than sixteen years of sharing one with my brother. And now the joy of having my own space was diminished since it meant that my grandmother was gone from our daily lives. We moved the piano into my new room, but we lacked the attentive, supportive audience my grandmother had once provided.

My brother and I left Milwaukee for Madison to attend the University of Wisconsin in the fall of 1978. Milwaukee, our childhood home, was a white working-class city of beer and bratwurst with the feel of a small town, despite its 1.5 million people. Madison, on the other hand, had a small but growing gay community. The Gay Center, located in the basement of a church on campus, would be the site of my first coming out—as a gay male. My brother would also come out later that year. Though we were close over the years, we had both kept this secret hidden from each other until then. It wasn't long before I realized, however, that my gay identity was incomplete because it didn't address my gender identity. There was no transgender community in Madison at that time and no openly transgendered people who could have served as role models for me. It wasn't until I moved to London in 1981 for a study-abroad program that I found the space to explore my gender identity. Interestingly, it was in London where I came to terms with my national identity as well.

I fell hopelessly in love with London, and I was determined to stay. During my first semester, I dated a young man named Stephen. I remember being swept away by a television broadcast of the Evelyn Waugh novel *Brideshead Revisited,* the story of a doomed homoerotic relationship between two young undergraduates at Oxford. Lord Sebastian Flyte and Charles Ryder were everything I wanted Stephen and me to be. I wanted their romance. And I wanted to be English. I realized later that this fantasy had more to do with my displacement of identity than anything else. Because I could not speak Korean, it was impossible to fulfill my expectations of what "Korean" might mean. In addition, the racial harassment I'd experienced growing up made it difficult for me to identify as American. But my attempt to live out this anglophilic fantasy with Stephen in London was a case of life imitating art. After two months, my relationship with him crumbled, just as Charles and Sebastian's had in *Brideshead Revisited.*

I stayed on another year in London to complete a master's degree program. My new lover, Bernard, invited me to move in with him just a few months after my relationship with Stephen had ended. His modest attached row house in East Acton (a mostly white lower-middle-class suburb in West London) would become my new home and my first and only experience of living with a lover.

I was twenty-two years old, and it was becoming increasingly clear that my gay male identity did not and could not adequately address my lifelong identification with women. While living with Bernard, I began going out dressed as a woman, much to Bernard's distaste. Though Bernard never confronted me, his best friend demanded that I stop cross-dressing because it was causing Bernard pain and straining our relationship. But I couldn't hide my need any longer. I began to go out regularly dressed as a woman, and it was the most liberating experience of my life. For the first time ever, I was presenting as I saw myself to be. My new public gender expression unnerved Bernard, who feared that I was going to seek sex reassignment surgery—something that I had already briefly considered but ultimately rejected.

I returned to the United States in October 1983 and experienced reverse culture shock. Ironically enough, it had been the experience of living in Europe that had made me realize how American I was. Now back in the country of my youth, I tried to reconstruct my identity once again.

I moved to Chicago and soon stopped thinking of London as home. My five years in Chicago would be the era of my identity as a guppie, a gay upper-middle-class professional. I was earning more money than I had ever earned before in public relations, forming with my brother a DINK (dual-income household, no kids) of sorts. Not long after moving to Chicago, the only tranny bar in town closed. I told my brother that I had been cross-dressing in London but insisted that it had just been a phase. My public corporate life had a good deal to do with my state of denial about my gender identity at that time.

It wasn't long before I realized that helping bad companies enhance their public image did not give me a sense of fulfillment. The year I decided to go back to graduate school to pursue a PhD in political science, my grandmother died. I became a poor grad student again. Days of wine and roses gave way to years of rice and beans. Losing my grandmother also cut off my last deep connection to Milwaukee, my first real home. I was starting anew yet again. At the music school building on campus, I had access to a piano for the first time since leaving Madison in 1981. I made a brief but ultimately futile attempt to play the piano; the pianos in the practice rooms were in such terrible condition that I gave up on it. Since my attempt to reestablish a connection with my past was fleeting, I looked toward my future.

The six years I spent pursuing my PhD at Urbana-Champaign would prove pivotal in redefining my identity in all its facets. When I finished my dissertation in December 1993, I discovered Foucault while taking a graduate seminar in political theory. Reading the work of this radical gay French theorist helped me rethink my lifelong identity complex. I had labored for years under the feeling that I was a "fake Korean," unable to live up to the expectations of others. In light of reading Foucault and other theorists, I came to understand that my pursuit of—or flight from—Koreanness was doomed to fail from the start, since there was no *essence* of Koreanness to pursue. I came to see myself as having a distinct identity as a Korean adoptee—neither ethnically Korean in the way that Koreans or recent Korean immigrants are, nor Korean American in the way that U.S.-born, English-speaking Korean Americans are.

Just as I came to reject the self-imposed label of "fake Korean" in favor of accepting myself as a Korean adoptee, I also came to understand "transgender" as distinct form of gender identity that challenges the false constructs of "man/woman." I would eventually come to call myself a "male-bodied woman," a concept radical even within the transgender community, because I reject the assumption that the presence or absence of the penis determines my status as a man or as a woman. While cross-dressers often find me *too transsexual* to relate to because I live full-time as a woman, transsexuals find me puzzling because I have not pursued hormone therapy or sex reassignment surgery. Even within the transgender community, I find myself *in between*. But I have found some transgendered people who understand me and the way that I have constructed my gender identity. And my activism and advocacy work on behalf of the transgender community has garnered respect even from those who do not understand my gender identity.

I also find myself *in between* the culture of my adoptive country and the culture of my birth, never fully at home in either. The most frequent question I am asked as a Korean adoptee is whether I have ever gone back to Korea. Though I hope to visit Korea one day, I haven't yet had the opportunity. As a Korean adoptee who never learned the Korean language, I cannot have anything but a complex relationship with the country of my birth. While I am proud of my Korean birth, I cannot claim that heritage easily. The question of where I am from has provoked different responses over the years. I usually respond with, "I was born in Korea but adopted by European American parents, and I grew up in Milwaukee." But I could just as easily answer the question with either "Wisconsin," or "the United States," or even "New York," depending on the context. Other Korean adoptees inquire about whether I've done a birth search. I made an attempt some years ago through a gay Korean friend to track down the orphanage in Seoul where my parents adopted me, only to discover that it no longer exists; instead, a high-rise apartment building now stands on that site. I am occasionally haunted by the possibility that one or both of my birth parents may still be alive and may actually be looking for me and my brother; but if so, they would be at least in their sixties. Even if I were to find my birth family, as a non-Korean-speaking, openly transgendered Korean adoptee, I would probably find it difficult to relate to them—and they to me.

I've come to reject the concept of "fake Korean." I am a real Korean adoptee; above all, I am the real *me*. And I no longer feel any need to apologize for my history, nor my lack of Korean-language proficiency. I can now locate my homeland in a way that does not diminish my own sense of wholeness or authenticity.

When I moved to Queens in 1997 at the end of my academic career, I revived my piano playing and brought back to life the best of my childhood memories. I bought a piano and thereby filled my little apartment with the music of my childhood and the spirits of those since lost to me. Sometimes when I play a Bach prelude, a Schubert impromptu, or a Chopin etude from my childhood or youth, the distinction between my past and present dissolves. And when I sing one of the German hymns from the Lutheran hymnal of my childhood, I realize how much music continues to shape my search for an authentic identity. My piano represents "home" in its fullest sense. It is not simply a musical instrument—or a decorative piece of furniture; it is an instrument of self-determination in the creation of my own culture of home; it is an instrument of the art of memory, a tool to be used in the archaeology of the self.

In Queens, I began my activism and advocacy work and came out as an openly transgendered woman. I also joined Also-Known-As, a group for Korean and other intercountry adoptees. In September 2001, I went to Washington, D.C., for the first international gathering of first-generation Korean adoptees. Being at a conference with more than two thousand Korean adoptees was an extraordinary experience. While a few of the attendees were initially shocked by my presence—most had never met an openly transgendered person before—they soon realized that my life story as a Korean adoptee was one that they could relate to. That same year, I began to work with other Queens activists to cofound Queens Pride House, a small LGBT community center in the borough, and I have continued to be actively involved in organizations that validate both my Korean adoptee and transgendered identities.

I have gone from one extreme to the other, having grown up in an all-white neighborhood on the south side of Milwaukee and ending up in New York, one of the most ethnically diverse cities in the United States. Only steps from my front door are the sights and smells of Little India and the culturally diverse neighborhood of Jackson Heights—the nexus of the Queens LGBT community, and home to the annual Queens Pride Parade and the largest collection of gay bars in the borough.

I now see myself as a transgendered Asian American woman with a distinct identity as a Korean adoptee. Through my active participation in many communities, I have found a place for myself in my adoptive country, as well as in the city that I now call home. Today, the United States is home because New York City is home.

Identifying with América

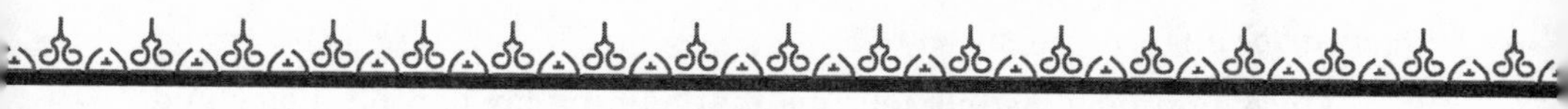

ERIKA MARTÍNEZ

"Mis padres son de la República Dominicana," I say in my crisp Spanish to another Latina after she asks me where I am from. It is 2005 and I still have to answer this question as a thirty-two-year-old graduate student. She is reluctant to respond as our classmates settle into their seats and the teacher begins the lecture on media and performance. Her eyes survey my face, my body, making me feel like I don't belong. I was born in the United States, yet she looks at me as if I can't possibly define myself as Latina like her. "Dominican Republic?" she asks. Can she hear the waves crashing on the *malecón,* the breezes rustling the palm trees? I wonder. If she could only imagine how soothing a *frío-frío* is in the humid heat.

Explaining where I'm from is something I always have to do. Even when I lived in Union City, New Jersey–the Latino Little Italy–as a child, many Latinos mistook me for African American. I wish I'd been born in the Dominican Republic. Maybe the explanation would be easier; maybe I would feel better whenever my origins are questioned because of my chestnut skin and my crown of black ringlets. To say that I lived in my parents' home country between the ages of three and six is a more detailed explanation. Perhaps it would be easier on my soul to know exactly what my homeland is so I could ease the discomfort of not being recognized for who I am: the smooth rolling of the *rr* from my tongue, the rhythm of a *perico ripiao* echoing between my ears, the hue of mahogany trees radiating from my skin, and the salt of *el mar caribe* lingering in my tears.

Once again my instinct tells me that naming my parents' homeland does not answer the question of where I am from, nor does it satisfy the requirement. The Dominican Republic is located in between Cuba and Puerto Rico, two better-known countries. Usually at this point in my explanation, I say that my parents' home country shares the island with Haiti. This fact would make my mother's sister-in-law, Tía Margarita, cringe. Like many Dominicans, Tía denies any ties with Haitians. According to Tía, Haitians are black and Dominicans are not. She likes to trace the family lineage back to *la madre patria;* she taught me to consider Spain as the mother homeland.

Tía Margarita never speaks of our African ancestry. No one does. Since colonial times, Dominicans have viewed darker skin as a sign of inferiority. Those who are dark are considered low class, poor, and unattractive. Like Tía, most people I know in Santo Domingo trace their roots to Europe to prove that they are white.

Whenever I go back to the Dominican Republic and stay with Tía Margarita, her mission as a host is to educate me on the Dominican Republic's history. My lessons began at the age of eight when I visited for summer vacation. She took me to the Alcázar de Colón to see how Columbus lived in 1492. We walked through the narrow cobblestone streets leading us to the plaza where the castle stood. Its facade was lined with archways twice as tall as the wooden shacks located on the other side of the Río Ozama. As we walked through la Zona Colonial, I acquired Tía's affinity for this section of Santo Domingo. I wondered if buildings in Spain really looked like this.

I bought miniature white houses with red-tile roofs and wrought-iron bars on the windows as souvenirs of my favorite place on the island to take back to New Jersey.

When I returned to Santo Domingo six years later for Easter and to plan my *quinceañera* party, Tía took me to the port to see *el buque español.* I heard about my cousin Carolinita's engagement to a Spanish sailor whom she met on a similar ship. Tía hoped I would have the same fortune of strengthening our Spanish bloodline through marriage, *"Hay que mejorar la raza."*

On my visit during Christmas break at the age of twenty, I was taken to El Faro a Colón, the new monument built for the Bicentenario—the five hundreth anniversary of Columbus's arrival in Santo Domingo. The government couldn't resolve the country's energy shortage, yet still constructed a lighthouse as a memorial. Its beams formed the shape of a cross in the night sky as countless neighborhoods remained without electricity for several hours each day. Tía's elite social circle believed that thousands of Spaniards would come to the island to celebrate this occasion. They prepared for the festivities as any country would if they were hosting the Olympic Games. But the crowds never arrived. Looking at the cross in the sky, I thought of how irrational their expectations were. Santo Domingo was a forgotten ex-colony. All of the Spanish history that Tía taught me to value was no longer important to the people of Spain.

I was twenty-one when I heard a broader history of the Dominican Republic from Papi in 1994. Two days before I left to do a junior semester abroad in Spain, I stayed with Papi in New Jersey, since he had offered to take me to the airport. I rested on his couch without much energy to move. Exhaustion from final exams and working during winter break penetrated my body. The fatigue was sweet though; I was going to Europe. Soon I would attend flamenco shows, drink sangria in *mesónes,* and see Picasso's *Guernica.*

The culture revered in my Spanish civilization, literature, and art history classes would soon surround me. I was going to study literature in the country where my mother tongue originated. I sat back and thought about how my hard work was paying off. I had more opportunities than Papi, whose life remained unchanged despite years of struggle.

Although comfortable among other Latin American immigrants in Union City, Papi still talked about his plan to move back to Santo Domingo. He lived in a basement apartment designated for the superintendent of the building and saw his maintenance job as a way of saving money on rent for his eventual return to the island. He worked the night shift for a division of Pfizer—at the same factory where he had worked for twenty years—to increase his income.

Papi looked nervous as he sat on the couch beside me. His eyes wandered from the industrial carpeted floor to the imitation Queen Anne coffee table and then to passersby shuffling in the dirty snow outside the half windows of his little apartment. He coughed and rubbed his chin with one hand. "We have to talk about something important," he said. His eyes did not meet mine.

I didn't mind his fatherly talks. He often told me he loved me, and had even said I could come to him if I ever got pregnant. The unspoken rule at Mami's house was that she would disown me if such a thing happened.

Our eyes finally met. "You have to be careful when you're in Madrid. You're going to meet people who are racists." His voice was hoarse, tired. He cleared his throat again and rubbed his hands together. He talked slowly, choosing each word carefully. "If you ever come across prejudiced people, you tell them that it's their fault you have that funny-looking color." He pointed to my hand and rubbed it. His brown hands were rough from years of factory work and his childhood on coffee farms in his small hometown of Padre Las Casas. He looked straight into my eyes and said, "The Spaniards went to Santo Domingo, raped the indigenous women, and killed so many of them. Then they brought the blacks and mixed with them, too."

"Yeah, Papi, I know." I pulled my hand away and shifted my weight. This was like having the birds-and-the-bees talk at the age of twenty. I didn't want to be reminded that people saw me as ugly or low class. I felt that I was bettering myself. Besides, I imagined that Spaniards weren't going to have more prejudices than people in the United States. Spaniards wouldn't see me as different since I spoke the same language as their people. I wanted to be excited about my trip, not worried. "I'm going to be fine," I reassured him, "I already learned all that stuff in my college classes." My brow furrowed. I would fit in. Papi was not going to take this hope away from me. I ignored him.

"You did?" He leaned back on the couch as if relieved. Did he think this speech could be my defense against racism? Why hadn't he told me this when I was ten years old and had moved to an all-white neighborhood? He didn't know how often I had to explain where I was from to everyone—including other Latinos. The hardest question to answer was whether I was black or white. I wanted to say I was white from the time I was excluded from a Girl Scout troop because of discrimination based on the color of my skin. No matter how much our family lineage was tied to Spain, what was evident was my African origin. Being dark kept me out of social groups. He didn't know that my biggest desire was to be treated and accepted the way white people were. It took years for me to begin claiming my African roots and to finally say that I was black without feeling shame.

I sat motionless, my arms crossed at my chest. Papi reminded me of Marina Fernandez in my Latin American Civilization class. She was a Puerto Rican student who dominated many class conversations. By midsemester, her contributions to discussions sounded like a rant against *conquistadores* and colonization. Part of her ancestry was tied to Spain; it was in her language, it was in her name. The only time I tried to enter into dialogue with her, she silenced me by responding that any relationship she had with Spain was not by choice. I couldn't confront such rage. Like Tía Margarita, I focused on the great things Spain had done for the Americas without looking at the costs. I didn't want to make those ancient losses my pain. At the time, I couldn't digest every part of this colonial history. Papi would have been happy if I shared Marina's views. She didn't reject her blackness the way I did. Back then, I didn't want to say that I was a descendant of African people, but I also didn't want to push Papi away. Still, I wasn't ready to accept all parts of my identity.

I considered the fact that Papi would not give my sister Melissa a preparatory speech if she were leaving for Spain instead of me. With her pale skin, light-brown hair, and green eyes, Melissa bears the evidence of our Spanish ancestry. In Santo Domingo, Tía Margarita always pointed that out. Upon our arrival, Tía would inspect us from head to toe. She would take us directly to the salon, where hairdressers forced my curls to fall straight down my back the way Melissa's did naturally. I'd often be reprimanded for being in the sun too long. "Don't get too dark," Tía would warn me. "People will say you're Haitian." I wished I could scrub away the darkness that made me feel ugly and unwanted. This reality was following me everywhere.

What I thought was going to be a warm moment together with Papi left my stomach turning. His speech reminded me about my "funny-looking" skin and how it kept me from feeling at home in the United States and in Santo Domingo—that my skin would again do the same thing in Spain. I grabbed the remote control from the coffee table and turned the TV back on. We watched the end of *El Show de Cristina,* the number-one talk program on Univisión. Credits rolled over the host's pale skin and bleached-blond hair. Her commercial success reminded me of the color preference resulting from Latin America's colonial past.

I thought I could forget Papi's warning, but his words haunted me once I was in Spain. One Sunday morning in Madrid, I called my friend Derek, who was studying in Granada that same semester. We talked about my roommate, Kate, who had moved out that week. Before her departure, she told me she didn't feel at home with our host family in Spain. From a public pay phone on the corner of Calles Guzmán el Bueno and Gaztambide, I recounted the details of the situation.

"Kate and I were so alike," I said. "We both study languages. We've been to Europe before. I don't know what went wrong."

"Just 'cause you both like to travel doesn't mean you're alike."

"But we worked so well together in Spanish Club, don't you think?" I looked down Calle Gaztambide. It was dead before noon. Just ten hours earlier, university students had pumped life into this street, which had vibrated with music that ranged from techno to *sevillanas.* Music, liquor, people—everything spilled out from the bars. On weekends it seemed like everyone flocked into this part of the city at midnight. Yet at that moment, storefronts were barred shut.

A young Spaniard dressed in a snug V-neck pullover sweater and imitation Levi's jeans smoked a cigarette and paced around the telephone booth. His messy auburn hair and bloodshot dusky eyes signaled that he may not have gone home after a night of partying. He walked a few feet away and leaned against the door of La Sal, my least favorite discotheque, eyeing me.

Suddenly, he left his post against the door and came right up to the phone booth where I was talking. *"¿Cuanto tiempo vas a durar?"* he asked. He lifted his wrist and tapped on his watch. His unshaved jaw line cocked upward.

I cracked the door open. *"Es mejor que encuentres otro teléfono."* I pointed down the street and let the door slip out of my hands. Telling him to find another phone didn't help. He didn't leave.

"Sorry, Derek," I spoke into the phone again. We resumed our conversation about Kate.

The young Spaniard finished his cigarette and put it out where the wall of the phone booth met the cement. His glare chiseled through the glass box encasing me. I turned to face the green and black Telefonica phone. Sunday morning was *my* time. This guy was not going to cut my conversation short. He knocked on the translucent door.

"Hay otro teléfono en la próxima calle," I said again as I signaled down the street. "I can't believe this guy can't just walk one block to use a different pay phone. Why does he have to wait for me?" I said as much for my own benefit as Derek's.

Derek talked as the Spaniard outside continued with his attempt to get me off the phone. I started circling inside the two-by-two-foot square of the telephone booth. A hundred *pesetas* remained on my card, and I intended to finish it on my conversation with Derek.

"¿Cuando vas a terminar?" The Spaniard's voice was louder, deeper. He kicked his extinguished cigarette onto the street.

Instead of telling him when I would finish, I covered my left ear in an attempt to shut him out. But no matter how hard I pressed the palm of my hand over my ear, I still heard him telling me to get off the phone. "This guy is going to keep interrupting me. Hold on Derek." I turned around and pulled the folding door open. *"¡Jódete!"* I shouted at the Spaniard.

"Jódete tu, y tu maldita raza negra." His index finger pointed directly at me. The anger in his words penetrated the glass doors, tensed every muscle in my body.

"You told him to fuck off," Derek laughed.

I was shocked to hear Derek's translation for *"jódete."* In Santo Domingo *"joder"* means "to bother." Derek hadn't heard the Spaniard telling me and my damn black race to fuck off.

I turned around and let the door close. He slammed the door with his fist and the handle hit my spine right between my shoulder blades. I exhaled sharply. Derek asked me if I was okay, but I couldn't respond. Pools formed in my eyes. Air reentered my lungs. Sound finally came out of my quivering mouth. "I have to go," I said, in between tears.

"What's wrong?" Derek asked.

"I gotta go."

When I stepped out of the phone booth, the Spaniard was gone. The gray '70s buildings towering above felt like they could tumble down on me as I made my way back to my temporary home. My sneakers squeaked loudly on the ceramic tiles when I entered the building. The floor numbers flashing above the elevator doors felt like seconds ticking on a time bomb. I covered my mouth with my hands so that I wouldn't explode. Remedios, my host mother, sat at the kitchen table when I walked into the apartment. I always greeted her when I returned home, but I walked right past her to my room without saying a word.

"¿Que pasó?" Remedios asked as she entered my room.

Samira, another exchange student staying in the house, followed right behind her. She pulled her bathrobe tighter over her sienna skin then sat on the bed next to me. Her teddy bear eyes gazed at me. "What's wrong?" she asked.

"¿Algo pasó con el novio?" Remedios wondered. If I had a problem, Remedios assumed it was with my boyfriend.

I shook my head but my voice was gone.

"No se apure, Remedios, yo me ocupo." Samira waved Remedios out of the room, promising to take care of me.

I sat up. Samira rubbed my back. My voice returned; words emerged in English. I told her what had happened.

Samira said nothing. She listened to me cry. Samira was Indian Muslim, and I imagined that she empathized. She understood that there was nothing she could say to stop the tears.

Papi had foreseen an act of violence against me because of the color of my skin. He had warned me, but he couldn't have prevented me from reacting to harassment. In that moment my instincts told me to protect myself without thinking about the possibility of a racial slur thrown in my face. The insult left me in shock, stripped of my defenses. People saw me as black. Why couldn't they see beyond color? What could Papi's speech have done? I didn't get angry, as Marina would have. I was afraid of what rage could do; it had already brought on the incident in the phone booth. I turned to tears as I usually did when feelings overwhelmed me—those could be controlled, muffled under a pillow. This time however, the hopelessness that I usually managed to keep deep in my belly was dislodged. It traveled through my core, up my throat, and out of my mouth—the tempest of despair I thought I wouldn't survive if ever it erupted. I thought about Marina's rage against the Spanish colonizers. She and Papi were right. The dehumanization of five hundred years ago still existed. I sobbed for hours until I fell asleep.

A few days after my telephone booth experience, I met up with Papi's cousin, América, and my perception of Spain wavered again. When visiting a new place where we had family, I was expected to make contact. Papi lent me his camera so that I could take pictures of the meeting.

"Erika?" América asked, approaching me at the Argüelles metro stop where we had agreed to meet. Her lips parted into a smile that was familiar. A short woman who wore a brown fur coat, her eyes were the shape of anise seeds like Papi's, her skin the color of sepia.

Like Spaniards, we kissed each other's cheeks twice. She led me to a bus that took us to the suburb where she worked and lived. During the forty-five minute ride I discovered that América worked as a live-in caretaker for an elderly woman. Her three children were still in the Dominican Republic studying—she sent them all of the money she earned. Her hope was to return for a visit soon, but she needed to make sure her papers were ready or else she could not get back into Spain; she had entered the country just before the Spanish government began to actively regulate the entry of people from "third world" countries due to a high increase in immigration.

Once we arrived in her neighborhood, América led me to a schoolyard where other women were already congregated. To my surprise, most were Dominican—all domestic workers who could not invite company to the place where they lived/worked. This little park was their gathering place. The sparse trees were barren, nothing was in bloom. The sky above was gray. We settled around a wooden picnic table. América introduced me as the daughter of Agapito Martínez. I was astonished when a few said they knew Papi.

The conversation turned into a remembrance of friends and family back on the island. A woman in a light-blue jacket described her sons back in Azua. Tears rolled down past the frames of her glasses as she spoke about not being able to go back to the island. Their sadness seeped into my pores.

On my way back to the city center, I realized that I never took a picture with América. It was never the right time. It would have been like taking a photograph at a funeral. Hearing América tell stories about her separation from her children and from her homeland made me sad. Still, I went to see her every other week for the remainder of the semester. Getting to know her connected me to Papi's family, whom I rarely saw on my returns to Santo Domingo.

During another visit I made to the park, nuns wearing traditional black habits invited the women into the school for a special meeting. We crossed the schoolyard and entered the building. Our voices echoed in the corridor until we reached the designated classroom. After we settled in, one nun delivered the latest Spanish immigration laws. It seemed like the nuns' mission was to help domestic workers gain legal status. As a member of the European Union, Spain needed to regulate immigration from all countries, including its former colonies. The government would no longer honor the treaty it signed with the Dominican Republic in 1966, which allowed Dominicans to enter Spain without a visa.

One year earlier, these women were free to board a plane from Santo Domingo to Madrid; all they needed was the money to buy the ticket. Upon arrival in Spain, they claimed to be on vacation. But they stayed on and worked without proper documentation. I later found out that in the '60s—when the Dominican and Spanish governments agreed to let their citizens travel freely between the two countries—professionals were the ones who primarily migrated. Spain changed its regulations after the '90s introduced a new wave of immigration: mostly uneducated farm workers from the Dominican Republic who were looking for any means to feed their families, and who were considered undesirable by the Spanish government.

I learned that it was easier for the domestic workers to get visas if they were political refugees, but they could only make this claim if their country was in a declared state of war. The women were warned about the police, informed about the latest arrests and deportations of undocumented immigrants. Copies of application forms were distributed. If anyone had unique circumstances or further questions, the nuns were available afterward to help them on an individual basis.

The distribution of papers reminded me of my internship at the U.S. Embassy. Instead of applications, I handed out advertisements to Disneyworld, maps of Hollywood, and flyers for ferries to the Statue of Liberty. I thought about the fact that no Spaniard would be barred from the United States, but both countries were trying to keep Dominicans out.

As we walked back into the cold winter day, the women murmured their concerns. A tall woman with her black hair tied back protested loudly, "I'll tell them I'm a political refugee. If the politics in Santo Domingo weren't so bad then we wouldn't have economic problems."

"They think we want to be here, but they don't know," remarked another woman dressed in black.

They all wanted to be home in Santo Domingo, but couldn't survive there because of the bad economy. In order to financially support the families they left behind, they had to work abroad. These women seemed more transient than the Dominicans in New Jersey and New York who, like other members of my family, gave up on the dream of returning.

"I don't carry my passport," I whispered to América.

"You shouldn't walk the streets without it," América responded.

"I have my student identification."

"You need your passport, and watch out for the police."

On the bus ride home, I made note to take my U.S. passport out of its hiding place in between my mattresses and put it into my purse. My birthplace gave me the privilege to travel freely and have better educational opportunities, but at the cost of displacement and an altered identity.

I recalled a conversation I had with a Dominican immigrant from New York on my last trip to the island. We talked about our previous travels and where we would go next. Since this was before my study-abroad trip, I told him how much I wanted to visit Spain. He said that if we covered our ears and our mouths while in Spain, we would see we had nothing in common with the people. I didn't want to believe him, but he was right. The strongest tie I had in Madrid was not to the Spaniards my Tía talked so highly of, not to the American students in my study-abroad program; it was to my dad's cousin, América, and her circle of friends who couldn't afford the cost of gathering at a café on Sunday, their only day off. I was like her, far from home looking for a better life, easily identified as "other," and discriminated against because of the color of my skin.

I was born in the U.S.; I've spent most of my life here. I used to wish I could say, "I was raised in the Dominican Republic." The years I lived in Santo Domingo between the ages of three and six are what I piece together when I need to feel at home. Even though Papi never saved enough money to return with us, it was where my brother, Francisco, was born. It was there where I learned to ride a bicycle without training wheels, where I took dance classes in *mangulina,* where I learned to read and write, where I first pledged allegiance to a flag in school. It was where my grandparents lived. It was a time before I recognized the preference given to those with skin lighter than mine. I was too young to understand my Tía's allegiance to Spain, too juvenile to lay claim to any land. The island was what I knew. No one considered me to be from anywhere else. I can't discard the years of my life on the island because my entire experience has been about straddling two cultures.

My parents' intention was never to leave the Dominican Republic. Hurricane David destroyed Abuela Macuya's house in 1979. Since Papi provided for his mother, it wasn't possible to reconstruct her house and maintain our family on a Dominican salary. Instead of returning to Santo Domingo, Papi decided that the whole family would move back to the United States in 1980 and join him in New Jersey.

When my Latina classmate in graduate school asked me where I am from, she didn't want to know that my parents are from the Dominican Republic. When someone asks about my nationality or where home is, what they really want to know is my race—not about where Mami and Papi came from. They want to know about my ancestors. A history beyond what Tía Margarita taught me.

I now claim the African roots that my family still denies. I don't reject my Spanish ancestors, but I contend with the slavery they established on the island. It is a painful past that mixes with the childhood memories I cling to, what my body holds on to. No explanation can ever stop a violent phone booth incident or keep Papi's cousin, América, safe in Spain. Now, I celebrate the question "Where are you from?" because my answer opens up a spectrum between black and white. I can finally declare all that I am.

Seeing Istanos

NANCY AGABIAN

Auntie Esther, my father's sister, left a message on my answering machine. "Nancy, this man, Levon Andonyan, has found Istanos, your grandmother's village. He's taking a tour there this September. I want to go, but not by myself. Will you come with me?"

Yes, I thought. It was 1998, and I had been living in Los Angeles, in self-imposed exile from my traditional Armenian American family in Boston for about eight years. The time and distance had given me space to come of age and become myself, partially through writing and performing about being a bisexual Armenian girl from Massachusetts. But after turning thirty recently, I had hit a snag: I could only get so many gigs, I was out of a day job, and my boyfriend had just moved to another city. Ever since I had moved to L.A., I felt intrinsically connected to the desert, which I attributed to my ancestral roots; I hoped that going to Istanos to stand on the dry land whence my blood evolved would give me a greater sense of clarity, of completeness.

"I don't understand why you want to go to Turkey and contribute to their economy after all that they did," my mother said on the phone when I told her the news.

"Because I want to see where my grandmother came from," I replied. My paternal grandmother had been driven out of Istanos decades before, in what was then the Ottoman Empire, now central Turkey. I had been close to Grammy, who had passed away four years before, and who had told me heartrending stories of losing her parents, sister, little nieces, and nephews during the death marches of the Armenian Genocide of 1915.

"I don't understand," my mother continued. "It'll just be so depressing. There'll be nothing there. Absolutely nothing there to look at but rubble."

"I'm not going there for a vacation. I'm going to find out about my ancestors, and Auntie Esther can tell me our history." Auntie Esther had retained Grammy's stories more than anyone else in the family. As a child, I had visited the artist's studio she kept on the top floor of the house she shared with Grammy (before she passed away) and my two other aunts. During loud family get-togethers, I would look at the landscapes she painted of Armenia and dance around to Armenian records.

"Your Aunt Esther just wants to go on this trip because cousin Tina went," my mother said. Cousin Tina had visited Istanos, from where her parents also originated, the year before. "And Tina hasn't talked to her sisters in thirty years. Is that right? She won't speak to her sisters but she'll write letters to Turkish villagers?"

"Look, Mumma, I'm going. Nothing you can say will change my mind."

"Well, I hope you'll be happy in the middle of nowhere, where there's nothing but rubble, and you can kiss the dirt where your grandmother stood!"

She eventually acquiesced, but the trip caused similar disagreements among other members of my family. When my father and I picked up Auntie Esther to go to the airport, we shared a contentious meal of *lahmejun* and iceberg lettuce salad with my two other never-married aunts, Margo and Sarah, at their kitchen table.

"Are you excited, Auntie Esther?" I asked. She was wearing chunky turquoise jewelry and a smart denim outfit stretched over her rotund body.

"I'm excited about going to Ma's village and finding the family bible," Auntie Esther replied.

"Why do you talk such foolishness, Esther?" Margo spat. "You have to be a nut to think that still exists."

"Ma said her mother left it with a neighbor for safekeeping before they went on the march. It might still exist."

"Yeah, and you might *not* exist if you go around that village asking for it," Sarah said.

"It's been over eighty years," my father said. "You don't think one Turk decided to burn it?"

"I believe in the good of man, Skippy," Auntie Esther said, raising her chin. "And I don't see the harm in looking. All the Koshgarian family history is recorded inside of that bible, all the births and deaths and marriages dating back to when the Seljuks pushed us from Van in the 11th century. Why not look for it?"

"Yeah!" I chimed in. Even though I knew the bible's existence was farfetched and that Auntie Esther's quest for it seemed partly due to her propensity for drama, I couldn't help fantasizing about snatching our history back. Given half a chance, I wanted to claim our ancestors' lives from beyond the destruction of the genocide, to see our existence, our ancientness, instead of feeling like a lost band of orphan-victims.

As we readied ourselves to leave, Margo completely lost her mind when Esther wouldn't take a twenty-dollar bill from her. "Just take it, Esther!" she screamed, and gave no other words of goodbye to her sister. We all laughed, having witnessed or performed similar outbursts in the past. A moment later Margo hugged me and, still twitching from her fit, warmly told me, "Nancy, this won't be a fancy vacation. You'll get to meet the people of the villages."

I took her to mean that I would visit people like my grandmother's family, like us.

During the quiet void of the flight, I reflected on how difficult it had been for my family to separate for such a controversial trip. I surmised that Armenians became crazy and controlling when they left each other or when they defied expectations because of an ingrained, possibly genetic, survival mechanism: If we didn't cling together as a group, we would get clobbered individually until extinction.

One reason I suspected these dynamics stayed with us was the lack of recognition for the trauma. The Turkish government refuses to this day to acknowledge the truth of the matter, that an estimated 1.5 million Armenians were massacred intentionally at a time when the Ottoman Empire was vulnerable and crumbling. An oppressed Christian minority living on their historic homeland for around twenty-five hundred years, Armenians were seen as a traitorous threat since they were demanding autonomy with the support of Europe and Russia. Under the cover of WWI, the Young Turk regime killed Armenian men outright and deported women and children hundreds of miles through desert under inhumane conditions—no water, no food, no protection from physical attack. Women were raped, and the dead could not be buried; corpses rotted along roads and rivers. Shame and guilt were instilled in anyone who survived, and when it came time to continue their lives, they tried not to think about it. It didn't help that the world didn't want to think about it either. And yet it was impossible for feelings not to erupt; the safest place to have them was with family. Fear and mistrust, enacted over and over again on mothers, daughters, siblings, and loved ones, with no resolution nor apology. You screamed your head off and then you moved on.

In my mind, I tried to fit together the pieces of the Armenian family puzzle into this historical, framework as the plane moved closer and closer, across the ocean, to Turkey.

After a short plane trip from Istanbul, we were in the village of one of our tour mates, a handful of elderly Armenian Americans searching for the villages of their parents. Half of Parchanj (pronounced "perchance") was out in the street. Kamal, our Kurdish driver who resembled Ringo Starr, dropped us off in front of a small tiled fountain where a pipe emptied water into a basin. A few kids filled jugs with water and carried them away, watching us. The girls were wearing skirts over pants and sandals. Covered in dust and dirt, their hair was in shambles, but they were all very beautiful, with bright eyes.

The mayor and a dozen men surrounded Levon, our guide, who presented an old map of Armenian homes and orchards. Levon, a retired architect with silver hair, a moustache, and a regal stance, had started visiting the formerly Armenian provinces of Turkey seven years ago simply out of curiosity. He lectured on his travels, showing videos at Armenian American churches and cultural events, which sparked interest in his trips. An Armenian who spoke Turkish, he was an indispensable guide and had been leading one or two tours a year ever since.

The villagers brought us to a grand old house once belonging to Armenians. The current owner, a young man, smiled and welcomed us into his back yard. His wife, a young woman wearing a floral-patterned headscarf, brought us watermelon. As we slurped and spit out the seeds, I recalled Grammy serving us watermelon on a TV tray in her wood-paneled den in Boston whenever we visited in the summertime. The village kids animatedly spoke to us in Turkish, pointing out a large garden, like the kind my father had recently planted in the back yard, of tomato and cucumber plants. Bulghur was drying on plastic tarps on the ground, and I tasted the cracked-wheat pilaf my mother had cooked throughout my childhood. Propped around the trunks of trees were large carved stone arches; they looked like the former pediments of an Armenian church. Our hosts gestured for us to sit on them, like benches.

Auntie Esther had to pee so the owner's wife led her inside to use the facilities. "You should have seen the beautiful woodwork on the ceiling," Auntie said as she emerged. "I'm sure it was from the days of the Armenians." I was curious, but I didn't want to see. Though the people were kind and excited, proudly showing us our common culture, it was all so sad to me. The only remnants of the Armenians were the stones we sat upon and the ceiling we stared up at.

A group of villagers followed us when we returned to the van. As I stood in the doorway of the bus, I passed out ballpoint pens to a group of overjoyed girls. A few old men then approached the van and held out their hands, but I didn't want to give them a thing. For some reason, they seemed culpable for their ancestors' wrongs, even though I did not know who their ancestors were. I was offended that they wanted something from me, and I felt an uncharitable urge to ignore or deny them.

I was about to turn around, but Kamal stopped me. He put his hand on one man's shoulder and said haltingly, "Miss, these are big children." I could not argue with his pure expression, so I gave them the pens. But I did not apologize.

On the bus, Levon spoke about the mayor of Parchanj. "The mayor's family arrived seven generations ago," Levon said, "when the only inhabitants were four Armenian families." Levon shared with us that when they had spoken of 1915, the mayor's eyes had glazed over. "The mayor told me that Turks and Armenians had lived side by side in peace before that time," Levon continued, "it was the government that forced the Armenians out and gave away their homes to Bulgarian, Hungarian, and Romanian Turks. And then twenty years later, the new owners sold the homes to locals."

Some part of me expected the mayor to give words of regret, but based on Levon's story they did not come. I wondered why his eyes had glazed over if he knew the truth. It struck me that the mayor of Parchanj was one of Kamal's "big children" too: blameless, powerless over the past, and ultimately unable to apologize. Perhaps he was sad, or the event was beyond his grasp, or, just maybe, he did not want to be a child anymore.

Kamal pulled off a highway and let Auntie Esther and me take pictures in front of the road sign. After I developed the film, I could see how nervous we were, arms around each other, shoulders hunched. ÇIMENYENICE, the Turkish name for Istanos, was stenciled in black on the white arrow behind us.

We slowly motored down a dirt road, through a pastoral setting. I could see goats, geese, and the Alis River, a calmly flowing stream. A man in a field pitched hay with a fork. We drove down the road a bit farther to another little village, where Kamal parked the van next to a dried-up field. This was Istanos, and my heart pumped as we stepped out of the van and walked by a pair of crumbling stone houses. "Armenians probably once lived in these ruins," Levon said. The walls were covered with circles of dung drying in the sun, to be used as fuel in the winter. I smelled an open sewer and spotted a satellite dish atop a roof.

As we made our way through the village, a few kids watched us, but they were not filled with wonder. Our hard candy made no impression—they wouldn't touch it. The sturdiness fell out of my stomach and I wandered about, hoping for a sign that we were in the right place. High walls surrounded us; there were very few windows and doors. Some men emerged to greet Levon, including a big stern man in his forties with a distinguished beard who seemed to be the village leader. He and his posse looked at us sideways, surly and suspicious.

We made our way up a hill, toward the houses that Levon believed belonged to my grandmother's family, the Koshgarians, as the villagers tentatively followed. We walked as far as we could, to a ledge overlooking miles of fields below. Levon pointed downward to roofless tiny rooms like monks' cells at monastery ruins. "Those were the Koshgarian homes," Levon said.

"No, that can't be," Auntie Esther said, her voice high. "My mother said our house was the largest in the village and that people had marriages in the courtyard. And the doors were so tall and wide a man on a horse could ride through them." I smiled at Grammy's grandiose description. "So this can't be it," Auntie Esther continued, gesturing to the ruins. "The house was on top of a hill, across the street from a church."

We happened to be standing next to a big house, on top of a hill, across the street from a mosque. "What about this?" Auntie Esther asked, looking up at it.

The house had wing doors, though not big enough for a man on a horse to pass through. As I took a picture of them, a smiling girl stepped into the frame of my lens. She was bright and lively, about ten years old, wearing an orange outfit and a headband over her shiny black hair. I looked out from behind my camera to smile at her and then snapped the picture. Many kids we'd encountered had been wearing clothes emblazoned with English words: BASEBALL LEGENDS and TWEETY-BIRD. The front of this girl's sweatshirt was divided into four sections, each with a cartoon character named L. C. WAIKIKI.

Auntie Esther asked the girl her name—it was Ana. She lived with her family in the house with the big wing doors. There was a car parked in front, a rarity in far-off villages. I looked carefully at the house, trying to determine if this had been Grammy's home, and found a date carved into a cornerstone: 1954.

After lengthy negotiations between Levon and Ana's father, a handsome man in his midthirties, we entered the building. It turned out to be a storage room the size of a one-car garage, with piles of wheat on the ground and old farm implements hanging on the walls. There was a diamond-shaped hole in the ceiling, framed with large timbers. "Look at that," Auntie Esther said, pointing. "This must be a very old building since this land has been deforested." She told me that, incredibly, oak trees once covered the arid plains we were traveling through. *So much for my theory on feeling historically connected to desert,* I thought.

"That hole was built to let the smoke out, from when people lived in here," Levon said. He pointed to a huge fireplace, about ten feet wide and six feet tall, taking up most of the western wall. “Oh my goodness!” Auntie Esther said. That must be the *tonir!*” she exclaimed. “My mother said she fell into the *tonir* when she was a baby!” I knew that a *tonir* was actually an oven dug into the ground, which would explain how a child could accidentally fall into one. Nevertheless, I said nothing as Levon shot some video of me and Auntie Esther standing inside the oven while Kamal, our traveling companions, the bearded mayor, Ana’s family, and a half-dozen village kids looked on.

“I could see a wedding party inside this room,” Auntie Esther mused. The light was soft from the skylight and the small windows high in the wall. There was an old TV in one corner, and underneath it, a carved trunk, just the sort that would hold an ancient family bible. In order to get a closer look, Auntie Esther pretended to wipe off the dust with a Kleenex. “It’s an antique,” she said.

Auntie Esther produced a chart of the Armenian alphabet and asked Levon to tell the mayor in Turkish that if anyone found a book with such writing, to let her know. “I pay you big money,” she said, playfully touching the underside of a boy’s chin. The mayor, via Levon, said it was unlikely, since the generation before had already found those kinds of things. Still, ever the optimist, she gave the mayor her phone number.

“I really think that was the house,” Auntie Esther said as we emptied outside. I didn’t have the heart to tell her about the 1954 cornerstone, that the room was probably built long after Grammy’s family had been banished. Even if the building wasn’t Grammy’s house, this place was still her home. I could imagine her as a child from the stories she had told me: stealing cream off the milk to give to her Kurdish girlfriends, playing with birds outside, and riding a horse in the plains below. I remembered Grammy’s wrinkled hands and her dark eyes ringed with gray, her short white hair and her scratchy voice, always insisting that people treat her with respect.

I turned around to get one last look of the site and waved to Ana. Later, when I looked at her photograph in front of the wing doors, I noticed on her American sweatshirt, appearing in the quadrant over her heart, the word MEMORY.

As we passed through the dung-covered ruins, where we had entered earlier, a Cimenyenice family invited us for tea. We were ushered into a small room with an upper ledge where men sat leaning against the walls and a lower level a step down for the women. There were rugs covering the seating surfaces and family pictures on the walls.

Levon turned on his camera. "This man's name is Sarkut. His grandfather was a Sarkissian who converted to Islam." I had heard that those Armenians who converted from Christianity to Islam were spared at the time of the genocide; the Turks saw it as Armenian compliance with the Turkish nation. "He's a distant relative of yours," Levon told Auntie Esther, pointing to one of the men.

"A second cousin of Boghos Sarkissian, I think. He looks a little like him," Auntie Esther said with awe. The man got out his photo ID, which read Neset Sarkut. It didn't give the date of his birth, but he looked to be around Auntie's age, perhaps a little younger.

Sarkut's two daughters served us tea. They were wearing colorful, mismatched sweaters and skirts and seemed to be teenagers or in their early twenties. Their headscarves were cotton and covered the buns on top of their crowns and at the napes of their necks, making their heads look like the shape of gourds. One of them, whose name was Cameh, had light hair, a soft voice, and a very sweet smile. Her darker sister, Esgu, was flustered with excitement, kissing us nervously on our cheeks in greeting.

I was feeling shaky. I didn't know what to say or do. *I should have Levon translate something for me, some questions,* I thought, but I didn't know where to begin. If one of my great grandparents had converted his or her faith, I wouldn't exist, and part of my spirit, I imagined, would be living here with the Sarkut family. Was my spirit here now? Was it ever?

After tea we posed with Sarkut and his daughters, our arms around each other, for a picture. "Esther," Levon said, "you're getting the royal treatment here. The father threw Tina out of his house after a few minutes." *So, these are the same Turkish villagers that cousin Tina has been writing letters to,* I thought. Overwhelmed and emotionally exhausted, I was sandwiched between Cameh and Esgu, whose warmth buoyed me.

The family walked us to our van, and Levon took yet another group picture. Auntie Esther disentangled herself from the crowd and kissed everyone on both cheeks, and I followed, smiling at people as I approached.

While Levon was panning his camera over the countryside one last time, I ran into a field to gather some dirt into a tiny film container. When I returned, he commanded me to do it again so he could get it on videotape.

"No, that's okay," I said.

"Yes, do it again," he ordered. "Dump out that container and refill it."

I considered telling Levon that I didn't want to be part of his ridiculous documentation that cheapened my experience in the home of my ancestry. But I couldn't. I knew if I said one thing, it would betray all the rage in my heart, and I didn't want to admit I had rage in my heart. I was angry because Levon wasn't available to translate for me, so busy having his own conversations with Sarkut and the other men, neglecting me and Auntie Esther, so I didn't communicate at all with these distant relatives who were friendly, who kissed both my cheeks and posed for portraits with me. I didn't know if I was having a *real* experience with them or not.

But the dirt was real. Back in America, I had imagined it would be so powerful to stand on this dirt, this land, which my mother had spitefully told me to kiss. All I wanted was to have my moment with the dirt, to feel its properties, to be joined with my heritage through its minerals, and here was Levon, exploiting my moment. I seethed while scooping up the soil my ancestors were composed of so that Levon could get his shot of a girl returning to her homeland, an advertisement for young people to take his trips, just as he wished.

When I was done with my faux film work, I turned around to find Cameh holding a plastic bag and a twist tie. She knelt down to the ground and helped me fill it with dirt.

I thought I understood why my cousin Tina would write letters to these people while she was estranged from her sisters. Who wouldn't like distantly related villagers who couldn't criticize you, who weren't acting out the particular rage and shame of Armenian American families? I realized I wasn't much different from Tina, living three thousand miles away from my family, now trying to find them in a village halfway across the world.

I couldn't communicate with Cameh beyond a smile, so I turned to watch Levon, who was still videotaping in the field where I had left him. Cameh turned and looked too, and then we retreated to the van. As I walked with her, I felt her gentle jitteriness, distantly related to the unsettling feelings I'd experienced while leaving my family back in Boston. I sensed by her kindness and emotion that she knew the significance of this moment: We were inexplicably, miraculously brought together for an hour on an ordinary fall day, decades after world events had torn our people, our family, apart. I'd come here to stand on the land, but it turned out that blood was more important.

Later when I watched the video, Cameh and I appear to be very tiny, just a couple of characters in an old country tableau of villagers and tourists, trees and chickens, and a wooden barn door. And then she and I turn our faces—two featureless ovals reflecting the sun—at the exact same time.

Waves:
My Haitian American Rhythm

PHOENIX SOLEIL

It is raining outside. With nothing else to do, Jeanette and I play in the hallway of her apartment building in East Flatbush, Brooklyn. I am ten. She is eleven and my best friend—my only real friend. Jeanette from Guyana never lets me into her apartment. I don't know why. I don't let her into my apartment either: the one bedroom, too many people, a strange language, and my crazy mom. How much of my interior can I reveal to her—their hurts, my helplessness—and still have her friendship?

She goes to get us a board game—probably "Trouble" or "Life." I am waiting for Jeanette by the stairs. From where I stand, I hear noises behind a door, fighting, in Kreyòl, insults I am familiar with like "*makak,*" "*malelve,*" "*djab*" ("monkey," "misbehaved," "devil"). The door opens, a young woman appears with suitcases, big vinyl bags, two in each hand. She's silent. Behind her, following her, comes a stream of insults; the young woman's eyes focus in front of her. She struggles her bags through the doorway. I see hands behind her gesticulating. As the young woman moves farther through the door, I see it's an older woman shadowing her, yelling at her.

The younger woman's back is to the older woman. The wall and I, her audience, watch the voiceless expressions on the younger woman's face—outrage, exhaustion, determination, and a brief, very slight smile, like: *How could you say something that ridiculous?*

She checks her stuff again. She looks ahead. She's leaving for good.

I can tell by the way she holds herself that she is Haitian correct, born and bred there. It always felt to me that real Haitians move as if in a private ocean. In New York African American culture, the poor urban black culture of the States, people move like the hip-hop dances, like the breakdances, like cutting through and making space, angular, and that always has seemed fitting to me, because American culture, New York City culture, is angular. You have to be the Terminator to get through. Smoothness is expressed with a war of movement—the smoothness of the running man, a dance where you run in place, reminiscent of technology: gears, angles, smooth delivery. But Haitians move as if in their own world; they move with a softness, as if water is always surrounding them—a rough ocean, but their own.

My third-grade teacher says that grandparents have great stories to tell. I feel bad: My grandmother lives with us but we rarely talk, or rather we talk but we don't have many conversations; sometimes we fight. So after school that night, I'm sitting on the floor of the bedroom, she enters, her walk is slow and heavy, she sits down on a bed, softly, heavily, she's still, and I ask her, "Do you have any stories? They say at school grandmothers are supposed to have stories." My mother and aunt chime in, *"Wi bay li istwa."* ("Yes, tell her stories."). *Wow,* I think, *so this applies even to my family.* What really surprises me is how she tries, really tries; her eyes turn inward. I wait. I watch as she peers inside herself. Finally she answers, *"non."* But her eyes are still searching, still trying. I wait, hoping she will find something she can give me. She dies years later, and I still wonder what was inside of her.

My aunt, she lives with us too, is the adult with the most joy: We take walks in the summer; she opens the drapes in the morning, both of us delighted when the sun fills our bedroom. My mother, on the other hand, insists we bring the drapes down when she is home; my aunt smiles at me in secret understanding. I watch my aunt stand in front of her mirror as she puts on her makeup, combs her hair; we work on word-find puzzles together, watch *All My Children*, go to *bals* (Haitian parties): food, drink, music, kids, watching the adults from the sidelines, scared that my aunt will drag me out to dance with them. The only relationship in my family where I saw affection and joy flow easily was a relationship outside the family. Every day, sometimes twice a day, my aunt and her best friend, Pascal, would lighten up the heaviness of our apartment with animated conversations sprinkled with laughter. *"Kouman ou ye?"* ("How are you?") *"Mwen la."* ("I'm here.")

On my second remembered trip to Haiti, looking out the airplane window, I see a soldier walk ten steps and then take a drag from a cigarette. The walk, the stride, the look, the expression, the posture, the motion—are all so Haitian. I search for the words to describe why. My cousin next to me, born in Haiti, raised in Haiti, agrees. She says, "I wish I could take a picture, he's so typically Haitian."

Features. Genetics. I can pick out Haitians. I have a friend whose features are so Haitian: a certain kind of wideness in the forehead, a roundness in the cheek bones, the lips. Language. Assimilated. Learned. Babies learning to walk, they watch others. How do you walk on the poorest land in the Western Hemisphere? With half of your body swimming in the water of dreams. Motion. How many ways are there to walk? Some of the dreadlocked men from Jamaica, tall men, you look for the sand behind them; they carry Jamaica with them, in them.

Haitian women shopping at the grocery store on Nostrand and Newkirk, tropical dresses with tube socks and sneakers—whatever works—stubborn expressions on the subway cars. Sundays: Haitians girls wearing ribbons and dresses with lots of frills; Haitian boys and men in suits; mothers in hats and formal wear from another time. Haitian Mass: the songs and energy; women with their arms open raised toward the sky, staring beyond the church steeple, begging, wailing. *Amwe!* (*Help!*)

The hallway walls are beige. The wooden stair railing is cracked and painted blue. The older woman's voice picks up in speed and pitch. The young woman is still and silent. She gazes ahead. I see relief on her face, followed by a stubborn expression. She checks her bags. Then her eyes focus straight ahead again. She walks quickly, carrying her bags down the stairs. I wonder if she has a long, thought-out plan or whether I am witnessing the final breaking point, where nothing matters anymore. Their tension feels old. It seems to be the young woman's decision to change the circular loop of their tension into a straight line out the door. The insults appear to be hurled after something that is moving away, not the smack that pushed it out the door. What made enough, enough? The older woman stands holding the brown metal door open. Her insults pursue the young one even after she is out of sight and the sound of her footsteps going down fades. Finally the older woman slams the door shut.

Does the young woman have a place to go or does she walk into a haze of hopes and fears?

It takes a lot to get the Haitian women I know to do something financially impractical. Bernadette, my cousin who is Haitian correct, left Haiti for a better life. She sleeps on the extra mattress in our living room. She tells us she was fired from a job cleaning a house for something she didn't do. She describes the white woman yelling insults, following her from room to room as she gets her stuff together. Bernadette says she stayed silent to avoid agitating the white woman—hoping she won't make an angry call to the placement office. Bernadette needs the work. I imagine the scene: the powerful one with furious expression shadowing the less powerful one with stubborn silence from room to room. In my family, my futile attempts to use words to break through their loud anger exposes me to more humiliation than absorbing the roar of a vocal attack. Silence is the only hope.

I can't imagine a hip-hop song about letting someone dis you ever becoming popular. Hip-hop celebrates a different kind of strength. The hate and violence in hip-hop comforts me on a visceral level—hearing the anger expressed, a loud space where you hit back at what hits you. And your dignity is worth any sacrifice including death. Hip-hop is the opposite of what I've had to do to survive my family.

I was silent when my mom *jouwe mwen* (cursed me). When I used to cry and argue, Bernadette and my aunt would say, "Why aren't you used to it?" Kids from the neighborhood, on the playground, laughing off their parents' tempers, whippings, crying, fear, and "Oh, I'll give you something to cry at." Why was I so bad at getting used to it? Annoyed at my tears, my mom only got angrier. I decided that dignity was in silence, my grief expressed, an object of ridicule. If I showed a shell, even if my heart was breaking, then I looked strong—and that was very important.

Maybe my shell would have been less hard. Maybe, in a different neighborhood. In my neighborhood anger and frustration spilled out onto the street, needing to be spilled, the way rappers need to drop lines. It was normal for thirteen-year-old girls to say, "I feel like beating her up," about someone they didn't know, proud of their reckless hate. I had to decide at age eleven how much I'd risk to protect my friend Kimone from teenage boys who wanted to feel her up on our way to the library after school. A six-year-old boy threw his desk on the floor in the middle of class. Sixth-grade boy aimed *bitch, hoes,* and *fuck-yous* at me. Jeanette told me to yell back. But I was always paralyzed, silent. How could language save me in the streets when it didn't save me at home? I went from one kind of pain to another—sharp to round. Cross, cross, cross culturalism.

I understood the tension, the young woman needing to leave. I understood leaving. She and the older woman, they are both Haitian and probably family, but that isn't strong enough. She has to leave because whatever connects them isn't enough.

Haitians fighting, how is it different from two Germans fighting, two Russians fighting, two Puerto Ricans fighting? I know the ocean they swim in, and it's an ocean I float in, swim in, struggle against, drown in.

The language, the roundness of French words mixed with West African languages and other pieces of what came and stayed. I tried to learn German, a semester of running away from French that never belonged to me the way Kreyòl did. And I understood that nothing is ever translated. Intellectually, I know that *"guten tag"* means "good morning," but in my gut, I know *"Mwen la"* doesn't mean "I'm fine." It means "I'm here and life could be a lot worse, often is, but I'm here, and that's enough, and you, my listener, understand that just being here is enough." Hearing Kreyòl spoken in the subway or on the street, I lean my head toward it, parts of me are pulled to it—a chaos of feelings bouncing on the sounds above the words, music echoing deep. Home. I wish I had happier memories. My most intense memories are of hurled insults, drowning in my mother's words thrown with hate. Freedom was running away from my family, walking out from under a barrage of insults much like that young woman—running from pain that I only understood later had little to do with me.

Darkness. When I walk into my aunt and mother's home as a twenty-seven-year-old, three o'clock in the afternoon, the two of them want the drapes down all the time. They yell at me when I try to open them. I expect this from my mother, but my aunt always brings in the light. Worried about my aunt's sanity, I ask her about Pascal. "Oh, I don't know. I haven't talked to Pascal in weeks." Flippant, this response about a friend she has spoken to nearly every day for the past forty years. "We're not family; she doesn't owe me anything." I keep pushing against the ridiculousness of that, finally stopping when her protestations grow to anger, accompanied by a couple of tears that she completely ignores. I always imagined that it was because Pascal and my aunt were free of familial chains and debts, that there could be such sincere affection.

She is becoming as dark as my mother. My mother always said, "Don't put your trust in friends," and yet I run to my friends for emotional sustenance and shelter. Like my aunt's calls to Pascal, my childhood calls to Jeanette are filled with laughter and excitement. Two poor black girls shift between accents and identities in our made-up adventures: English lords, Hollywood movie stars, Southern belles. We share our fantasies but we don't share our realities until decades later, after drifting away and then back together again. Far away from East Flatbush Brooklyn, our mostly Caribbean neighborhood—when our need and pain were less—Jeanette and I finally let each other in to our private pain. Escapees, we sit in my kitchen, the light flooding in, shocked by what we reveal to one another, at what we don't know about each other, laughing at the past. We realize our secrets had cut us off from a lot of love.

Except for the bedroom, the home I live in now is without shades, without drapes. I forgot to open them when I had them. Worried about how easily I could slip into darkness, I keep the windows bare, so that sun can always come in. Don't want to sacrifice even a little bit of the sky, don't want to block even a little bit of the light for the respectability of drapes.

I know more Kreyòl words for "hate" than "love." Could I tell someone how much I love them in Kreyòl? Not just I love you, but the size and shape of the feeling? Can I create beauty with the language that ripped me into pieces? I try to write poetry in Kreyòl.

Mwen renmen ou, (Mommy I love you mom,)
Pou tout sa ou eseye fè, (For all you tried to do,)
Pou tout sa ou pat kapab di, (For all you couldn't say,)
Mèsi. (Thank you.)

I visit my mom thinking I've finished the piece, this poem marking the end. I don't tell her about it. When I give my mother my words wrapped with bits of my soul, she takes them and fashions them into a rope. She wraps them around my neck and strangles me with them. Then she asks me why I don't visit more often, and the answer is stuck in my throat. But I love her. I've been taking care of her, developing my forgiveness. She's mellowed some, but I'm not myself, the animated person I am with my friends. I am very careful. I speak to her in English and broken Kreyòl. I half ask it: *"Fanmi nou pa pale de emosyon."* ("Our family doesn't talk about feelings.") I don't expect much, and she says, *"Non."*

I ask, "Why do you think that is?" She says, *"Mwen pa konnen."* ("I don't know.")

Long pause.

"Nou pale de chanson damou." ("We talk about love songs.")

"Songs of romance?"

"Wi, mwen ekri pwezi." ("Yes, I wrote poetry.")

Shock. "You wrote poetry?"

"Wi."

"How old were you?"

"Vingt-ans." ("Twenty.")

"What inspired you?"

"Litèrature Français."

"What about French literature inspired you to write?"

Her eyes widen in dismissive surprise. With a "like duh" expression she answers.

"Litèrature Français li très bèl." ("French Literature is very beautiful.")

I didn't know the woman who often called me ugly and could go on at length about how much she hated me was once fascinated with beautiful words.

Literature. *Pwezi.* It's not as if I never asked my mom about her past. It was one of the safe things to talk about, the thing that made her happy. As a little girl, I'd roll up in her lap and listen to her stories of climbing trees, eating mangoes in Les Angles, her childhood in the country, a tomboy with her brothers. I knew she loved to read. She became a teacher in Haiti. She loved dancing and often went to *bals* and danced until the early morning. From the family, I heard stories of a striking woman confident in her tall heels who sewed her own clothes and dressed well. It's always a shock looking at pictures of her then—beautiful and happy, the brightest black eyes. She seems like a movie star in those pictures.

"Did anyone else in the family write *pwezi?*"

"De kouzin." ("Two cousins.")

She, Roget, and Jean would stroll and discuss French literature and their own poetry.

Once, when I told my mom that I wanted to be a scientist, she said, "No, don't dream like that, it's not possible." I was five. Eventually, I kept my dreams, my loves, to myself—to keep them safe.

The first time I got published, I decided it was safe to tell my mother. She told me she was proud, but she never told me about her own writing.

"Mom, we're both writers; I didn't know we had this in common."

She looks at me. Silence. Sometimes I see my grandmother in her–the face and the expressions. As I ask her these questions, she waits with a long pause before giving me the answers. They are short sentences, bullets from her soul. It's like a mountain had always been in my land and I didn't know till it erupted molten lava that it was a volcano.

"When did you stop?"

"Apré mwen vini America, ou vinn disoriented." ("After coming to America, you become disoriented.") *"Ou chè che travay."* ("You search for work.) *"Fanmi yan te pòv."* ("The family was poor.")

In Haiti, my grandmother struggled to get my mother and her six siblings, plus some nephews and nieces, through school. When my mom was growing up, there were times when there was only one meal a day. She'd describe being very hungry, but knowing she had to wait.

I admire my mom for being the first to come to America, sending money back home, and then bringing everyone else. Like my cousin Bernadette, her first jobs were cleaning houses and taking care of other people's children. In the photographs from after she came to America you can see the change: She stopped caring about fashion. Her eyes took on a dead look. Everyone in the family is shocked at what she's become. Growing up, I felt like she hated fun.

"Do you still have your poetry?"

"Mwen vini avec mwen kouti e kaye dans bagaj mwen. . . . Mwen te konn koud tou tan. . . . Mwen koude rad la pou maman. . . . Mais mwen jeter sa paske pat gen plas." ("I came to America with my sewing stuff and notebooks in my bags. . . . I used to sew all the time. . . . I made that dress for my mom in that photograph. . . . But I threw them away because there was no place.")

"You threw them away?"

"Wi."

"Was that hard?"

"Pat gen plas. Apatman te two piti. Fanmi yan te pòv." ("There was no place. The apartment was small. Our family was poor.")

"You worried a lot? You were scared a lot?"

"Wi."

In America, even when she finally had a safe job, she never could let go of worrying, never let go of fear.

I understand now what I was going through growing up. Walking from the angularity of the streets to the water of my home, the borders, and the bitterness that crashed on either side, hard to articulate, hard to navigate. Haitians and African Americans found different ways to walk with pain. My home was a fog of unshed tears. It wasn't until later—now—that I understand the emptiness, unspoken desires, resigned suffering, the weight of always feeling fearful. Love and laughter were constantly sacrificed for practicality, for necessity, the seriousness of people who are used to the idea that laughter is extra and not needed.

"Mom, I'm proud of you. *Mè si.* I have a life where I can write. I don't worry."

She looks at me and asks, "You don't?"

I say, "No, I don't." Which isn't honest, I think, just after I say it. I do worry about money. Did the poet in my mom die in the same battle that threatens the life of the poet in me, battles against the armies of poverty, self-doubt, and too little time? Her dead eyes are the tombstones left on the battlefield—the sacrifices from the mother I never met, the mother who put me in a better position to win my war.

Mom! Did you have to die? Life is so hard and nothing has been as hard as you. Throw away my notebooks? They will have to pry them out of my dead, cold hands.

I felt soft after that conversation, like molten lava, like melted rock.

I have a legacy. How did it get passed down? The silences were so loud. What had been bouncing above the insults and the emptiness? I didn't know I carried her *kouti* and *kaye* in the bags I struggled out the door with when I left.

Leaving. Was I just dancing the running man? I got something from the motion, the movement. I needed to leave in order to become who I am, but I didn't go anywhere. Tides—waves recede back to the ocean; I wanted to be different from her. I thought I was running away from her; instead I ran into her. With a stunned voice, a loud voice, I say *I am a writer like my mother before me.*

This essay is dedicated to the next wave of my family: Anika, Anouck, Audrey, Axelle, Ivan, Jessica, Justine, Jonathan, Jovanna, Jovanka, Karim, Linzi, Namazzi, Samantha, and Soraya. Crest!

Leaving Battambang, the City of Answers

SOKUNTHARY SVAY

Sometimes what's left unsaid can contain the most power. I recall English teachers emphasizing that students learn to "read between the lines," to see the written words as representations of a deeper meaning. The unearthing of silence symbolizes my personal history. I was born in a Khmer refugee camp in Khao I Dang, Thailand. My family crossed over to Thailand shortly after the Khmer Rouge—the brutal communist regime that reigned in Cambodia from 1975 to 1979—was expelled by a Vietnamese "liberation."

For most of my life, the details of my parents' past in Cambodia and how their lives have been affected by the regime have been a mystery to me. For so long, my parents have been silent about their struggles. In reading between the lines of my family's silence, I am slowly learning where I stand in relation to my three worlds: Cambodia, my parents' homeland; New York, where I grew up; and, Thailand, where I was born. It should be as simple as identifying as Khmer American, but although my parents are from Cambodia, I still feel awkward calling Cambodia home.

My picture of Cambodia consisted of scenes from *The Killing Fields*—

from the historical depiction of the exodus of Phnom Penh to the traditional red scarves worn by the Khmer Rouge—and from my attendance at numerous Khmer weddings. I was introduced to my distant relatives by looking at photographs of their grim facial expressions. Early on, I knew that if I wanted to learn anything about my family's background and how and why they ended up in the United States, I would have to learn it on my own. My limited exposure to Khmers and our homeland, combined with my parents' silence, left me with a strong desire to uncover the truth of our history and experiences.

My curiosity about Cambodia burgeoned in college, where I was eager to discover something new. Hidden in an obscure corner of the library with stacks of books on Cambodia, I pored through Cambodian memoirs published in the 1980s that hinted at what my parents survived. My family was disconnected from this self-discovery. If they sometimes saw books with Cambodian titles in the house, they never inquired about them. One of the first memoirs I read was by Haing Ngor, the Khmer actor who won an Oscar for his role in *The Killing Fields.* When I read his book, I replaced the faces of his parents with my own; I recreated the experience in my mind as though it were my family's story.

Once I had asked my father, "What happened to you during the Khmer Rouge regime?" The result was an evasive but somewhat promising answer: "One day I'll tell you our story and you'll write a book about it." I have been writing about this topic since college.

Although both my brothers did not finish high school, I managed to write my way to a free education. I received an English Literature scholarship that paid for my schooling, and later received a humanities fellowship. Both awards were given to me based on the context of Cambodia, which was the focus of my writing. Poetry, particularly prosody, also became my platform to begin etching out answers or interpretations to my own feelings of displacement. I wrote lines of verse to bring down personal barriers of silence. I was particularly inspired by U Sam Oeur, the first accomplished Khmer poet both in Cambodia and America who used traditional Khmer poetry to speak about his life.

My mother was married to my father at an early age, and they had Thy, their firstborn son, within a couple of years. Sothea, my second brother, came shortly afterward, but died of dysentery during the regime. My younger brother, Jammy, was born later. Writing this is painful because I do not know the full story of Sothea's death or my parents' loss during the regime. When I was born a few years later in the camps, I was born with a birthmark on my knee shaped like my country. Cambodians believe that birthmarks are signs of past lives. My mother must have made some peace with herself when I was born, believing that Sothea was reincarnated in me.

During my first trip to Cambodia in the winter of 2002—my father's third trip and my mother's second since they left Cambodia to make the United States their home—it was a smorgasbord of catching up with relatives, alive and dead, as well as deciding on a bride for my older brother, Thy. My father rented a van for a slew of our relatives to journey in. Seeing the ruins of Angkor Wat is practically a required Khmer pilgrimage. Sadly, most of my relatives, who have spent their entire lives in this country, could never afford to see the temples of Angkor, the ancient city of the Khmer Empire, at its height. The outline of the three-tiered temple appears on everything in Cambodia as a source of national pride, and it's also the emblem on the country's flag. Close to twenty-five of us packed ourselves into a van blatantly marked TOURISM on the side, which I lovingly dubbed the Tourismobile.

But after the weeklong excursion to see the temples, something else on that road trip had more of an impact on me: revisiting my parents' home during the Khmer Rouge regime in the province of Battambang to find the remains of Sothea.

In most cities in Cambodia, the streets are filled with dusty *motos* (motorcycles), bicycles, and small but increasing numbers of hand-me-down Toyotas. We finally reached Battambang, marked by a statue—a deity with several arms—in the middle of the road, remnants of Cambodia's past Hindu influence. We relied on memory to find the shacks my parents called home. The Cambodian countryside can be difficult to navigate since houses are demarcated only by man-made plots or ponds. Past the several-armed deity, most shacks in this area were indistinguishable.

In my father's impatience to find Sothea's burial spot, he stopped the van in front of a roadside restaurant. He flagged a *moto* taxi and then rushed off without a word. Meanwhile, my mother and the rest of us panicked. Worried that he would get lost, my mother instructed her younger brother to go after him on another available *moto* taxi. The twenty-something of us waited on the roadside, scattered outside the tourism van. Within minutes, my uncle returned with my father, who safely found his way back to us but seemed as lost as ever. At this point, we piled back into the van. My mother took over and instructed the driver to take us through different roads in the city until something looked familiar to her.

Finally, my mother asked the driver to stop the van. Our clan jumped out and followed her, perplexed at the story unfolding before their eyes. Walking into the boundary of a person's property, my mother immediately introduced herself to the owner, an elder woman, and began asking questions. My mother spoke from her memory: "I buried my son's body in a spot between two coconut trees." My mother made shuffling motions in her sandals and pink sarong toward the tropical bark. Meanwhile, the resident followed her, just as mystified as we were.

"I think it was here," my mother continued, implying that she wanted to dig up the ground. And then the elder spoke as if channeling from the local spirits: "How are we to know what is left of him? It has been over twenty years. Sometimes our memory changes to fit with our desires. For all we know, the wind may have blown his bones away along with the rest of the dust in this country." My mother took the hint and dropped the idea of digging up the woman's land.

I took a photograph of my mother at that moment. Her eyes crinkled with pain, drawing her forehead inward. Her face was covered by her *krama,* a traditional Khmer scarf. It was hard to tell if she was protecting her face from the airborne dirt in the road, or if she was holding in the sob that threatened to escape. My father's back was to the camera, hands on his hips. His arm was larger than anything else in the picture, and he seemed determined and yet hopeless at the same time. Oftentimes, I found him falling into silence with a wistful expression on his face. I know that expression so well; it has plagued me as much as his thoughts have plagued him. At that moment I wanted to comfort my parents, but instead I continued taking pictures.

We thanked the woman with *riel,* the local currency, and went on our way. The vagueness of the land and my mother's memory were not grounds for overturning the old woman's property.

On the way back, we hiked Phnom Sampov, the "ship hill" of seven hundred steps. Phnom Sampov, once a torture and prison facility during the regime, is now a home for monks and nuns. After some prayers and a libation, we went inside a cave to burn incense and pray some more. My family and I prayed, not only for Sothea, but also for the souls left to die in that cave.

I snapped a blurry shot of my cousin as he stood near the cave's opening. Light shone on him at an angle, and he appeared to be an apparition in my viewfinder. The blurriness of my digital camera only magnified the spiritual presence of this city within a hill. We eventually fumbled and felt our way out of the cave to an elevated opening. I didn't know until I conducted research three years later that this was one of many caves where victims were pushed to their deaths. The blood that once covered the caves has since been scrubbed off. There were bones scattered where people were pushed off. I learned that the Khmer Rouge committed such acts to save bullets. Learning that Phnom Sampov was actually a place of death (and enlightenment) was a startling discovery.

Toward the end of the day, we headed back to the local temple, where the entire family sought forgiveness from Sothea, who had been left twice by his family in this land. We bought sticks of incense, soda, and other foods to give as offerings. We inscribed his name on the incense as if without the inscription, our offerings would get lost among those from other families. I snapped a photo of my parents in front of the temple. *We stayed here too, when they first came.* We did not need to call the oppressors by their names anymore, as though doing so would give them power.

Before the night was over, my father revealed his emotions to me; this was unusual. "It was like it just happened yesterday," he said. His tears fell on the ends of his eyelashes. I wanted to ask him right then and there about the entire story. What led up to Sothea's death? What happened from the moment the Khmer Rouge invaded till my family's arrival in the United States? And why are these answers kept from me? But it seemed too vulnerable a moment for him, and I could not exploit the pain he was feeling, not when he had hidden it for so long, kept it so far buried that he had almost forgotten it.

I probably lost my chance to hear that story. But maybe there will be a day when their reluctance to remember will be outweighed by the need to pass on the truth to their grandchildren. When they realize that history will be lost with them, then the importance of submitting to the reality of their events will be even more cathartic than they realize.

When we left Battambang, we left the city of answers. We left Sothea, knowing that these answers were not ours to be found and would be aerated in the dust that fills the roads and the cities of this beautiful and tragic country. We left with reminders of the pain that Cambodia holds, ready to rebury them once more.

My mother had told me that Sothea's last words when he died were "Mother, I'm so hungry. Please find me food . . . Mother . . . I'm so cold now." After which he shut his eyes.

Triggered by some event or smell, I look back on that trip now and then. Being there brought to life all the images and stories that Thy confessed to me in the stairwell of the Bronx building, our first apartment in the States, when we were kids.

Even now I have difficulty calling my brother "Thy," and often revert to "Sothy." After passing his citizenship test, he shortened his name with a lackadaisical air. My younger brother, Jammy, is actually Sokuntharith on his birth certificate (it's common for Khmer children to be named alliteratively). My younger brother and I would often be mistaken for each other on paper. For the standardized tests given in New York City, preprinted electronic sheets with our names would only display six out of the many letters in our names. Finally, my mother dubbed him Jammy, after the lead character in the 1980s TV show *The Bionic Woman*. Like many immigrants, we learned English and picked up American culture through television. Since then, his nickname has mutated into various forms and appearances—Jammy, Jimmy, Jaime, Jim—changes subject to mood and trend.

It has been a little more than three years since my first trip to Cambodia in 2002. In the midst of looking for Jammy's birth certificate in June 2006 (as a favor to him, since he recently moved to another state), I came across papers documenting my family's refugee resettlement when we were accepted into the United States in 1981 under the sponsorship of the International Rescue Committee. Uncovering my family's story revealed a drawn-out saga.

From what I've read in Khmer memoirs, upon applying for relocation, refugees had to go through a very thorough interview process; this included listing past occupations, family members, and so on. In the refugee documents, my mother's entire family is listed, and in the status section all were claimed as MISSING. The reality of 1981, when the whereabouts of my mother's entire family were unknown, filled me with a grief I'd never known. However, upon closer inspection, the family names brought me solace—my mother had made contact with some family members after her resettlement in the United States and was reunited with many more upon her first return to Cambodia twenty years after she had left.

Often, I think about my family's history of name changing and its relationship to our identity. My father's real name is Pheng Nget, not Chy Svay, as it appears on all of his documents. I was told that the name change was done to protect our family. Before he married my mother, he was in the Cambodian army. In addition to many other things, being affiliated with the prior Cambodian government was grounds for extermination under the Khmer Rouge.

Photos of them at the time of the interview were included in the documents. In spite of these photos, I still have no idea what my parents looked like when they were younger since their wedding and family photos are lost. Without concrete documents or pictures, my reliance on our story and who we are had, up to this point, been verbal. These resurfaced mug shots of my parents' terrified faces, and the outstretched hand of a refugee-camp worker holding an identification number, were a revelation. I was starving for this information, and I brimmed with tears of triumph and relief at recovering something hidden from me. In that picture, my mother is the most beautiful I've ever seen her; she's the age I am now, making this discovery either well timed or eerie, or both. It makes me wonder about the importance of being twenty-five, for her as someone surviving a regime, death, and separation, and for me as someone who has lived a life of secrets and is now unearthing this significant connection. For once, I have something tangible to include in my parents' re-created past, one that has no room for the errors of memory.

However, the discrepancies between my parents' ages, along with my birthday, did not add up to what I had been told: that there is a ten-year age difference between my parents, despite the paper indicating five, and that my birth date, which I'd believed to be July 31 all my life, was listed as July 21. There have been too many mistakes, either rooted in great coincidence or in incompetence.

These changes point to how our identities are not grounded but floating across borders. With my attempts to learn my parents' past without them, I was left to interpret, re-create, and imagine their scenarios. With snippets throughout the years like a time lapse, I have created a picture of their experience. But that was all dependent on their passive storytelling. And now faced with the bluntness of these documents, I cannot trust that the answers lie here. To do that would be denying the discrepancy between my parents' verbal storytelling and the conflicting facts of these refugee documents. At least they confirmed my father's original name, Pheng Nget. Still, if our names and identities can be stripped of us, what is the value in being attached to these identifiers? More importantly, why has there been silence from my parents about the reasons behind this and everything else they have hidden?

Silence can become a means to an end. In their silence, my parents have kept their truth of Cambodia; in my own silence, I have kept my connection to Cambodia from them. We are hiding behind our aliases, either through fear or through tradition. Where can I begin to draw the lines between my parents' destroyed identities and their current ones? Their documented ages and their real ones? The name changes symbolize how I feel about the nature of my relationship to them, of hiding who I am in an American identity as they hide themselves in their Khmer identity, and of the assimilation through the two letters left behind in Thy's name and the morphing of Jammy's moniker. Ultimately, I feel robbed of permanence in name, in country, and in personal history. When can I begin to trust in my parents and how they display themselves to the world?

In my parents' living room during one of my many trips to the Bronx this past year to see my family, without any prompting, my mother and father disclosed stories from their time in the camps in Thailand. My father spoke about an incident in which some Cambodian refugees were herded onto a bus, believing that they would go to another camp. Upon stopping, the soldiers forced them out of the vehicle and designated a spot for them to walk. They innocently walked to their deaths in an area laden with land mines.

My mother told me that during our family's stay in Khao I Dang from late 1979 to early 1981, the soldiers' trucks would stop every night before a refugee's home. Although the trucks stopped nearby, they never stopped at our home. She said that I was the reason they did not stop at her door, that the noise of a crying newborn prevented any unexpected "visits." My parents calmly told me about their traumatic experiences, and I speculated that the distance of so many years was a factor in their controlled storytelling. Walking to my apartment later that evening, I went over again what my mother said about the soldiers not stopping at her house. In essence, she was saying that *I* saved her life. In that realization, I lost my composure on the sidewalk. *I saved my mother's life.*

After my first trip to Cambodia, I had great respect and appreciation for my parents' every sacrifice and worry. Each decision they made for me seemed to be colored by their experience of living under the regime.

The danger of creating a journey in the mind is that we may keep it so abstract that it has no credibility in reality. I was faced with cultural and familial barriers in my attempt to create a homeland in Cambodia. The books I read about Cambodia dealt with a limited time in the country's history—the Khmer Rouge regime. Because of this limited perspective, I envisioned Cambodia as only a place of death and tragedy.

My trip to Cambodia gave me a broader picture of the country outside of the tragedy. Now, I have images of collapsed and tarnished colonial buildings in my head when I think of Phnom Penh; the countryside is filled with rice fields and coconut and palm trees that provide sustenance to the surrounding residents. I'm convinced that Cambodia has the most beautiful children I've ever seen: round and brown, cherublike faces expressing that joy of simply being alive. I will remember my family's pleasure in Khmer dance, when they fan their fingers in gestures reminiscent of lotus blossoming nearby, as they swing and grin at one another in the dance circle. This is Cambodia to me, a place of my heritage and a wallpapered landscape in my mind.

While the challenges of being bicultural are a pretty common experience for hyphenated Americans, I feel envious. At least there's something more definitive about being American-born. I was born in a country neither of my parents' origin nor of my upbringing. Early on, I knew that nationality—the place of your birth—had something to do with who you are. I knew other children my age who were born in the same camp. Somehow we felt distinct from those born in Cambodia. We weren't just Khmer; we were refugees. In addition to that distinction, we similarly shared conflicted feelings of being less Khmer because of our birthplace and, later on, because we weren't fluent in our native language.

Khao I Dang, the camp where I was born, contained an influx of refugees en route to other destinations. Unlike in other Thai camps, refugees in Khao I Dang were eligible for resettlement in another (or third, as they put it) country. Some who were associated with the Khmer Rouge were turned down for resettlement and repatriation. Eventually the camp closed in 1992, and its residents were moved to another site where they awaited (what many inhabitants felt was a forced) repatriation.[1] The camp's progression embodies my own shifting identity and how our personal truths are impermanent and constantly evolving.

My father and I recently conversed for an hour about family. Eventually, I pulled out the resettlement documents I found and asked him to explain the inconsistency between his own words and the text before him. We spent the next half hour solving the puzzles I created in my mind. As it turns out, my father did not change his name to save the family. He took his cousin's birth certificate and birth date so he could enroll in school (back then in Cambodia, proof of age was required in order to sit for school entrance exams). My mother's lack of a birthday is simply because she forgot her birthday, as did my father who had assumed the birthday of his cousin. My mother's May 5 birthday, as explained by my father, was a date conjured up that my mother could easily remember because of its repetition of fives. Since Cambodia observes the lunar calendar, it is difficult to decipher their actual birthdays. My father told me that on the day he was born, his mother unceremoniously scratched his birthday in chalk on the wall of their home. That was *his* birth certificate.

In asking my father these questions, I challenged the silence in my family. In doing so, I've gained, for the first time, some semipermanent truths. There's no doubt of the atrocities of living under the Khmer Rouge regime, but the uncovering of aspects of my parents' personal history has taken away its mystique for me. I credit part of it to the act of writing. Through writing, I have created my own documentation of my family's history. The realities I experienced through books prepared me and gave me an appreciation of our history, while the unpredictable trip to Battambang, learning about Sothea and the victims of the cave, showed me that stories develop on their own. My parents needed their own time and distance in order to relay their stories. Questioning my father about the documents showed me that I was ready to find the truth in the lines of my own creation, a truth that cannot be contained any longer. Like the three worlds I inhabit—Cambodia, New York, and Thailand—my truth contains multiple realities. Across borders and between the lines of my family history, in my parents' stories I've created a homeland in my own words.

Heartbroken for Lebanon

LEILA ABU-SABA

In the summer of 1974, when I was twelve, my Lebanese uncle took me into Ain el-Hilweh camp for a quick tour. I was the American cousin who arrived without my parents to spend the summer with my family in our village, Mieh-Mieh, on a hillside overlooking the port city of Sidon. Ain el-Hilweh lies between Sidon and Mieh-Mieh and contains the largest Palestinian refugee camp in South Lebanon. Uncle Adib stopped the car at a crowded intersection, where low concrete block buildings stretched as far as I could see.

"That building on the corner is on our land," he said. "These used to be fields belonging to your grandfather and other villagers." His hand moved across the crowded street. "But when the Palestinians fled Palestine in 1948, they came here, and the Lebanese government asked us if they could stay. The government said it would only be two weeks." Uncle Adib had large brown eyes and a gentle face; he looked at me expectantly, eyebrows slightly raised.

I'd heard the story of the Palestinian Disaster, the events of 1948, for as long as I could remember. This was the first time anyone had taken me to see our property in the camp. I knew from watching TV news and from my family's stories that this camp had been bombed heavily by Israel in the previous month.

Children milled around the car, staring at me, the exotic American. My uncle showed me an apartment block on the main road that had buckled in the center from an Israeli bomb, dropped in retaliation for the terrorism at Ma'alot that spring, when members of the Democratic Front for the Liberation of Palestine instigated a school massacre in northern Israel. In America just two months before, a Jewish school friend accused me of being complicit in this crime. I hated that she would lump me, an Arab American, in the same category as the armed guerrillas of the Palestinian movement. But nothing I said could break my Jewish friend's conviction that all Arabs were terrorists.

Now, looking at the devastated building, everything seemed hopelessly unfair. I was frightened of the buckled concrete, the empty floors, the way an enormous apartment block could crumple like a flimsy box.

Not long after that 1974 visit, Israeli planes bombed Ain el-Hilweh. I stood on my uncle's balcony and watched the jets dip and turn, while mushroom clouds billowed over the apartment blocks. I felt outraged that people were being killed before my eyes and I could do nothing to stop it. I was positive that if my Jewish friends could stand with me and really *see* what was happening, they would be just as distraught. My family members convinced me to come downstairs to the orchard with the women and children. The earth shook beneath our feet every time another bomb dropped. The neighbor held a baby in her arms who looked at me curiously as I wept.

"The baby doesn't cry," the mother said. "She did the first time they bombed, but now she is used to it. You will be, too."

Born and largely raised in America, I am of the first generation of jet plane immigrants; unlike previous generations who took long boat trips to their new countries, we have not been content to stay in the new land forever.

My Lebanese father flew to the U.S. in 1956 for graduate school. He met and married my American mother and took her to Lebanon for their honeymoon. Just after my birth in 1962, we returned to Lebanon to live for two years. I lived there again when I was eight, when I learned to read and write in Arabic. In the thirteen years until the onset of civil war in 1975, we returned to Lebanon four times, not including the two-year sojourn, and have been returning at intervals ever since.

My sense of homeland was shaped not only by the intense family life of my father's clan and the love of Arabic suffusing the culture, but also by my passionate, emotional connection to the soil. My father was born a peasant and spent his youth plowing and harvesting alongside his brothers. After he emigrated, Lebanon prospered and our relatives took jobs that allowed them to treat the family farm as a sideline. When I was born, the cycle of crops still ruled daily life. Figs, almonds, and grapes ripened in their time, and I was instructed on how to pick and preserve them. My grandmother's storeroom supplied olives and olive oil to several families, and I helped her as she baked bread, dried tomatoes, and gathered wild thyme for the winter.

In the U.S., I was accustomed to playgrounds, lawns, orderly suburban childhood pleasures. In Lebanon, our fields and village were my playgrounds. My cousins and I climbed trees, threw rocks, went on hikes into the hills, wandered the village square. When I was twelve, the summer of the bombings, my cousins organized a folk dance troupe, and I danced the *dabke* with them to the thrilling strains of proud nationalist Lebanese songs. Our days were filled with social calls, feasts, poetry recitations, weddings, and for me—the American visitor—trips to ancient ruins.

From the age of five, I was aware of Lebanon's history and felt a personal connection to it. From my uncle's balcony, I could see a seven-hundred-year-old Crusader's castle on an island in the harbor, which we visited often. My American home was decorated with pictures, posters, and artwork depicting these and other Lebanese antiquities. In kindergarten, I found a picture of Sidon's castle in a history book and brought it to class for show-and-tell. I explained that I'd toured this castle, that it was near my grandparents' home, that we had flown to Lebanon in a plane. To my surprise, my teacher hustled me back to my seat. My mother later told me that my teacher thought I was lying. The teacher told my mother that children who read books above their grade level had trouble distinguishing truth from reality. This was the first of many instances in which my personal connection to Lebanon struck Americans as implausible and possibly a lie.

Throughout my school years in America, I always looked for references in books or news reports about Lebanon. I learned early how to use an index and would look up Sidon and its sister city, Tyre, in the Bible. But as the Lebanese civil war of 1975 took over the news, my homeland became all too visible. Bombs, invasions, broken buildings, screaming women–the images repeated incessantly, and I began avoiding the TV news. The civil war got worse in 1982 when the Israelis invaded Lebanon–now the papers printed pictures of Ain el-Hilweh, of unimaginable destruction and loss of life.

I went to college in New York City, wishing I could go to the American University of Beirut instead; I watched the civil war progress from afar. When it got really terrible I felt overwhelmed, and yet I had to keep functioning: go to my summer job, study for classes, have a social life. As I grew older, the civil war dragged on.

In 1985, Mieh-Mieh was sacked as part of the sectarian fighting of the civil war. My relatives fled to Christian areas of Lebanon, to America, and to Australia, where they made new lives for themselves. My connection to the homeland was truly broken. The house where my father was born, and all the other houses of my uncles, stood empty, abandoned.

Then in 1991, without warning, the civil war ended. I was twenty-nine. The war had been going on for half of my life. My uncles returned to our village. Villagers came from across the world to rebuild. My parents returned to Lebanon as well, and my mother found a job at the American University of

Beirut. Lebanon went from a disaster on television—a place cut off from me permanently—to a country I could visit almost as easily as visiting Europe. All I needed to do was buy a plane ticket.

In 1995, I returned to Lebanon. Landing on the tarmac at Beirut made me weep. I was sad for the long years of death caused by the war, but I was overjoyed to see the mountains and the sea again. People on the plane looked at me with curiosity—most of the other passengers were Lebanese, and they seemed nonchalant about flying in from Paris.

During that trip I walked all over Beirut and my village, trying to cram in a lifetime's worth of sights and sensory experiences. I wanted to make up for all the years I had lost; I spent hours with my cousins: chitchatting, eating, dancing, going to church. On one walk I pointed out the location of the old chicken coop behind our grandparents' home.

"You remember things we have totally forgotten," one of my cousins said.

"I used to dream about this place," I said. "You don't know how much I walked here at night, in my sleep."

I hiked through our orchards, and I walked around the rubble of downtown Beirut, then in the very early stages of reconstruction, trying to piece together my broken dreams.

After that two-week visit, I returned to the U.S. but kept my close connection to Lebanon. My parents emailed me regularly and came to the States for long visits. The rise of the Internet made the connection easier; by 1996 there were countless websites devoted to Lebanon and the Middle East. My village itself is documented extensively with photos. I could sit at a computer in California and browse roads and houses I had known since childhood. I could read the *Beirut Daily Star* online, the same paper that would arrive on my parents' Beirut doorstep every morning.

After marrying a Jewish American and having our first child, I returned to Lebanon with my husband and baby for a family wedding in the summer of 2000. It was a hopeful time since the country was rebuilding. I delighted in showing my husband the magnificent antiquities and bustling cities of Lebanon. However, while we were there, fighting broke out in Palestine, the start of the Second Intifada.[1] The end of our visit was shadowed by a new mood of fear and uncertainty in Lebanon.

Exactly a year later, on September 11, 2001, the attacks on the World Trade Center and the Pentagon took place. The tragedy affected me not only because I am an American and an ex–New Yorker, but also because I feared the start of a new age of war. All my parents' hopes for Middle East peace were set back for another generation. However, they still moved back and forth between the U.S. and Lebanon for another two years, while my Lebanese American relatives continued to travel with their children to Lebanon for summer vacations. I had hoped one day to join my Lebanese American cousins in our village, to harvest olives on my grandparents' land, bake Arabic bread, and tell stories. I wanted to show my young sons my ancestral homeland.

Now, in July 2006, Israel is bombing Lebanon in a devastating war, ostensibly against Hizbullah. Thousands of foreigners evacuated under fire. The infrastructure of Lebanon has been demolished, and civilian deaths are already in the hundreds. The end is not yet in sight. The progress Lebanon had made in the fifteen years since the end of the civil war has come undone. My family members in Mieh-Mieh call my cousins in America, who tell me the latest news. Our village is largely cut off, the water supply is unpredictable, and hundreds of refugees are sleeping in the local school. People don't know how children will attend classes now that the school is full of refugees. They don't know if the refugees will start breaking in to the empty houses of absent villagers. The specter of civil war looms.

A week into the bombing, I broke down in front of my husband. "I will never go back with our children," I said. He nodded with certainty. He would never let our children venture into a war zone.

A large TV above the counter of the donut shop in Oakland shows a stark image: a row of children's coffins in Tyre, Lebanon, each coffin spray-painted with a number in red. Tyre is the sister city to Sidon; I was there six years before, eating lunch at a beach resort next to the magnificent Roman ruins. I watch the carnage, feeling slammed by images of disaster from my homeland, while my fellow Californians order tea. I am caught in the schizophrenic disconnect of living my peaceful life in America, while my Lebanese life is destroyed before my eyes as this new war in 2006 rages on. I feel desperate, frantic, and slightly insane. I am so visibly shaken that a man in a booth nearby makes a sympathetic face at me, and I know he can't imagine why I'm distraught. I'm tall, light-skinned; I don't look like the countrywomen of the Lebanese people on TV. I cannot explain myself to him; he will never know or understand why seeing these images hurts me. It's maddening, and yet it's my fate as an Arab American who can visibly pass as a white woman.

Thirty-two years after I first watched Israeli planes bomb the Ain el-Hilweh refugee camp from my Uncle Adib's balcony, my Lebanese homeland is again under attack. My American homeland, where my mother and a dozen generations of her ancestors were born, is complicit in the violence. When I see death in one homeland while living safely in another, I feel incredible torment. I felt this way while I lived in America as the 1975 civil war inflicted Lebanon. When the civil war ended, it took me time to recover. Just when I think I've worked through my feelings about it and put it all behind me, a new war blasts it open again.

My father's country and village are in peril. Once again, I must negotiate this duality of war happening far away in a beloved place, while peace exists in my Californian home. My children are growing up American, and I have little hope of them seeing their grandfather's homeland. Conflicting feelings of grief, loss, and anger disturb the calm of my family's daily routine. To cope, I reach out to my cousins. We comfort each other, send each other pictures, talk gossip, share news. I also reach out to the Arab American community in my town, attending cultural and civic events. Fellow Arab Americans from the Berkeley peace movement have called me in recent days, and my contacts in the Arab-Jewish dialogue movement have reconnected with me too. Jewish and Israeli friends have gotten in touch to ask after my family in Lebanon. Now, I can only assuage my loss and grief by appreciating the life I have right here in front of me. Working to build bridges for peace, no matter where I am, is the only solution I have left. Because my heart, once again, is broken for Lebanon.

American Viking

SARAH MCCORMIC

In college, I studied history—other people's histories. I focused on cultures with ancient, epic timelines: China, India, and the Middle East. American history seemed too new, too familiar. I didn't think of history as something that could relate directly to me. Unlike my Asian American or African American friends, whose status as "hyphenated" Americans served as a daily reminder of their heritage, I had always had the privilege of being considered—and of considering myself—as that bland, modern creature that has no past, existing only in an eternal now and a perfect tomorrow: the generic white American.

That all changed one day, in my early thirties, when I caught the genealogy bug. I was wasting an afternoon surfing aimlessly on the Internet when I came across a family-history website and learned that I could look up my ancestors in their online database. I found one branch of my family in census records from a century ago and tracked them, decade by decade, watching as they trudged west across the country, had children, lost children, got jobs: painter, miller, corset salesman, laborer. In a single afternoon, I was hooked. There was suddenly so much I wanted to know: What mix of genes had combined to result in me? What concoction of cultures and peoples had come together, passing on to me their likes and dislikes, their wisdom and prejudices, their fears and dreams?

I started researching my family tree. I consulted second cousins. I joined the local genealogical society. I purchased a subscription to an online family-history database, which zipped back through the centuries with the click of a mouse. One moment, I wasn't German; the next moment, I was (6.25 percent, through Dad's father's mother's mother). The results, though exciting, were also a little depressing. I learned that I was even more of an American mutt than I had originally thought: I had known that I was Norwegian and Irish, but apparently I was also Scottish, English, French, German, Swiss, and who knew what else. Even my Irish last name—McCormic—didn't represent any larger share of my genes than dozens of other surnames, those of generations of women whose identities had been cancelled out by marriage certificates: Mosier, Cooke, Bjorge, Pixley, Aarsby, Tardif, Madsen, Morencey. . . . It was too much. I needed to focus.

Scandinavia seemed like my best bet. Mom, it turned out, was half-Danish. And I knew that my paternal grandmother's parents were both from Norway, which made Dad half-Norwegian. This meant that I was 50 percent Scandinavian. It seemed like a respectable chunk, giving me a fairly solid claim to a heritage.

I started to think about all the obvious clues I had been ignoring. There were the carved wooden trolls on Grandma's mantelpiece. Grotesque but kindly in appearance, they had forest green skin, bulbous red noses, and goofy grins that watched over every family gathering. There was the Norwegian grace Grandma had taught us to say before dinner—a melodic chant that only she and the trolls understood. There was the endless supply of buttery cookies with exotic names—*krumkake, kransekake*—that flowed out of Grandma's kitchen at Christmastime. And there were the tall blond visitors who filled Grandma's house every summer. I was told that these attractive, blue-eyed strangers were my Norwegian cousins. Dad joked that we shared the same "Viking blood," but it had always seemed unlikely to me that we were very closely related. The tallest member of our family was Dad, who barely hit five foot six inches and was a vocal admirer of both Napoleon and Danny DeVito. I am just more than five feet tall, don't know how to ski, and have eyes that are pond-water brown. Could I really make a legitimate claim to a Norwegian heritage?

For answers, I turned to Grandma. I found her alone in her condo on a rainy winter afternoon. "Tell me about your parents," I said.

She wiggled in her easy chair, picking invisible sweater lint off her chest and dodging my questions with her own. "Why do you want to know all *that?* Aren't you hungry?"

I insisted and she eventually gave in. "She was just seventeen when she came, you know." Grandma's eyes held mine, gleaming with pride. "Seventeen years old and *all alone.*" Within a few hours I had formed a mental picture of my great-grandmother, Karen Anderson Aarsby Bjorge, the intrepid teenager who left behind everything and everyone she knew, puking her way across the Atlantic on a third-class boat ticket, and landing in the middle of a frozen Midwestern prairie, which, according to Grandma's description, was buried year-round in twenty feet of snow. Karen boarded in the drafty attics of distant relatives until she married a poor fisherman named Waldemar from the north of Norway because "she wanted a home of her own." Waldemar brought her to the far Northwest, "in the direction of the fish," where they set up house on a small, rain-soaked island. He made a living pulling salmon out of the Columbia River until he died suddenly, barely forty, leaving Karen alone with three children, a house that smelled of fish, and the Great Depression.

"Why did she leave Norway?" I asked. "Was her family very poor?"

"Poor?!" Grandma looked offended. "Dear, my mother had *servants!*"

I sat back in my chair, mulling over this surprising fact. Why would the daughter of a wealthy family leave for America to become a poor fisherman's wife? I scooted to the edge of my chair and waited for her to explain.

"Honey, the eldest brother got everything in those days," she said, sucking in her cheeks like someone resisting the urge to spit.

I assumed Grandma was exaggerating. "But there must be some keepsakes," I said. "Special family things she brought from Norway?"

Grandma rolled her eyes. "I just *told* you—her brother got *everything*." She shook her head and picked at her sweater lint.

"But what about the trolls? Did she get them when she went back to visit Norway?"

"Went *back*? Mother never went back. Your grandfather and I got those things when we went in 1978."

When I decided to go to Norway with my husband, Ben, Grandma was pleased but solemn, like I was finally going to the dentist to take care of a bad tooth. She taught me how to pronounce the strange names of the distant cousins I would be visiting, the ones who lived on the farm that her mother had left more than one hundred years ago. Rangnild, Haakon, Ingeborg, Arnhild. Silje, Olaf, Edvard, Mette. I prepared a genealogy chart and memorized polite Norwegian greetings. *"Røkelaks er deilig!"* (The smoked salmon is delicious!) *"Hjertelig hilsen fra mine foreldrene."* (My parents send you their best wishes.) *"Husker du min oldemor?"* (Do you remember my great-grandmother?) I had a homeland in my sights, an ancestor to find and get acquainted with, a heritage to claim and to make my own—all in just two short weeks. When I said goodbye to Grandma, she hugged me so hard I couldn't breathe.

On the long flight to Oslo, while the rest of the passengers slept, I indulged in somber thoughts, letting the last part of Great-Grandmother Karen's story sink in and make me as sad as it should. "She planned a trip back to Norway once," Grandma had said. "In 1962, I think. It would have been her very first airplane ride. But she was elderly by then and got sick at the last moment. She had waited too long." Grandma shrugged. "I had to go in her place."

I would go in her place, too, I thought, feeling a guilty thrill at the profound nature of my visit. My journey was now infused with vague yet grand themes: lost homelands, lifelong partings, missed chances, and—I hoped—momentous returns.

My first glimpse of Norway wasn't too promising. My distant cousin Haakon, a sullen teenager who introduced himself as "Arne-Otto's son and slave," picked up Ben and me at the airport and spent the long, dark drive to the farm lecturing us about our bad timing. "The snow is very late this year. It is a pity you come now." According to Haakon, we were six months too late for the "really good fun" of the summer months, when the sun doesn't set and "the big party is never ending," but too early for the snowy Nordic wonderland I had hoped for when I booked our tickets for mid-January.

After hours of dull driving along a generic, modern highway, triangles of light appeared in the distance, illuminating one half of a plain white house, the tall red doors of a barn, low dark blotches that might have been cows, black earth pocked here and there with snow: farm country. "Welcome to Toten," Haakon mumbled, turning the car abruptly.

We stopped at the center of a ring of dark buildings. The door of the largest one opened, and Arne-Otto walked out to meet us. I had vague memories of him visiting when I was very young and being a little afraid of his massive size and his thick, dark beard. Dad had described him as "part troll, part Viking, and part teddy bear." He was still a vast person, but his beard was laced with gray now, and I was surprised at the low, gentle voice that welcomed us.

Arne-Otto herded us inside and into a huge farmhouse kitchen, where we met his wife, Lise, who was delicate-limbed and shy, the elegant half of this odd couple. We all sat at a long, battered table made of dark, ancient-looking wood that stretched down the middle of the room and could easily have seated twenty farm laborers or servants. Arne-Otto poured an amber liquid into glass tumblers and passed one to each of us. *"Akevitt!"* he said, grinning. "You know *akevitt?* If you are Norwegian, you must know it!" He winked at me, then threw his head back and emptied his glass. Eager to be Norwegian, I copied him. The drink scorched the back of my throat, and I coughed and gasped. Arne-Otto whacked me on the back with his giant Viking hand. "Not bad for American girl!" he exclaimed.

Their large house, like all of the homes we visited those two weeks, was as lean and neat as the people who lived in it. Its rooms were paneled with blond wood planks dotted with dark, mole-shaped knots—exactly like the bookcases I had bought at Ikea. In fact, the homes were not unlike the rooms in Ikea catalogs: bright, tidy, and uncluttered, furnished with sleek furniture in primary colors. The only difference was the antiques, which infiltrated every room: ornate cast-iron stoves that they still used to heat the houses, benches in the entry halls decorated in hand-painted floral patterns, silver and china monogrammed with the family name. These people lived surrounded by the past, by the kind of beautiful old things I had hoped Grandma could unearth for me out of some musty closet.

Arne-Otto showed us to our bedroom, another wood-paneled room with floors that creaked soothingly beneath the weight of our suitcases. "Good night. Tomorrow I show you the mountain," he said.

"Which mountain?" I asked.

"*My* mountain, of course," he said, winking at me. "You will see."

The next morning I looked out our bedroom window at Arne-Otto's mountain. It was actually more like a very large hill, shaped like a mashed cone that rose gradually from the back edge of his fields. Fir trees collected around its base, got thicker around the middle, and thinned out again just below the flattened top, giving way to a long green bald spot. I wondered whether Great-Grandmother Karen had ever climbed up there to meet a sweetheart, get away from her large family, or simply admire the view.

After a breakfast of bread, cheese, and a startling assortment of pungent meats and fish that we politely avoided, Arne-Otto led us outside for a tour of his farm. We stood in the muddy grass outside his front door, at the center of a circle of plain, upright buildings with steep rooflines, each one painted red or white—just like the houses in the "Memories of Scandinavia" calendars cousin Solveig sent Grandma each Christmas. Beyond the ring of buildings, Arne-Otto's farm stretched out in all directions. The entire landscape was tilted. From Arne-Otto's mountain, the fields poured gently down to the edge of a massive lake whose shoreline stretched out of sight in both directions, disappearing behind low hills. Collections of buildings similar to Arne-Otto's dotted the edge of the lake at respectful distances.

As I surveyed the surroundings I made a conscious effort to connect to something: *This* is where I am from, I thought. *This* was where my ancestors toiled and loved and died for centuries, perhaps millennia. Did I look like them? Think like them? Maybe one of them passed on to me the cowlick over my right eyebrow, or my hay fever, or my tendency to get a stomachache when I'm anxious, or even this very propensity to seek a connection to my past. And if my great-grandmother had been the eldest boy instead of the youngest daughter, then this would be would be *my* farm, *my* fields, *my* hand-painted benches, in the shadow of *my* mountain.

But even though it was not mine, a piece of what eventually became me had once walked on this same frozen ground: Karen, a teenager with big dreams and small prospects. I tried to imagine how this place had been when she left it. I raised a hand and blocked the view of Arne-Otto's Volvo and Haakon's motorbike. Was this the same view that Karen gazed upon more than a hundred years ago, when she walked out her front door for the last time?

I imagined women, their heavy wool skirts swinging off thick hips, scurrying across these frozen fields, chopping potatoes at that long kitchen table, knitting stockings in the flicker of firelight, carrying oil lamps across dark, chilly rooms. But these images weren't based on anything real. They were generic pictures of "olden times," gleaned from a lifetime of watching *Little House on the Prairie* and *Masterpiece Theatre*. I had no real stories of my great-grandmother's life here. She had died long before I was born, and Grandma's stories of her mother all started after the boat landed on the other side of the Atlantic. I had never even seen a photograph of my great-grandmother as a young woman. She was always the pudgy old woman in 1950s cat glasses, posing in front of my grandparents' suburban ranch house, surrounded by her all-American family, no trace of Norway in sight.

Arne-Otto nodded at a building at the distant edge of one of his fields, a tall, slender white house that tilted forward. Its roof sagged in the middle. "That's the old Aarsby place. Where your grandmother's mama lived, I think."

I stumbled on a frozen clod of dirt and stopped. My ears buzzed a little, my whole body primed and focused by the thoughts: *Pay Attention. This Is Important.*

"Karen?" I said.

"*Ja, ja*. Yes. Karen."

I squinted at the sagging building. "Who lives there now?" I asked.

"Oh, no one, I think," Arne-Otto said, "it is very old and cannot be comfortable. We sold it to the neighbor." It was my first real glimpse of Karen's life in Norway, and it was of a building too old and decrepit to be of any value to those who now owned it. The sky seemed suddenly grayer. Grandma's words ran through my mind: "*Everything*."

That evening, I spread out my genealogy charts on Arne-Otto's massive kitchen table. Printed in neat black lines on white computer paper, they looked reassuringly official. I wanted to determine, once and for all, my exact relationship to Arne-Otto, to this farm, to Norway, as I asked Arne-Otto to fill in the blank spaces on my family tree. On one side of the page, a branch climbed from me to my father to my grandmother to Karen, where it gave way to blank lines and question marks. "No problem," Arne-Otto said, sliding the paper toward him. He wrote down the names of his parents and grandparents, consulted with Lise in Norwegian, scribbled two more names at the top of the tree, and handed the chart back to me. I could see that Arne-Otto was a direct descendant of Karen's eldest brother, the one who inherited the farm. I studied the names he added and made some quick calculations. "Oh! That means we are . . . " I paused, "third cousins!" I beamed meaningfully at him.

The next morning at breakfast, Arne-Otto laid a fat yellow folder, bulging with papers, among the plates of cheese and stinky fish. "More cousins!" he said. When I looked up at him, confused, he gestured to the folder with a hunk of cheese.

It took me a few minutes to understand what I was looking at. Inside the folder were handwritten letters, all in English. There were also Christmas cards (tacky ones, featuring cartoony Santas or oil paintings of Mary and Jesus in the manger) and envelopes with return addresses in Iowa, North Dakota, Minnesota. Arne-Otto reached over and pulled a piece of paper from the middle of the pile. It was a printout of a web page with phone book listings for a town in Minnesota, all of them with our Norwegian family name—Aarsby, Karen's last name. There were dozens of Aarsbys. And this was just for Minnesota. Apparently there were hundreds of us scattered across the U.S., all descendants of this farm, all able to claim this place as I did.

There was a pile of photographs, too. In one of them, a pale, fleshy family posed in front of a Christmas tree: two teenage daughters in matching red Christmas sweaters, a mother with a frizzy perm dyed an unnatural shade of orange, her bosom straining the front of a leopard-print pantsuit, the father in a Packers football sweatshirt. The typical, tacky white American family.

"Suzie and Dave," Lise chirped, pointing over my shoulder at the photo. "We go . . . Iowa!" She blushed and looked to Arne-Otto.

"Yes," said Arne-Otto, "We visit them in Des Moines. Two years ago."

I felt more than a little betrayed. I wished I could return to the blissful naivete of a moment ago, when I was ignorant of the existence of these horrible Iowans. Ignorant of their equal claim on this place. Ignorant of the fact that I was not as precious to Arne-Otto as he was to me.

Now, my attempts to connect to my Norwegian past felt feeble, even pathetic. I had found a history for myself, but it felt generic, overcrowded, and too diluted by time and distance to have any special place for me.

The next day consisted of an exhausting round of visiting–breakfast with Arne-Otto's family, lunch next door at his mother's house, afternoon coffee with a young couple who arrived at Arne-Otto's house on cross-country skis, dinner at a neighboring farm owned by yet another distant cousin. The days that followed brought more of the same, until a week had disappeared in a blur of visits with tall, fair relatives. Some I remembered from Seattle, some I had never seen. Each evening, we raised our glasses of *akevitt* to share a toast with a new set of friendly faces, reminisced about their visits to Seattle, and politely compared notes on the differences between our two countries: food, work habits, school systems, weather. At each visit, I asked a few questions. Had they known Karen? Had they heard stories about her? Were there any photographs? What was life like on the farm when she lived here?

There didn't seem to be a trace of Karen anywhere. Apparently she had left as little behind as she had brought with her. Everyone who had known her was dead. Her youngest nephew, Anners, would have known her, but he was gone, too. "Anners got cancer in the head. 1995," one of my relatives informed me. I was ten years too late.

At the end of our fifth day, Ben and I lay sprawled on our bed at Arne-Otto's house, snatching a few quiet moments between visits. We were both exhausted.

Ben sighed. "Are you getting what you wanted from this?"

"I'm not sure." Through a window with tiny wooden panes, I watched Arne-Otto's mountain blacken in the early-afternoon twilight.

"It's funny, but you really don't look like any of these people, do you?" he said. "No offense, but it's hard to believe you're even related."

I couldn't argue with this. I looked as much like Arne-Otto and Lise and Haakon as the Iowans did. Like them, I possessed no real connection to any past older than Grandma's spotty memories of her mother's secondhand stories. Just like the Iowans, I was a motley mix of the genes of countless peasants, laborers, and servants who had slipped, practically unnoticed, out of the old world and into the new, severing most of their connections to their homeland somewhere in the middle of the Atlantic.

I thought about Grandma's first bittersweet visit more than fifty years ago. The middle-aged American housewife going "home" to Norway for the first time, seeing all the places her mother had described, hugging the elderly aunts and uncles she had never met, the wrinkled faces who had hoped for one last look at their sister but had to settle instead for her daughter. I remembered Grandma's words: "She had waited too long."

That must have been the first painful slice through the long, frayed strings that still stretched—barely—between us and Norway. With each generation, we were becoming a little less enthusiastic, a little less Norwegian. Every Christmas Grandma had followed us around the house, carrying a tray of Norwegian cookies before her, shoving it under our noses, begging us to eat them. "Don't you want just one more?" she'd say. "Just one more, dear. I made so many!" They were her mother's recipes—the only heirlooms that Karen had brought with her from Norway—and I had no idea how to make them.

Yet, here I was in Norway, trying to lay claim to something. What was I looking for? What did this place really mean to me, this farm that I might visit a few times in my life? When Grandma visited Norway, the connection was still a close one: She visited her aunts and uncles and first cousins. Even my dad could feel this direct family connection—he had vivid memories of Karen, the beloved grandmother who came from this place. All I had were their stories, my genealogy charts, and distant cousins who were kind to me but otherwise might have been strangers. I felt burdened by my position. Would I maintain the tie? Would my children feel any connection at all or would I be the one to let the strings snap completely?

I sighed and closed my eyes, blotting out Arne-Otto's black mountain. "You're right," I said to Ben, "we might as well be part of some international exchange program."

Arne-Otto called up the stairs. "Ready to go for dinner? Dagmar is waiting for you!"

I didn't know Dagmar. When Arne-Otto dropped us off at her house—another large plain box in the middle of frozen fields—the door opened before we had a chance to knock. Dagmar, a surprisingly short, thick-hipped woman in her forties, hugged me to her big, soft chest. She led us into a cozy living room and deposited us on a couch on either side of a tiny old woman. "My husband's mother, Gerd," she said, introducing us. "I must go make food now." Dagmar stepped out, leaving us alone with Gerd.

Gerd took my hand into her lap and peered into my face. "Aah, Sarah," she said. "*Ja, ja, ja* . . . Sarah." Her face reminded me a little of the trolls on

Grandma's mantle—eyes bright with mischief, smile-lines carved deep into her cheeks, a healthy red glow to her skin.

Gerd told me she hadn't known Karen, but she remembered my grandparents visiting and my father bringing my mother to visit when they were newly married. "You mother so, sooooo pretty." Gerd smiled so hard her eyes disappeared into slits; she chuckled silently, her shoulders bouncing up and down. I forgot about Karen. I had fallen in love with Gerd.

Dagmar came back with a tray of cheeses and bread. She looked at me and then turned to Gerd, saying something in Norwegian. They both examined me again, talking, nodding.

"Excuse me. Very bad manners," Dagmar said. "We say that your hair is nice this way. It was more shorter before, yes?"

"Umm, yes, but . . . you've never met me before!"

"Oh, we *all* know you." Gerd and Dagmar smiled at me, possessively, like doting aunts. "From your grandmother's letters. Photographs also, of course. I think you have new job now?"

I had heard about the letters. They had been crossing the Atlantic in both directions for nearly a century. Karen wrote them all her adult life. After Karen died, Grandma kept on writing them. And the Norwegians kept on writing back. Even now, in her nineties, Grandma keeps on exchanging these letters, sending her children and grandchildren and great-grandchildren "home" to Norway year after year, keeping a place for us there, keeping the frayed string from snapping completely.

Listening to Gerd talk about my grandmother's letters, I am struck by the tenacity of Grandma's grip on Norway, but I am not surprised. This tenacity is as familiar as the trolls on the mantel, as Grandma's ice blue eyes, as my own reflection in a mirror. Here in Dagmar's cozy living room, I finally start to see the thread that hasn't yet—quite—snapped: the thread of relentless ambition that enabled Karen to leave for America, Grandma to abandon that fishy island to make her way in the city, her children to attend college, her grandchildren to attend even better colleges, all so we could live up to the risks her mother had taken, demonstrating that Karen's century-old gamble was worth it.

I think of those Christmas cookies that Grandma spent weeks baking, year after year, even when she got old and the work made her fingers ache. When we dropped by her house, the air would be hot and buttery, the kitchen covered in flour, and Grandma would rub her sore hands, sweat pouring down her neck, her face tired but satisfied. On Christmas Eve, her hard work finished, the complete array of edible delights was laid out before us. Alternately crispy and chewy, nutty and buttery, shaped like rings or cones or little sugary logs, they were like precious old friends: the same every year and each one more tempting than the last. We stuffed ourselves until we felt sick. But no matter how many we ate, it was never quite enough for Grandma. "One more! Have just one more of these!" She wasn't going to let us off easy. She wasn't going to let us stop halfway through the job. Or forget who we were, and that the very best things—like her mother's laborious cookie recipes—come after effort and struggle.

Of course, it wasn't really about cookies. I thought of the story Dad had told me about Karen's insistence that her daughter get a good education. There was no school on their soggy little island, so each day Grandma crossed the wide, fickle river in a small boat, even in the wind and rain, amid waves that made the young girl seasick and gave her mother nightmares. I remembered Grandma's parting words to me when I left for college. They were simultaneously a command and a promise: "You'll do well." And I had. It hadn't come easy. I had studied as hard as anyone I knew. But Grandma had been right.

Dagmar passed around generous glasses of red wine, and we toasted our visit in the traditional Norwegian fashion, the way Grandma had taught us when we were kids: Say *"skål,"* raise glass, take a drink, raise glass again. "But you *must* hold one another's eyes while you drink," Grandma had said.

"But why?"

"If you break the gaze, it will cause offense." Grandma's tone had been solemn. Since then I had felt this gaze was sacred, that it ignited something far more powerful than any of us was capable of creating alone.

I turned and held Gerd's merry eyes in mine for a long, sweet time.

Never Gone Back

LEAH LAKSHMI PIEPZNA-SAMARASINHA

We never went back to Sri Lanka. "Why would we?" my mother would say. "Your father was raised in Malaya and Singapore. And anyway, it's all so different from how it was." She'd shake her head, sigh. "The country he grew up in just doesn't exist anymore."

Mom always said the old names: Malaya and Ceylon. She even said them with a trace of my father's Sri Lankan British accent. I couldn't find them in the atlas or on the globe at school. I thought they were like places from my Greek mythology book, islands that had sunk into the sea like Atlantis. Was Ceylon the same thing as Sri Lanka? Malaya the same name as Malaysia? My mom's forehead furrowed when I asked, so I dropped the subject.

I was eight, ten, fourteen, twenty. The only thing I could picture when I thought of where my father was from was the poster of the Raffles Hotel in our living room. Nothing but white columns and palm trees, but you could picture ladies and gentlemen having a gin and tonic on the patio. When my parents talked about Malaya and Ceylon, it meant pictures like that: colonial charm, elephants, my dad shimmying up coconut trees.

My mother had meticulously researched her family history. She had all the stories: her grandmother walking out of Galicia in the Ukraine with seven children, taking three years to make it to the sea; her mother forced to leave school at fourteen to work in the textile mills in Webster, Massachusetts; her aunt who married the mill owner's son, who filled her with child after child until she died of breast cancer in her thirties. But my father's history stayed in the shadows. My father's parents lived in Sri Lanka in the 1920s, the same time that my Ukrainian grandmother was a girl. My mother had no problem researching her family, but my father's history was always too long ago and far away to remember.

And my father wouldn't talk about Sri Lanka. He didn't want to talk about why we were thousands of miles away. My father would laugh and say he was Portuguese. He was gone so much of my childhood, and when he was around, I didn't want him to be: He yelled, drove too fast down one-lane streets. He did try and tell me some things, sometimes, but I was seven; I watched *He-Man* on TV; I had no context. When I was finally grown, I wanted his stories. But then he wouldn't tell them.

When I was grown and when I was growing up, my mother didn't want me to ask about being brown. But it was too late. She'd raised a baby genealogist when she'd taken me with her to Webster graveyards to dust off the stones, and she told the family stories her parents didn't want anyone to know. I would grow up to be a woman fond of going into libraries, doing Google searches, tracking down family members. I would call myself South Asian, Sri Lankan, mixed race, queer. She had no idea what she was in for.

In the books I read, in the stories I teased out, Sri Lanka became concrete, not myth. Sri Lanka was saris, string hoppers, ocean. Export Processing Zone factories, a civil war, Amnesty International special alerts, jaggery[1], bitterness, endurance, love. A feminist and LGBT rights movement, ID cards saying you were Tamil or Sinhalese.[2] Sri Lanka was always love cake triple-wrapped in foil sent in the mail for Christmas, auburn red cardboard packages of Jaffna curry powder and vegemite from Australia. Sri Lanka was my father, my cousins, and me.

My life has always been about the stories I had to dig for. The stories I tried to dig from my parents, and the stories inside my body. I had to dig for my abuse story, my Sri Lankan story. When I did, I dug myself out of the ground.

"You should say you're Pakistani and wear *salwar kameez,"* says the half–Sri Lankan, half-Indian investigative reporter who I am chatting with at the Asian Pacific Islander American Spoken Word and Poetry Summit in Boston in 2005. "Me, they think I'm a South Indian businessman when I go back. You . . . they'll think you're from someplace else." I'm planning my first trip back to Sri Lanka to perform at the second-ever Lankan pride festival in May 2006. I'm nervous as hell.

I know he's trying to do me a favor. I'm a mixed-race, light-skinned girl whose clothes and attitude scream North American. Passing as Pakistani sounds like a good deal to him: I'd still be seen as *desi* but escape the Sri Lankan gauntlet that every returning Lankan faces: Are you Tamil, Sinhalese, Muslim, Burgher, mixed? What are your families' names? Where are they from? How much skin are you showing, how weird do you look, how long has it been? Maybe it'll help me escape the special gauntlet waiting just for me: a single girl at thirty-one, traveling alone, wearing a BROWN, BOLD, AND BEAUTIFUL T-shirt with a giant, freshly done Tamil arm tattoo.

I think about what he says for a minute. But I can't do it. I can't picture pretending to be someone I am not as I walk on my heartline for the first time.

I have always longed for Sri Lanka and been terrified of Sri Lanka. Been afraid not so much of going home and not being recognized as Sri Lankan, but that all the fragile Sri Lankanness I've cultivated in North America will dissolve as soon as I step off the plane and go home to the *real* Sri Lanka. I'm too smart to expect that I'll step off the plane and think, *Yes, I am one with the people!*, but I still want to feel home settle in my chest. Mend all the distance that my family's assimilation and rejection has hurt my heart with. I want to find out that the Sri Lankan home I've made up out of scraps and hard work is really true.

We were always the family that never went back. And we're far from alone. Since the Sri Lankan civil war broke out in 1983, millions of Sri Lankans have left as immigrants and refugees, fleeing the land mines, truck bombs, and rape. Close to sixty thousand Tamil and Muslim people have been living in refugee camps in South India for two decades now, and there are huge diaspora communities in Canada, the U.S., the U.K., and Australia. In 2002, when a Norwegian peacekeeping team brokered a tentative ceasefire between the Sri Lankan army and the Liberation Tigers of Tamil Eelam (the paramilitary group fighting for a separate Tamil state), people began to return after decades of being away. There are plenty of other reasons why people haven't gone back: round-trip plane tickets that cost $1,600, being queer or trans, or being a target for political violence or assassination.

Dad left Sri Lanka in the 1960s. He grew up mostly in Kuala Lumpur and Singapore, and after he flunked out of his first year of college in Australia, he went roaming. There are pictures of him traveling the world in his Queen's Scout uniform. He was a six-foot-tall Sri Lankan Boy Scout moving through Australia, Southeast Asia, and Europe before he finally ended up in London in the late '60s, sharing an apartment with David, a slim, pretty brown man from Trinidad. Dad held down one of those three-pounds-a-week civil service jobs and was a partying coffee-drinking intellectual the rest of the time. He loved London. He wanted to be far away from his family and Sri Lanka, from all the generations of people who knew his business and the parents who never forgave him for being the second, dark-skinned son—the one who survived when his light-skinned, blond older brother died of bomb shock during World War II. He wanted to be free.

My father was a beautiful brown man vogueing in front of a VW bus in

1969. In 1970, his British Commonwealth status—the citizenship once granted to all brown people who were born in colonized British lands—expired. He was stateless. He could go back to Lanka, where he was born but had left as a child, and do compulsory military service. He could move to Australia and be with the family he'd gone thousands of miles to get away from. He wanted to stay in London, but it was impossible—he was brown and stateless, and my mother was on a student visa. Canada looked good but didn't work out after immigration lost their applications and didn't tell them for a year.

My parents decided that the easiest thing to do would be to get married and move to America. They moved to Watertown, a small town outside of Boston. When my father lost his job in the late-'70s recession, they moved to Worcester, Massachusetts, the dying blue-collar city my mother had lived her twenties in. The place she'd never, ever wanted to go back to, but you could buy a house there for $20,000. I am a Worcester girl. I grew up in that fucked-up city—red bricks, dirty river, factories, projects, and triple-deckers. Industrial landscapes are in my blood—old warehouses and steel beams, the eastern edge of the rust belt. I am the first generation of white working-class mama/brown father Sri Lankanness who grew up in a steel New England city.

When I turned twenty-two and my scholarship to college in New York was about to run out, I visited Toronto and fell in love. Yes, with that one crazy queer Latino ex-punk boy, but also with a city where Sri Lanka was on the map. Of all the Sri Lankan exile communities in the world, Toronto has the biggest one. For the first time, when I said I was Sri Lankan, people didn't say, "Where?" I could pass the Tamil housing co-op on my way to the subway, buy fish cutlets at the corner store, see brown men and women pushing strollers and buying groceries. It was the closest thing to home I'd seen yet. When my last classes finished in New York, I packed two backpacks and got on the Greyhound to Toronto.

Switching countries didn't feel like a big deal. It felt like a family tradition. But I wasn't prepared for the ache that would come. I had never had a home that grounded me before, and everything I stood to gain in Canada looked so much better than what I didn't know I would be losing in the U.S.

I left because of love and Sri Lankan community, but I also left to put a national boundary between my family and me. In Toronto, with friends more real than any I'd been able to find in New York activist culture, with a back yard, and a therapist who took barter, I turned around and opened the door to the violence I grew up with. I could see into those body memories I'd never had words for. The nonbody memories. The being out of my body when I was three and when I was trying to go to sleep last week. The ways I could close my eyes and drift to the yellow-painted wood room I slept in from ages one to three. How I could feel nothing during sex, but how depression and rage was a fist clamping me down to the ground.

1997 and 1998. Twenty-two and twenty-three. Years spent in that fucked-up apartment on Dupont, with the skinny gray wall-to-wall carpet and busted fixtures, but a back yard and my own place for $525 a month. So many days curled up in that cold apartment, listening to that same tape over and over again, burning cheap incense, walking everywhere. But happy. I was so happy to be alone, to have a door I could shut, to be able to cook and sleep and breathe. Years when I was alone with the ghosts in my body, my craziness, my abuse history, my dreams. Years when I held on to my memories and followed the path out that only I could see.

At the end of 1997, my mother's cancer came back. My parents called. They wanted me to move home to Worcester. I knew if I did, I would never be able to leave. I wrote them a letter. Saying, this is what happened, this is what I've been dealing with. This is what I need to never happen again. I was praying that since my mother was close to death, they might finally, finally be able to get real.

Instead they called and told me that I was crazy, needed help, needed to come home. I heard that voice in my heart I'd been hearing since I was little:

I love you guys, but you're really fucked-up, and when I grow up I'm going to do something different. I didn't go back. I stayed in Toronto. Stopped picking up the phone and curled up in my house. They sent cheerful cards that talked about the weather and what they were eating.

The years piled up. Things got better. I still walked scared up to my apartment, scared for the day when their car would be parked outside, ready to drag me back. But it didn't happen. Instead, I really did heal. Felt my body. Stopped getting triggered all the time. Breathed peace. I published, performed, paid the rent on time, and always had a full fridge. Memories full of good things piled up: Christmas 2005 with my lover, the thick June Jordan anthology under the tree, that time we blew up smoke bombs on the railroad tracks, that trip to San Francisco, the Minnesota writer's residency.

For long-term survivors who can't be in touch with their family, home is always a question. Mostly it's a blessing that I am grown, alive, and safe, and that I never, ever have to go back. I visit my lover's family on national holidays, and they are weird and normal but no one is hiding in the basement or getting crazy drunk. I feel guilty because I have calmness and space, because I'm here and not with the crazy people I love and fear—my family.

Mostly I feel blessed. But the years pile up, and I wonder what is happening in Worcester without me. Sometimes I feel like a ghost, like this is my afterlife. No one from back home knows where I am, and I ache for the family I don't and won't have. I need to know more than what *The Courage to Heal* tells me about being a long-term survivor. Please, the only thing they say is that things get better—and they do, they have. But what do I do with my unanswered questions? I wanted to transform not just myself, but my whole family. Will that ever happen?

I chose the best of many imperfect options to save myself. The home I made glows open. Lavender walls and red bed open to the sky. No screaming. But the homes I left do not disappear.

Since I wrote that letter to my family, I have never gone back to where I grew up, except nightly in my dreams, and always in my heart. I walked around for years with the road map of Worcester behind my eyelids. I'd be walking down a Toronto street or taking change from a Bed-Stuy bodega clerk, but inside I was seeing flashes of Chandler and May Streets, the abandoned toy store near Park Ave., the Salem Square library that was my drug growing up.

But I know I could never move back to Worcester. Despite Boston and other cities now being majority people of color, New England's mythology is still of a place that is tight and white, where Irish and Italian are still ethnic. I could never live somewhere where people don't wear bright colors, where the subway stops at midnight, where there's one queer bar and everyone there wears khaki. I can't imagine living in the same city as my parents, where everyone knows me and everyone knows them. I daydream about going back, doing some amazing art or organizing about all the POC and working-class histories of the town, but I also know that being a working-class artist and a survivor artist means having to leave. No matter how much I hate it.

I make my first trip in ten years back to Massachusetts during the summer of 2005. My friend Sarwat picks me up from the Toronto–Rochester ferry. When I get in the car, she says, "I hope you don't mind, but I like to drive fast." I don't, and we make it across the whole state in an hour and a half. At the rest station in Williamsburg, I am all eyes, watching out for my parents who will just happen to be in that rest stop at eight thirty on a Thursday night. They're not, but I still stare at the ranks of puffy lobster-red tanned white people wearing the entire L.L. Bean catalog at once. There is one mixed-looking black kid at the Ben & Jerry's with a poofy fro who stares at me and Sarwat oohing over the ice cream display, like we are the only sexy young brown girls with shaved heads and cleavage who have been here for years. Maybe we are.

All week, I shuttle between the friend's house in Jamaica Plain, where I'm staying, and the South End community center, where the conference is. My body is always on edge. When I ride the T, I carry a newspaper to shield my face and scan the subway car for my father every time I enter. Would I recognize him? Would he recognize me? Would he recognize his daughter without the look of terror and misery on her face—in big pink sunglasses, wearing colors? Would my mother? Would god make it so we just had to be on the same subway car at the same time?

I think about taking the commuter rail home, but a friend, also exiled for years from her family, warns me. "There's no public transit, right? Be careful. Even if your folks don't see you, somebody who knows you might. I'd wait till I could go back in a car." I take the commuter rail north instead of west, to the one town with a public beach that's walking distance from the train. I eat fried clams and drink a Sam Adams. I feel the ocean we went to on summer vacations pulsing inside me, smell the maple trees. I'm as close to home as I can be and still be safe.

For the past five years, I've wrestled with whether to write my parents another letter. A few years into our separation, they found my address and sent truly messed-up letters now and then. My mother left messages, ones bristling with rage and ones slurred with painkillers, on my voice mail until I stopped picking up the phone whenever UNKNOWN CALLER, INTERNATIONAL appeared on the call display. She would sound confused, slurred with lots of Vicodin, or would bark, rage hitting every syllable. I would slam down the phone and want to vomit. Disassociate right away and have to sit in my basement room, edge of the bed, trying to call myself back. But my mother was sixty-eight, my father sixty-three. I didn't even know what they'd look like now. I knew they could die, and this story would end unfinished.

I dream that my father would be able to meet me in Toronto, go for Sri

Lankan food, stroll through the comic book store with me drinking coffee. I want my mother to say: *Yes, I touched you when you were a kid. You're right, I didn't let you shut the door to your room long after you should've been able to. I'm sorry.* I know that probably neither would happen, that they would die without being able to face any of it. The joke about False Memory Syndrome is that it's much easier for people who perpetuate violence to create false memories about what happened. Survivors mostly do anything we can to not remember. We remember when there is no other choice.

When I finally write my father five months before my trip to Sri Lanka, I know what to say. I tell him that there are some things I need to say before either of us dies. That I love him, but I hold him accountable. That I know it is almost impossible for people to believe in female perpetrators of sexual or physical violence, but what happened to me is true. That I never meant to walk away forever, but I was not going to go home and "get help" either. I tell him that the original meaning of the word "forgive" is to reopen the possibility of a relationship with one who has harmed you. The survivor must risk opening a connection to someone who wounded her, and the abuser must choose honesty and accountability over denial and violence. I tell him that accountability and honesty are all I've ever wanted. That I never intended to never speak to him again.

When I go back to Sri Lanka, I go with no expectations. Before I leave, I talk with my Sri Lankan best friend about the trip she is planning, her first trip back ever since her parents fled the war for London and Texas. "I'm afraid," she says. "I'm afraid I'll get there and find out just how American I am." I have that fear in me too.

As I get up at 6:00 AM to get the car service from Bed-Stuy to JFK, and as I sit on the twenty-three-hour Emirates flight from New York to Dubai and then Colombo, I do not picture a grand, perfect moment, a diasporic *desi* girl kissing the soil. I just sit there, watching movie after movie, writing in my journal, feeling the prayers I know my friends are sending me. I feel like I'm waiting for a multiple orgasm or a nervous breakdown, or both. When I pray, I ask the land to give whatever she can spare.

When I walk out of Negombo Airport after twenty-four hours in the air, one in a line of tired-eyed brown people, the humidity hits my face. In the back of my friend's car, I ride staring open-eyed at everything. Red mud road, hopper and cutlet shops. Piles of bright, cheap T-shirts and plastic buckets. My hair curls up in the heat like it's been waiting for Lanka forever. It has.

And as my browning arm hangs out of a freezing-ass AC window, Lanka takes me back. Takes me back with no word about how long I'd been gone. The kirtal and mango trees wave a greeting. I am home in forty-five minutes from Negombo to Borella, past the cemetery and the train tracks, to the small house behind a high metal gate. The land wraps its red-brown fist around my muscular heart. A lover who takes me home. A lover who has been waiting for me.

Two days later, I walk up Galle Road, past eighteen-year-old soldiers guarding barricades in front of embassies, all the way to Galle Face Green, the beaten-down stretch of grass in Colombo 7 facing the sea. I sit on a bench drinking Elephant brand ginger beer, staring at the Indian Ocean. To my left is the Galle Face Hotel, not the Raffles, but one of those same grand colonial buildings. Buildings that sneer at the land, like an argument they think they've won. I stare at the palmyra trees, couples strolling and kissing under umbrellas, the relentlessness of the sea.

I have my father's letters in my backpack. Unopened, because I need a space where it will be okay to fall apart if they tell me what I don't want to hear. Thousands of miles away from the people who know me, this isn't it. But I brought them with me anyway, so at least that man's words on paper could come home. Even if he is not here on the bench next to me.

And I think: *It's still here, Dad. It's still ours. This land that is our home never stops changing, but neither do we. Neither do the stories. The ones we know, the ones we work for years to unearth out of our bones. The new ones we are brave enough to dream.*

What Is Home after Exile?
An Iranian Greek American Homecoming

APHRODITE DESIREE NAVAB

With spit on my face and the taunting words, "Go back home, you dirty Iranian!" I was welcomed into the United States. It was 1980 on a New York City public school playground. I was nine. I stood there in silence. Ever since then I have been asking through my art and my writing what I could not ask my taunter: "Home? I've lost my home. Can you tell me where it is?"

I am Iranian Greek American. I joke with my parents that I am the peace child of the ancient Persian-Greek wars. I was born in Isfahan, Iran, to an Iranian Muslim father and a Greek Christian mother. During the 1950s my father completed his residency in cardiology in the United States. He met my mother in New York and began a love that spanned three countries, a revolution, stretches of time spent apart, and a close encounter with death. They were the first in their families to marry outside of their cultures and religions.

Within the first year of their marriage, my mother agreed to go to Iran, where my father was appointed vice chancellor and dean of the medical school at the University of Isfahan. In the end, it was the Iranian Revolution fourteen years later that unexpectedly compelled my parents to leave the world they had created for their four children–*forever.*

My first language is Persian, but Greek language, food, and music enveloped my childhood memories.

I was eight years old when the Iranian Revolution of 1979 altered my childhood. I saw protesters marching in my neighborhood near the Pol-e Khaju (Khaju Bridge) with tanks and soldiers behind them. For weeks there was martial law and no electricity. When my parents discovered that the schools in Iran were teaching children how to load and use guns, they decided that we would be safer in Greece. This decision had a horrible price: At the airport we discovered that my father had been placed on forbidden passage and would have to stay behind in Iran.

If you would permit me, I will take your hand and place it on the scars that mark my body. They stand in remembrance of an encounter. Through them we can travel to the homes in my memory. The first place we will go is the line under my left eye. My siblings–Pericles, Alexander, and Demetra–and I were playing catch with my mother's high heels in the living room of our house in Isfahan in 1973. I missed a throw. The heel hit the skin under my eye, making a large, jagged tear. I was two years old. My mother rushed me to the hospital and begged that her daughter's face not be marred for life. The scar remained, however, but I am grateful it has stretched and faded as I have grown. People no longer ask why it's there, but I still see it every day. In this, my first house, I remember my siblings sitting in a circle on the Persian carpet while my mother played Greek music. We laughed and joked in Farsi. The smell of Persian kabab and rice was in the air. In

1980, my family left this home that held the fabric of our childhood, our first language, and our relatives and friends. We were never to return.

The second place I will take you is my right hand, where the remains of four long stitches crisscross my middle and index fingers. It was the year we left Isfahan. I was nine years old. My brothers went shopping for groceries. My father was still in Iran. My mother, sister, and I were at our temporary home in Athens, Greece. The five of us lived in a one-bedroom apartment. From our terrace we could see a small mountain in the distance to our left and the ocean to our right. We lived near the international airport. Countless planes passed over our heads with deafening sound. Each plane that came and went without our father marked our home with longing. On the day I received the scar, I thought I heard the doorbell ring. I ran to the front door, opened it, but found no one there. I leaned against the door's frame, wondering and waiting. A strong wind blew from the opened doors of the terrace inside the apartment, slamming the front door on my fingers. After my scream, my mother came to the rescue. She hailed a taxi. The driver took one look at my blood-covered arm and refused to take us, fearing I would stain his car. My mother cursed him in Greek and threatened that if I lost any more blood, she would tell the police that it was his fault. I remember the pain and that it was mixed with feeling intense pride in my mother's fearlessness.

After leaving Iran in 1980, my mother, siblings, and I waited in Greece for my father for twenty-one months. Finally, my father was allowed out of Iran for medical care as a result of a close brush with heart failure. Reunited as a family, we arrived in New York City in 1981, when anti-Iranian sentiment was at its peak. After the overthrow of Muhammad Reza Shah Pahlevi, the Iranian king, by an Islamic revolutionary government, the American embassy in Tehran was seized in 1979. The Iranian revolutionaries were responding to the United States' granting medical treatment to the deposed Shah. Fifty-two Americans were held hostage for 444 days until a deal between the United States and Iranian governments secured their release in 1981.

The next place I will take you is below my elbow on my right arm. Several dark, splotchy spots run in different directions. They are the result of second- and third-degree burns that I suffered after a bike accident while living in Cambridge, Massachusetts, as a Harvard undergraduate. I was cycling too fast on a bike path that ran alongside the Charles River. I was wearing a tank top and shorts on a hot summer day. In order to avoid hitting an elderly woman, I stopped short. The bike dragged my body along the dirt road for several feet. I took myself to the infirmary, and the doctor tried to scrape away the rocks that were mixed with blood and skin on my palms, hips, and arms. He wanted to put me under general anesthesia to clean the wounds better. I refused. He warned me that one day I would regret this because it would scar. "Let it," I responded. I was twenty years old. I had completed my sophomore year and was living with roommates in a garden flat on campus. I was making photographs for my own art and working as a research assistant for a neurologist at a local children's hospital. I was debating whether to follow my father and become a doctor or follow my heart and make art. The accident decided for me. My mother came and brought me back to New York City, where she stayed with me for one month, changing the dressings on my burns. During the process of healing, the only thing I used was art—not medicine.

Another place on this journey is low on my abdomen. Stretch marks stand in remembrance of my two pregnancies. They remind me that my daughter Shahrzad was once inside of me, pushing her growing body against me. Ten years later, my son Bijan left his marks as well. My screams during labor were followed by their screams at birth. The first birth was during a heavy winter snowfall in Boston, Massachusetts. It was a year after traveling and photographing throughout Central Asia, and three years after graduating from college. My husband had just completed his PhD in Middle Eastern Studies at Harvard University. Shahrzad spent her first months of life in arctic conditions, swaddled in a snowsuit in a front sling against my body, moving through a landscape covered in a blanket of snow. The second birth was on a hot early-summer day in Gainesville, Florida. A diaper and an undershirt were all Bijan needed as I carried him against my skin on campus. He spent his first months in a subtropical swampland, among alligators that sunned themselves on Lake Alice and surrounded by storks, cranes, and ibises. It was 2005. I had just completed my first year as an assistant professor of art at the University of Florida. The stretch marks left from each birth remind me of the contrasting homes and lands where I received them; the scars are similar in how sacred they are to me. When I don't believe that my growing children who walk and talk in front of me were once nestled deep within me, these scars remind me of the stretching of the self that is necessary to bring forth life.

Time moved on in its indifference. Old wounds healed with new truths revealed against the landscape of adjustment. I feel pain and shame each and every time I travel and they see my American passport marked BIRTHPLACE: ISFAHAN, IRAN. The airport officials in Europe and North America look me up and down and then shuffle through the passport for something to shrink or swell their suspicions. Never have an airport official's eyes in the West looked at me with any sign of recognition for Iran's two thousand five hundred years of civilization. It's a mixture of pain and joy, shame and pride, this triple inheritance of being Iranian Greek American that I carry inside. I am not ashamed of my scars. They are marks of memory. When memory itself fades, they will remain and they will remind me of home.

There are two incidents in my life that I wish to recall. The first is a memory of me living as an immigrant in the United States. I am sitting and having my breakfast. The same old combination I had since my childhood in Iran—black tea with lots of sugar cubes, bread, sheep's milk cheese, green onions, and a cucumber. I'm looking at an article on the front page of

The Salt Lake Tribune: "Tehran Vice: Iranian Dancer Forced to Stop Giving Lessons." I learn that Mohammad Khordadian, a fellow Iranian American artist, wanted to visit Iran, his first home, to reconnect with his ailing father and his relatives after being away for twenty years. His official welcome by the Iranian government was being sent to jail for two months. When he was released, Khordadian was slapped with a ten-year suspended jail term. His crime was being a dancer and teaching dance. *How can dance be a crime?* I thought to myself. His offense, as Ali Akbar Dareini from The Associated Press reported, was a "court ruling that teaching traditional Iranian dance corrupts the nation's youth." By holding dance classes in the United States he was "promoting moral corruption" and therefore barred from leaving Iran for ten years and from giving dance lessons for life. He is also barred for three years from attending public celebrations or weddings of people who are not his relatives. In other words, he cannot continue doing public dance—his performance art, his livelihood. The report further stated that he had been released from jail, but if he continued being who he is and doing what he does he would be imprisoned for ten years—entering one jail to avoid another.

Like Khordadian, I had the pressing need to see my homeland and relatives for my sense of self, history, my art, my research, and my life. The stakes were very high. Like Khordadian, I am an artist who is public about her art.

I had to renew my Iranian passport. What a yearlong bureaucratic nightmare of form-filling! In the process, I learned that my mother's existence did not count, only my father's did. There wasn't a line naming my Greek mother on a single form of identity or citizenship. I also learned that I did not have the right to travel anywhere without the written permission of my husband. I was thirty-one years old!

Despite this mother-erasing and self-effacing, I went back to Iran. But I feared facing the same fate as Khordadian's—of being arrested upon arrival or departure because of my public art. This paralyzing fear has prevented me, along with thousands of other Iranians, from communicating and having a relationship with our homeland. We have been disrupted and disconnected from the land of our language, culture, and relatives. How much longer can we move forward while dragging this dislocated limb? We know we can go home, but we might never leave again.

I took the risk and returned to Iran in 2002. I wore the covering against every pore of my body in 110-degree heat. I gave up some things in order to gain others. From this trip alone, I have more than a thousand photographs of reencountering Iran and rewriting myself into its history—photographs of my family, friends, new people, myself, and places that have shaped my old and new conceptions of my first home.

The second incident that I would like to take you to is when I had just finished presenting my paper, "I Am Not a Persian Miniature: The Art of Iranian Women in Exile," at the Society for Photographic Education's annual conference in Austin, Texas, in 2003. I was thirty-two. I took the first cab outside the hotel and headed straight for the airport.

Instinctually, I heard Iran in the driver's accent. "Ver vould you eh-like to go?" he asked, hitting home. I took one look at the name on his identification card: Mahmad, the Iranian nickname for Mohammad. I had never met an Iranian taxi driver in the United States. I was not prepared. I felt cornered, frightened, and distrusting of my fellow countryman. I decided not to tell him who I was and where I was from because Iranian fundamentalists have occasionally been sent abroad by the government to kill Iranian activists and public dissenters. I was afraid and, like many Iranians, preferred not to disclose my identity.

"To the airport please," I responded.

"Very traffic. I try to get you dere soon as possible."

I studied his face and clothes. He did not have the short beard of the religious right. He was clean shaven, wearing a T-shirt and jeans, an appearance more similar to the irreverent left.

"Vere you from?" he asked, looking at my equally dark hair and skin.

"Greece," I lied, "how about you?"

"I don't know if you know Iran, vere I come. Greeks. I love Greeks. I vork many years in Greek restaurant in Canada. Good people. Treat me good, even teach me Greek. *Yasoo, ti kanete?*" ("Hello, how are you?")

"I know about Iran," I interrupted. "I have seen movies by Kiarostami. It looks beautiful."

"Ma'am it is more dan dat. How can I explain? The vhite people here knows noting about dere. Dey tink ve terrorist. Dey tink ve have no culture. No beauty. Vhite people can't separate government from people."

On and on I let him go. He told me he escaped Iran so as not to be drafted into the Iran-Iraq War, which lasted from 1980 until 1988.

"Now I'm taxi guy in Texas. I'm not e-happy. All dis vorking and I don't have e-time for learning good English. My English, it's e-broken. And my heart it's e-broken for Iran. I go back and dey kill me. I stay here but go around like a ghost. Vhite people don't see or hear me. I must tell you dat de most beautiful vomen in the vorld are from Iran. Not de men, of e-course. See how ugly I am?"

Little did he know that I could translate his English words into Persian, that I understood his simultaneous praise of Iranian women and self-insult as the Persian tradition of *ta'rof* (an elaborate system of social discourse with intricate rules of appropriate verbal exchange), that if I were speaking Persian to him I would have immediately responded with "No, please forgive me, but you are mistaken. Not at all are you ugly."

Fishing for a compliment, what he was really saying was: *Iranian women are beautiful and I am too, don't you agree?* I would reply back: *No you are not handsome but you are full of soul.* What I couldn't say aloud is: *And being Iranian, I would never say that to your face in public and humiliate you.* But I could not give up my disguise so late. It would have made him suspicious. Like me, he too would worry whether I was an informant for the present Iranian government.

This was the first time I denied my Iranian identity. At first I did it to protect myself from his scrutiny. But as the game of self-effacement continued, I realized that it enabled me to observe him from inside out, as a fellow Iranian, while not being asked to account for my history and myself. Instead, it allowed me to attend to *his* story. It gave me the space to observe while not being observed. I was invisible, but only for the purpose of trying to understand how invisible he felt in the United States. Sitting in the back in the dark, my heart went out to him. It was my choice to be invisible, whereas he had no choice. Our racial features portrayed a Middle Eastern or Mediterranean origin, but our command of English separated us. Because of my olive complexion and dark hair, I can pass racially as either Greek or Iranian in the West. I can speak both languages with native proficiency, but in my English there is no trace of an accent. In his accent was still Iran, and Iran was forever erased in mine. All I could say was "Thank you." All I could do was pay him a large tip. His eyes widened in shock. "I don't deserve twenty-dollar tip," he said.

As I was about to shake his hand, his eyes shifted from shock, to confusion, and then recognition. Something became warm and clear in his face. My Persian gold and turquoise rings and bracelets had betrayed me. I turned around and ran off as the taxi drove away.

"What's your destination?" the curbside check-in man asked, looking down at me from his counter. I stared up at him, still panting from the escape.

"Ma'am, what is your airline?" he repeated, impatiently. "Plane? Which Plane? Ticket. Show T-I-C-K-E-T," he repeatedly enunciated. "These foreigners, really, why don't they go back home?" he asked the other curbside man, under his breath.

Finally I had the words that I didn't have when I was first told to go back home. "This is every bit my home as it is yours," I said as I searched for my plane tickets. Tears fell and slowly slid down my face. At that moment my different homes collapsed into one, provoked by the memory of the taxi driver's look of recognition and by the cruel words of the curbside porter. I realized that home for me would always remind me that I was *not* at home. I would always have the ambivalent consciousness of being at once inside and outside, native and foreign, visible and invisible.

I get intermittent urges to fit into one culture completely. I feel beauty and longing when I hear Persian music and Greek music, but among an Iranian crowd I am not at home, and among a Greek one I am not at home either. A Greek relative of mine once looked me straight in the eyes and said in a matter-of-fact voice that I should highlight my Greek heritage, which carries with it the greatest civilization, and hide the embarrassing inferiority of my Iranian background. He thought he was complimenting me by saying I was more Greek. At that moment, I never felt less. But sometimes I do find a home within the tales of my photographs and writing, tales of longing and belonging, part myth, part reality, but always with the hope that the tales will be taken up by others. My art is an invitation for others to take up the tales of survival.

The final place I will take you is a scar that swims beneath the surface. It is a mental one, a kind of unwelcome guest who stays long after the others have gone. Like my parents twenty-six years earlier, I left a form of tyranny. With one suitcase and my two children, I fled from my husband in Montreal, Canada. My daughter is now the same age that I was when I first left Iran. We left a house I co-owned and all of our material possessions behind—this time, as a result of a psychological revolution, not a political one. But we are not homeless. When you have lost your homeland once, you pitch portable tents thereafter. We are in New York City again. I am thirty-four. For my children, I am home.

Yiddishland

ELLEN CASSEDY

A soft rain was falling as a white-haired woman slowly made her way to the microphone in the courtyard of Vilnius University. *"Tayere talmidim!"* she began. "Dear students!" I leaned forward to catch her words through the pattering of drops on my umbrella. The old woman was a member of the tiny, aging Jewish community in the capital of Lithuania. Her name was Blume. "How fortunate I am," she said in a quavering voice, "that I have lived long enough to see people coming to Vilnius to study Yiddish."

Seventy-five of us huddled together on wooden benches under the heavy Baltic sky. We had come from all over the globe to spend a month at the Vilnius Yiddish Institute. Some were college students looking for credits; others, middle-aged like me, had arrived in the former Jerusalem of the North in search of something else.

Years earlier, when my mother died, I'd developed a yearning for the language of my ancestors—the Jewish ones, that is (my gentile father's family hails from Germany and Great Britain). My mother had used the old Jewish vernacular only sparingly, like a spice, but when she died I found myself missing the hints of the Old World that I used to hear in her pungent Yiddish expressions. At the window on a rainy day: "A *pliukhe!*" ("A downpour!") In the kitchen: "Hand me that *shisl.*" ("Hand me that bowl.") On the telephone: "The woman's a *makhsheyfe.*" ("The woman's a witch.")

When my mother was alive, I could count on her to keep hold of the past. Now that she was dead, not only had I lost her, but all those who'd gone before seemed to be slipping out of reach, too. I hadn't been able to save my mother from cancer, but maybe by joining the Yiddish revival I could help to save *mame-loshn,* the old mother tongue. Maybe Yiddish, which has been called "the linguistic homeland of a people without a home," could offer me the comforting sense of continuity that had been ruptured by my mother's death. In helping to keep that cultural homeland alive, perhaps I could find a way home myself.

I started with an elementary Yiddish phrase book, then tried an evening class at the Jewish college near my home in Philadelphia. The Germanic sounds felt comfortable in my ears and mouth, and the Hebrew alphabet was daunting but not impossible. I listened to tapes, copied out grammar exercises, and thumbed my dictionary till the binding broke. Bit by bit, I began to feel a connection to the language once common in lanes, meeting halls, and market squares on both sides of the Atlantic Ocean.

Now in Vilnius, or Vilna, the former capital of the Yiddish world, I hoped to deepen that connection. Lithuania, in my childhood, had always seemed utterly inaccessible, as if it existed in another dimension, like Atlantis or Narnia. No one from my family who'd made it across the Atlantic from there had ever been back. Yet here I was, looking up into the same sky that had sheltered my great-grandmother Asne and her dairy farm and my great-grandfather Dovid and his study house. Under this sky, my grandfather Yankel had been a *yeshive bokher* (student) and then a socialist before running to America to escape the draft. Here, during the Nazi era, my Uncle Velvl had been confined behind barbed wire in the Shavl ghetto. And here, after returning from Dachau, my Uncle Aron had been arrested and exiled to Siberia. As the rain continued to fall and the damp courtyard darkened, I shivered. It was a hard place, this land of my forebears—a country where Jews and their culture had been systematically exterminated—a curious place to come looking for a sense of belonging.

The next morning I hurried through the courtyard and up a steep stairway into a classroom that was crammed with four rows of battered wooden desks. The Yiddish instructor, a bearded scholar, did not actually carry a stick, like a *melamed*—a teacher in the one-room Jewish schoolhouse of old—but his rules were strict. Before every class, we were to study the assigned text with care. Questions would be allowed only about words that did not appear in our dictionaries—and having written one of the dictionaries himself, he knew exactly what was in them. Not a word of English was permitted.

As we took turns reading aloud, I kept a finger glued to the page. If my concentration faltered for a second, I was lost. When the teacher spoke, whole paragraphs went by in a blur. For some reason, my hand kept flying into the air with questions and comments. The moment I opened my mouth, however, I realized I had no idea how to get to the end of a sentence. In this language that was not really my own, it was as if I were two people. One was an impractical idealist who set off with supreme confidence into the unknown, while the other was a benighted worker who ran ahead, frantically trying to build a road for the journey.

Outside the classroom, amid the pastel facades and crisp spires of 21st-century Vilnius, traces of the old Jewish world were few and far between. But the last Yiddish speakers of Vilnius led us on long walks that began on cobblestoned Zydu *gatve* (Jewish Street). Blume returned with Fania and Rokhl—stumpy, tireless women with strong, short legs. Standing in the scuffed grass of a vacant lot, they described the centuries-old Great Synagogue that had once towered over the surrounding study houses, the famous Strashun Library, the schools and theaters that had crowded the narrow lanes when they were young. Back then, they said, the streets resounded with Yiddish, as learned rabbis brushed up against fish peddlers, and young people like my grandfather engaged in fierce debates over politics and religion. Then came the Nazi invasion and the ghetto. Some seventy thousand Jews were jammed into the old Jewish quarter on this very spot where we were standing amid trash bins and dusty playground swings.

"One night," Rokhl said, "I was awakened by the barking of dogs. Outside my window, the police were driving long columns of Jews. The people had their children by the hand and their belongings tied up in bed sheets, white sheets in the black night."

More than 90 percent of Lithuania's 240,000 Jews died during World War II. Some of our elderly guides on this tour had fled to safety before the massacre began; others, like Rokhl, had escaped from the ghetto and joined the Red Army in the forests. Now, sometimes weeping, sometimes radiant, they talked and talked—about the world that used to be, about the people who were no more, about their own miraculous survival.

The flat where I lived with my roommate, Shirley, a retired kindergarten teacher from California, was located in the middle of the former ghetto. In the evenings, we used an old-fashioned key to open the creaking wooden door into our courtyard and then climbed the stairs to our rooms. Bent over our books at the kitchen table, we did massive amounts of homework, whispering under our breath as we riffled our dictionaries. Oy, those verbs, with the *umge*-this and the *oysge*-that, the *aroysge*-this and the *farge*-that! Every paragraph was an ordeal. On top of each sentence I penciled a spidery layer of interpretation, dividing the verbs and the compound nouns into their component parts, underlining words I didn't know, double-lining those that should be stressed when reading aloud, enclosing phrases in parentheses, numbering and rearranging the elements of especially convoluted expressions. As I grew tired, the letters swam before my eyes until the page of sinuous Hebrew characters resembled a sheet of matzoh. At times I was near tears. Why couldn't I understand? Why wouldn't this language—this comfortable old-mother tongue—reach out to embrace me?

In the mornings, I began to awaken with Yiddish words on my tongue, which I would savor with a slice of dense black bread topped with butter and cheese from Rokiskis—the very town where my great-grandmother had operated her dairy—and little knobby cucumbers. One week the market offered tiny apricots, and the next, small purple plums. Here in the old world, there was no abundance. Only the *shabes tish*—our weekly Friday night celebration at the Jewish community center—was lavish. The long tables spread with snowy cloths were loaded with candles and wine and platters of fruit and nuts, cheese and kasha and challah that tasted just right. Late into the night, we sang endless *nigunim,* old wordless melodies full of joy and sorrow.

Day after day, our teachers guided us into the most intimate linguistic nooks and crannies. One morning we pondered the mysteries of verb "aspects": the difference among "I kiss," "I am kissing," and "I keep on kissing." Another time we ran our tongues over long strings of adjectives formed from nouns: oaken door, woolen glove, golden ring, clay pot. On yet another day we learned that *krenken* is to get sick, but *krenklen,* with an added "l," is to fall ill again and again in a less life-threatening way. Later on, we were tickled by the playful variety of Yiddish diminutives: Blume, Blumele, Blumke, Blumkele. More and more, I found words emerging suddenly from the mist, shining and clear, or whole sentences popping out of my mouth fully formed. At the end of every session, we sat back and listened as the instructor read from his favorite texts in a sonorous and elegiac voice. A *mekhaye*—a great pleasure.

In the evenings, as I worked my way through my assignments, vivid scenes began to come into view:

One story I read ushered me into a snug wooden house on a chilly *shabes* afternoon. The cottage was sunk in deep snow—just as, for me, the meaning of the text was buried under the blanket of a difficult alphabet.

Inside, a beginning reader named Yidl opened a holy book. As Yidl used a thick index finger to sound out the words, the two of us made our way down the page together.

Another story in my textbook took place at the turn of the 20th century in the courtyard of the Great Synagogue—the very courtyard where Blume, Fania, and Rokhl had told their tales. On the first page, thousands upon thousands of Jews were gathered for the funeral of a famous Talmudist. Slowly, in an upper story high above the crowd, a window began to open, and as a curious little boy leaned out to survey the scene, I leaned out with him.

A third text brought me to a dark corner of the Vilna ghetto during World War II, where a writer sat scribbling, imagining himself to be a bell whose somber tones shattered the silence of the black ghetto night. How privileged I felt to be able to catch the tolling of that bell.

Halfway through the month, along with these literary characters, I began to sense another set of characters beside me as well: my mother with her love of a tasty turn of phrase; my grandfather with his old-age devotion to Carl Sandburg and Mark Twain and other giants of American literature; my great-grandfather Dovid, whose beard had quivered over the Talmud; and finally, perhaps not a reader at all, my great-grandmother Asne, the dairywoman and mother of nine, who must have been possessed by a fearsome persistence. Even more than I'd hoped, learning Yiddish had linked me to my ancestors and brought the past to life.

On weekends, I visited the grim headquarters of the Soviet secret police, now a museum, where Uncle Aron was imprisoned before being sent to the gulag, and the tumbledown alleys of the old Shavl ghetto where Uncle Velvl had been confined. I traveled to the tiny hamlet where my grandfather grew up—not even a crossroads, really, just a stand of trees and a scattering of houses and barns and marigolds nodding in the sun. In the town of Rokiskis, I walked down Synagogo *gatve,* where three wooden study houses used to stand—the green one, the red one, and my great-grandfather's yellow one. On the outskirts of town, I stood in the green glade where the Jews of Rokiskis had been lined up and shot. As the wind stirred the leaves of the birch trees overhead, I listened, and in my head I answered. *Ikh bin do,* I whispered, *I am here.*

Back in Vilnius, at the urging of my Rokiskis guide, I paid a call on Ida, an eighty-three-year-old woman with strong features and penetrating eyes, who had grown up not far from the three colorful study houses. "*Kumt arayn,*" ("Come in,") she said as she ushered me into her parlor, where a table was set with cream cakes dotted with red currants and sour cherries in a silver bowl. A visit from a Rokiskis *landsman*—a fellow countryman or descendant like me—was clearly a special occasion. Ida was one of only two in her entire family to have survived the war, she told me in Yiddish as we sipped tea from delicate china cups. Every September, she said, she travels to the mass murder site in the forest near Rokiskis, the same place I had just been, to honor the memory of her loved ones.

There was something she wanted from me, something I couldn't figure out. Again she explained, and again I strained to understand. After a while her meaning became clear. She wanted to know if she had been visiting the right place all these years. Were the bones of her mother and father, her brothers and her aunts and uncles and cousins and grandparents, truly buried beneath the grassy tufts of this particular clearing? Or were they in fact lying in another killing field, in Obeliai, a few miles up the road? Was there a list somewhere?

I shook my head. *Neyn,* I said, I didn't believe there was such a list. And no, I couldn't answer her question. But what I could do, as her attempt to tend to the dead touched my heart, was hold her hand. I could hear her words, and I could respond, however haltingly, in soft syllables of *mame-loshn,* our mother tongue.

As our month drew to a close, my roommate Shirley began to relax over her books at the kitchen table. She dreamed of her swing under the orange tree back in Los Angeles. But I kept going full-steam, still wrestling with every line of every assigned text, still looking up every unfamiliar word in the dictionary, then walking for hours through the city, taking in the pink walls that glimmered in the last light, the squares where young people—the inheritors of this land with its huge and complicated history—sat in the outdoor cafés under the stars.

On the last day of class, we finished a story written after the Holocaust in which the narrator finds himself pulling a wagon piled high with dead bodies. *So it is for all of us,* I thought, *as we go forward, lugging our past behind us.* It was our hardest story yet, a thicket of obscure words and fiendishly complex constructions, but I didn't mind. I'd come to feel that in Yiddishland, this place of love and of pain, it was the effort itself that mattered. Simply trying—to listen, to understand, to speak—brought a deep satisfaction and the sense of connection I'd been seeking.

At the graduation ceremony, the sun shone in a blue sky, and there were flowers and herring and vodka. Alas, Blume was too ill to attend, but Fania and Rokhl were there to send us on our way. We gave a kiss, we kissed, we kept on kissing, and crying. It was hard to leave.

Queer Heart in a Red-State Body

C. L. CARLTON

As a little girl, my sense of identity was simple: I was me, and the land I lived in stretched no farther than the distance between my house and my best friend's. Home was my mom, dad, brother, and my back yard, where I played on the jungle gym. Growing up naturally complicated the picture. Identity became about things like being a good student and being popular, as well as things I took for granted like gender and skin color. As a white person, I enjoyed white privilege for years before realizing that racism existed and had an impact on my consciousness. By the time I was in graduate school, I identified not only by my course of study (English) but also as a feminist and a lesbian, not to mention a musician, writer, reader, and photographer—to which today I could add wage slave, gardener, bird-watcher, and all-around nature lover. At the core of all of these identifiers, however, is another, deeper identification, one that I carry ambivalent feelings about yet wear more easily than ever before: Southerner.

My family's roots are Southern, but my parents took a different path from their families before them. After years of traveling and living abroad, my folks returned to their roots in Tennessee, building a house in a small town near both their families when I was a mere ten months old. The bulk of the town's population was white and lower middle class, though the entire economic spectrum from the housing projects to the country club was represented. We were middle class; my mom stayed home with me while my father went to work. When I entered kindergarten, the other kids thought I was different not only because I could already read and write, skills most of them were just beginning to acquire, but because I "talked funny"—I lacked the country twang so many of them spoke with, as my speech was modeled on my parents', whose own accents had become less prominent from years of life outside the South.

The library of our elementary school occupied part of the cafeteria, and the most popular book there was a gigantic atlas of Civil War battlefields. If my classmates and I had time after lunch, we would go and turn the pages of this magic book, kept reverently apart from the other books (probably due as much to its size as to its content). It was always open, sitting on its own stand above the card catalog. We examined with great interest and little comprehension the placement of blue and gray batteries and entrenchments. Some of the boys fancied themselves experts on "The War" and cited ancestors who fought for the Confederacy, declaring that the South would rise again. I wasn't sure what it would rise from, so I did a little research of my own in the shiny new set of World Book encyclopedias my parents had bought me.

What I learned in the encyclopedias made me thoroughly embarrassed and ashamed to be Southern. How could anyone believe that slavery was right? How could anyone want a culture based on such an abominable institution to have emerged victorious or, as my classmates said, *to rise again?* How could my parents have brought me here to live among white people who thought they were superior to black people? It seemed weird to hear my classmates brag about the greatness of the Confederacy and then sit down and eat lunch next to one of their black friends. At such a young age, they may not have fully understood what the old South, with its slave-driven culture, really stood for; I'm sure I didn't understand it.

I don't remember talking with my parents much about race. The meaning of the word "race" had yet to enter my consciousness. In hindsight, it seems to me that there was a disconnect between what some of the kids were learning at home and how we all acted in school, as if the seeds of racism were being planted in some but had yet to propagate. I knew there were black people and white people, but I had no concept yet of the oppression and privilege so linked to this. Later, there were those who used the N word or made racial jokes, and in those times I clung more fiercely than ever to the fact that I, thankfully, was born in the North. I might have to live among these Southerners, but I was by no means one of them. By the time I was ten, being different had become a point of pride.

I kept quiet about my Union sympathies, a rebel among the Rebels. I was different enough already: a smart girl who wanted to be an astronomer and, gasp, believed in evolution. At the age of thirteen, I took part in a debate in which I championed Darwinian evolution against creationism. After being told I was going to hell during the course of the debate, I was shunned in the lunch line. I was surprised by their intense reaction against Darwin and, more particularly, was amazed at the hostile way my classmates–some of whom I knew to be intelligent–regarded science. Over the next few weeks, things returned to normal for me socially, but I had learned to keep my beliefs largely to myself. It wouldn't have been prudent to be both godless *and* a Yankee-lover in such a hostile climate, and I had to make it through high school here. Despite our Rebel image, Southerners, especially Southern women, are schooled in not rocking the boat. So I soldiered on in silence, quietly plotting my escape, applying to not a single college in the South. Deliverance came in the form of an acceptance letter from the University of Chicago, and I readily took the offer.

While watching Tennessee disappear in the rearview mirror as my family and I drove north, I had a feeling of real liberation. Part of it was the hope and anticipation all college freshmen feel about leaving home for the first time to test themselves against the world, but it was more than that for me. For the first time, I would live my life on the "right" side of the Mason-Dixon line; I could finally come out of the closet wearing the blue I had always favored instead of passing in the dull gray of the rightfully defeated. My father maintained that I would miss the South, but I knew, as eighteen-year-olds often do, that he was dead wrong.

By the end of my first quarter at the University of Chicago, my perspective changed. The Chicago natives did not recognize me as one of their own. They laughed at my Southern accent, invisible to my ears but loud in theirs. They could barely conceal their surprise that I was admitted to such a prestigious institution when it is considered a well-known fact that Southerners not only cannot talk "right" but cannot cipher, much less think, well either. I was no longer me; I was a stereotype. The realization hit me full force the very day I moved into the women's dorm. We had a house meeting and played an introductory game in which we introduced ourselves and then recited the names of all the girls who had already introduced themselves. When my turn came, I was afraid that I wouldn't remember the names correctly and would make a fool out of myself. To my delight, I made it through the fairly lengthy list with no mistakes, but despite how well I was playing the game, people were laughing, some uproariously, and then it hit me why: To their ears, I sounded like a buffoon.

No one appreciates being reduced to a stereotype, and I was no exception. Of course not everyone did this; I made many friends in Chicago whom I still keep in touch with today. I always felt a sense of otherness, and once again it was pointed out to me in firm and undeniable strokes. This did not sit well with me, especially since most of the assumptions were wrong.

After a winter full of snow and ice and without fried okra and crowder peas, I had discovered that dear old Dad was right: There was much about my homeland that I missed terribly. Though financial considerations and a change in major were the primary reasons I decided to leave Chicago after my freshman year, there was also an undeniable element of homesickness—not just for my parents' home and my friends but for the South. It took leaving the South to make me realize that I was, whether I liked it or not, a Southerner.

For the last twenty-plus years, I have been coming to terms with my Southernness, defusing my own stereotypes about what this identity means and its relationship to me. Most stereotypes contain some core of truth, and I can cite firsthand examples of practically every facet of the stereotype. I walked the halls with good old boys in high school and heard them make racial slurs. I had neighbors wax rhapsodic over the good old days of moonlight and magnolia when the "darkies" were happy "in their place" and taken care of by a benevolent master. But in my experience of the South, these are the aberrations and not the rule. I would be lying if I said race wasn't an issue, but my parents never exposed me to vitriolic racism, and my white privilege prevented me from seeing and experiencing its effects. Now as an adult I feel I am continuously learning what this privilege means, particularly in the South. I am certainly aware that racism, ignorance, and intolerance exist here, but this doesn't mean that all Southerners are complacent about these issues or that we wish for them to continue and don't work for change. Our schools are underfunded, many of our people live in grinding poverty, and our healthcare system is inadequate. But all of this is true of America in general and not the South in particular.

In coming back to my homeland, I came to see it for the first time. I listened to the differences in cadence and drawl of Southern speech and to the stories told by my family and strangers. And I began to see, really *see*, the South, often through the lens of a camera, taking in the landscape and its denizens and realizing a beauty in the natural world to which my web of prejudices had previously blinded me. I discovered a love of the land that my suburban self had never imagined and began to yearn for some chunk of it to call my own, delighting in even the hundred-degree summer days and the ten-degree winter nights. The beauty all around me opened me up, and I realized I was a part of it and it was, irrevocably, a part of me.

Then, in my early twenties, I discovered something that forced me to transcend my old boundaries and reinvent myself, something that shook my identity to the core: I was a lesbian. It took about a year for me to come to terms with this "new" facet of myself, a part of me that, like hands and eyes, had been present since birth but that I had somehow managed to ignore or deny for two decades. Coming out to myself was not easy; applying the words *lesbian* or *queer* to me was like a slap in the face, and I flinched accordingly each time I said it. Nice girls aren't dykes, especially nice Southern girls. What would my parents and friends think? Would the Southern Baptists and the Church of Christ unite to burn me at the stake?

I couldn't help but think how much easier it would be to come out somewhere like Boston, New York, or San Francisco instead of Tennessee, an area often called, and deservedly so, "the buckle on the Bible Belt." I had awakened to my sexuality only to find myself demonized by the community at large. I began to make undercover forays into Nashville, not to bars but to bookstores, where I was amazed to find entire sections of gay and lesbian books. I hated taking them to the register; I was certain the clerk was sitting in judgment, possibly even taking my name and address from my check and passing it on to some homophobic rednecks who would rape and/or kill me. *Paranoia* became not just a word in my vocabulary but part and parcel of my existence. It never dawned on me that the clerk might be gay too or simply open-minded and open-hearted. In my mind the stereotypical Southerner became real again, but this time the stereotype stretched to include homophobic, a quality that had always been latent in the description—and one I ignored because I assumed it didn't apply to me, just as I had assumed racism and other qualities of the stereotype didn't apply.

Of course, I had internalized homophobia. I had to work to defuse my own prejudice against myself as well as learn how to deal with the rest of the world's prejudice against me. Frankly, I was terrified. The prejudice I have experienced as a white Southerner is unpleasant but usually not life-threatening: people either assume I'm an ignorant bigot or hick and dismiss me out of hand, or they find me funny, perhaps quaint. But being gay threatens the hell out of many straight people. I find that the hatred that fuels racism in the South and throughout America, for that matter, is rooted in a mentality of violence and ignorance that is similar to homophobia.

Surprisingly, being a Southerner actually helped me come to terms with being a lesbian, largely because having come out and accepted myself as a Southerner had made me very aware of what it was like to be the other. I learned that identity is dynamic and changeable, not necessarily fated and inflexible. Just as I had shaped my identity as a Southerner, I could also shape my lesbian identity.

First, though, I needed to have some clue about what it meant to be a lesbian. There was the obvious, but I knew there was more to it than sex. Ever the good student, I studied. I visited those bookstores and bought shelves full of books: collections of essays and coming-out stories, queer theory tomes, naiad potboilers, erotica, even the occasional piece of literary fiction. I read and digested everything I could get my hands and eyeballs on, and I spent a great deal of time thinking and writing about what I was learning. There is not one lesbian identity but many, much like there are many Southern identities. Each lesbian is unique, her background and experiences shaping her lesbian identity as much as the rest of her identity.

I was also fortunate. My parents were liberal, not just politically but religiously. I didn't have the burden of religious guilt to weigh me down. We went to church occasionally, a liberal Protestant sect, then dashed home after the sermon to watch football. I stripped off the hated pantyhose and dress as soon as I hit the back door. Science and mathematics were the cornerstones of my education, and I was always told that I could be anything I wanted to be—my options weren't limited because I was a girl. Further, my skin color and class background gave me access to many things beyond my public school education.

Like most gay people, when I took my first tentative steps out of the closet it was to come out to friends. The first person to whom I came out turned out to be lesbian also, and one of my best friends turned out to be gay, so those two were pretty easy. My oldest and dearest friend, though, was Southern Baptist, and I was shaking in my shoes when I finally came out to her, fearing one of those god-awful "you'll burn in hell, sinner" speeches. But again my friend showed me the untruth of stereotypes: her heart, not her religion, governed her, and she embraced me as she always had. When I came out to my parents, my father was okay with it, my mother less so, but both made peace with it because they love me for who I am. In this respect, I've been lucky too.

But still, luck only goes so far. I don't advertise my queerness, and I fear—perhaps justly, perhaps not—that my house will be burned down or my car blown up. Would this be different if I lived somewhere else? Would I be less fearful, more willing to simply be who I am if I lived, say, in New York City or Seattle, where there are larger queer communities? I don't know. Hatred is a widespread sickness, and the South has no monopoly on homophobia. Still, I do dream of that happy paradise where people accept each other for who they are rather than what labels they attach to themselves or to one another. As a lesbian, I feel every day the consequences—fear, disgust, hatred—of this label, yet I don't feel that the hateful qualities society has ascribed to this label in any way reflect who I am as a human being. And if the labelers are wrong about me, they're almost certainly wrong about other people described by other labels. The ideal, of course, would be to eschew labels altogether, but the best I can do is remember my own humanity in the face of the label and ascribe it to others regardless of the label(s) they wear.

Even so, the adult me is multifaceted, and two of the parts that compose me are undeniably the Southerner and the lesbian. Ensuring that *Southern lesbian* is not the oxymoron it might seem has been one of the central exercises of the past several years of my life. Being both of these things—not to mention being a woman, an intellectual, an artist, an environmentalist, a daughter, a sister—is, at times, like being on two roller-coaster tracks that rise and fall, twist and turn, loop upside down, and, occasionally, intersect in the strangest places and ways. It appalls some people when I say I am proud of being a Southerner. In their minds, I should hang my head in shame for being a racist and an ignorant hick. It never dawns on them to question their stereotype, to understand that ignorance and prejudice are as much on their end as on mine. Or perhaps they might see me as an exception to the general rule, the same self-congratulatory posture I used to assume in my younger days when escaping the South was my primary goal. I have learned, however, that I am not particularly exceptional, that many Southerners share, to some degree, my background and my viewpoints, and while we may be in the minority in our homeland, we seem to be the minority throughout the United States as well.

Moreover, I have family, friends, and a history in Tennessee. I was raised in a subdivision in a small town. Our back yard abutted a pasture that was sometimes home to cows and horses and always to wildlife and wildflowers. I learned to identify the birds and trees. I caught lightning bugs and terrapins and June bugs and crawfish. I shelled peas and lima beans and spent countless afternoons reading and rocking in the patio swing. I learned to name the constellations and respect the power of an electrical storm. The rhythm of the seasons and the roll and the pitch of the land became as much a part of me as the skin on my body and the blood that moves beneath it. I learned the idioms of Southern speech and the peculiarities of the people. I went to school here, played flute (badly) in the marching band here, learned to drive here, had my first kiss here. I went to college here, became a writer here, fell in love with literature here. My mother is buried here, and my father and brother live within thirty miles of my house. I eat here, I drink here, I think here, I dream here. I became who I am—as a white woman, a lesbian, a Southerner, and much more—here, and I am still becoming who I am here.

No homeland can be discharged from its political dimension, nor can its cultural freight be unloaded. It has a history and a geography that are inexorable and that shape the people who live there. I could elucidate all the flaws and failings of the South, but they are failings I am familiar with and that, to some degree, I share—even if sharing them means that I define myself against them.

And so here I am, the once-reluctant Southerner who has come full circle, back where I started, more or less, but with a perspective vastly different from the one that drove me growing up. I see things, I hope, more clearly, which means I am both more critical and more accepting of humanity and its frailties. In optimistic moments, I like to think I'm part of the growing-up process, causing others to come to terms with their own prejudices as I have done (and still do on a daily basis). My roots here run deep. I may not stay in the South forever, but for now this queer heart beats more or less happily in a red-state body.

Home, Adopted

JILL KIM SOOHOO

An unnamed pregnant Korean woman goes to an adoption agency in Daegu, South Korea, with the intent of relinquishing her unborn child for adoption. It is 1977, and this practice is uncommon; most women go to the adoption agency *after* their child is born. She gives up her baby immediately after birth, and after three months of living with a foster family, the child is successfully adopted by white American parents living thousands of miles away in the United States.

I am that child. I was born Kim Sae Bom in Daegu to an unwed birth mother who wanted to remain anonymous. I've never had the option to locate her even if I wanted to. The whereabouts of my birth father have always been unknown. Having no knowledge of my Korean birth parents and growing up in a white family in the U.S., I never felt very Korean. I often wondered why my identity had to be such a mystery—something I had to solve on my own. I've always wished that some pieces of the puzzle could come more easily.

My Korean identity died the minute I arrived in the U.S. I was absolved of my Korean name and slapped with an English one: Jill Elizabeth Morneau (my premarried name). Having been raised in a New England suburb that is 90 percent white, I learned nothing of Korea or Korean people until college. There, I met people from Korea for the very first time. "They eat dogs" and "If you'd stayed there you would've been begging on the streets for rice," were common laments I heard from my parents about my country of birth when I was young.

I grew up thinking I was white. I was so sure I was so white, in fact, that when someone called me a "Jap," I thought it meant Jewish American Princess. The suburb I grew up in was so white that a boy I went to school with once asked me, "Are you black?" I only realized how white I *wasn't* when I moved to New York City after college and found myself suddenly surrounded by people of color who were aware of their ethnicities in ways I never knew were possible.

It was a shock for me to realize that the country I was born in—Korea—had thousands of years of history, accomplishments, and a thriving, rich culture. I learned about this more intimately in 2001, when I had a chance to live in Korea for four months with a newly created program for adoptees to learn about their heritage. I lived at Inje University in southeastern Korea in a school dorm with Korean students, and also had access to a local host family.

Most nonadoptees think the highest priority for an adoptee is to meet his or her birth parents, a concept that had always eluded me. My connection to my ethnicity had always stemmed from a desire to know about my culture rather than my biology: I needed to know what being Korean meant for my identity's sake—how it played into and influenced who I was. I needed a cultural awareness so that when people asked, "That's Korean food, isn't it?" Or, "What does Korean sound like?" I'd actually have an answer; I'd know for myself, and I'd have control over the situation. I needed to know so that I wouldn't feel stupid when people asked me things *they* thought I should know. After being asked these questions, professing ignorance for the umpteenth time, I longed to know the answers and ward off the questions.

Three months into my stay in Korea, I made up a list of things I wanted to do before I left. Visiting Daegu, the city I was born in, was at the top of my list. I imagined I would feel an automatic connection to Daegu, similar to how I'd felt when I moved to New York City after growing up in New England. "Home" for me was an undefined concept, especially given the resonance of the word among Asian Americans who are constantly bombarded with the question, "Where are you from? No, where are you *really* from?" I'd gone to Korea to figure out what being Korean meant to me, how it affected my life thus far: Seeing my birth city seemed to be part of my necessary identity-solving puzzle.

My host father, Professor Chang, an economics teacher in the adoptee program, offered to take me to Daegu when I told him I had been born there. He suggested we go as a family—along with his wife, my host mother, and their seven-year-old daughter, Yuri. They'd never been there before, so it would be a new experience for all of us.

"Jeel," my host father told me, "I want you call me 'Apa.'" He spoke with a smile, his eyes large in his thick glasses, his body tall and skinny and his back slightly hunched.

"Okay," I said, not quite settled with the idea of calling him "dad."

It didn't surprise me that he considered me family. When I spent time with them over Korean Thanksgiving, Professor Chang insisted on taking a "family photo," which included me. After three months in Korea, I'd learned how deep kinship runs, how being part of this ethnic group was like being part of a secret club. Many people in Korea had urged me to call them "older brother" or "father" or "sister." But it was still a hard concept to get used to.

When we arrived in Daegu we passed a few groups of people: old men sitting on small, worn blankets in the middle of the sidewalk playing cards; *ajummas* with tanned skin and baggy mismatched clothing, squatting or sitting on the ground, trying to sell their farmed vegetables and fruits.

I was disappointed when my host father led us underground. I'd been through submerged streets in both Seoul and in Busan, where my host family lived. I wasn't fond of these underground areas where whole neighborhoods of clothing stores, restaurants, fountains, music stores, hardware stores, and eyewear shops stretched on for what seemed like miles. I wished we were aboveground rather than below like sewer rats. We passed countless glass storefronts displaying jeans, T-shirts, and belts. We walked down hallways and floors covered with dirty, faded tiles. Groups of young people and families strolled by, walking and talking, creating a human slalom course. The subterranean passages seemed so endless in part because the jam-packed population had swelled its landmass.

When we finally exited we were in a different neighborhood entirely. The dirty garages were replaced with a wide brick street bordered by clean modern buildings.

"Jeel, we are going to a ginseng market," my host father told me as I trailed behind. "It is largest medicinal market in Korea. Second largest in all of Asia." The way he recited our purpose conjured up for me an image of him standing in front of one of his economics classes. He sounded as if he was reading from a brochure.

He motioned for the family to stop for a moment as he seemed to be trying to get a sense of where we were headed. I was grateful for a brief break to look around and absorb the surroundings. I saw street carts holding everything from batteries to socks. Throngs of people, families and singles alike, stopped to buy items from the carts and browsed outside stores.

After a quick conference with his wife, my host father told me, "Jeel, we eat lunch first. Normally we eat Korean food, but today we go to Pizza Hut." I knew this was intended to be a special treat for me, but I was disappointed. Koreans had offered me this slice of Western life in the same way that Americans take foreigners to the places in the States that might remind them of "home." In actuality, this was the last thing I wanted. I was in Korea to eat

Korean food with Korean people. But I kept quiet and pretended Pizza Hut was the same treat for me that I knew it was for them.

"Jeel, you try and speak Korean," my host father instructed once we were seated in a booth. "I translate for you if you cannot."

"Nay," I told him, feeling self-conscious. The Korean I knew wasn't enough to string together into a sentence. Even though I'd been studying for four hours a day and was working with a tutor, there wasn't much I could say. It was as if my brain were closed off to the idea that I might be able to learn the language that would have been my native tongue, as if in punishment for having become too Americanized.

Yuri's small fingers pointed to menu images that depicted greasy food options. I got my own menu while the three of them shared one. I spent extra time looking over the choices; I didn't want to order anything too expensive.

"We will get pizza and salad, Jeel," my host father said after conversing with his wife.

I'd already discovered that salad was something I'd taken for granted in the States after I'd tried the salad bar at the Pizza Hut near our university. I wasn't looking forward to trying it again, but out of politeness I obliged.

"Jeel, we know that in U.S. people have their own bowls," my host father said, smiling as he beckoned the waitress toward me.

"Oh, it's okay," I said as the waitress handed me one bowl and placed another one on the table for the family to share. *If I were really part of the family, I'd share too,* I thought. I felt myself blushing, feeling embarrassed by being selected out as somehow more deserving.

When I went up to the salad bar with my host mother and Yuri, it was exactly the same display as my previous experience: an odd assortment of pineapple and other fruits, corn, broccoli, and bacon bits. There were none of the vegetables normally associated with salad bars back home, such as lettuce or cucumbers.

The family bowl quickly became a goulash of pickles, pineapple, carrots, and corn. Back at the table they picked up their forks and dug into their shared salad while I ate mine with deliberation.

"Mah-chee-say-yo," I said, telling them it tasted good.

My host mother beamed a smile that lit up her whole face, her cheeks suddenly round and wide. *"Ma-chee-say-yo,"* she echoed.

I felt a sudden connection to the family in that moment. "Apa," I said, opting to see how it felt to take my host father up on calling him dad, "you can call me by my Korean name, 'Sae Bom.'" I always liked the way these two words—"new spring"—sounded. The way he pronounced my name, "Jeel," meant vagina in Korean. I didn't like the idea of my esteemed economics professor host father yelling "Vagina!" across the room.

"What is 'Sae Bom'?" he asked, confused. I could tell he didn't understand my pronunciation.

"Sae Bom," I said again, trying to make it sound more "Korean" by turning the "s" sound into more of a "th," and trying to make the "Bom" sound longer and deeper.

"Ahhh, Sae Bom," he said, putting accents on the words that my mouth couldn't make. "Okay, I will call you Sae Bom."

When our pizza arrived, I eyed the bacon, corn, peppers, ham, and hamburger—toppings chosen by Pizza Hut—with skepticism. This Korean impression of Western food had puzzled me on previous occasions; such odd ingredients, but at least it wasn't a kimchi pizza.[1] I ate my share, thinking maybe I'd miss this strange concoction after I left Korea.

"You should try kimchi more," Apa said.

"I don't like the taste," I said. We'd had this conversation several times before.

"My children, they don't likes kimchi often, but I still maked them eat it. They want to eat things like pizzas, but I maked them eat it at least once a week," Apa said.

As if we were really father and daughter, this was our familiar argument. He'd tout the benefits: good for digestion, full of vitamins and minerals, and even effective at preventing diseases and some types of cancer.

"I just don't like way it tastes," I responded every time he raised the issue. At times it made me feel even less Korean not to savor this oh-so-Korean food, until Apa finally admitted that the younger generations didn't like it either. Maybe I had something in common with my Korean peers after all.

Our next stop after lunch was the medicinal market. I saw ginseng roots the size of office spring water dispensers, some hanging in store windows, others on display in clear, capped bottles, suspended in transparent liquid. They looked like octopi with long beige tentacles.

I peeked into one of the stores to see metal shelves against a far wall filled with clear flat plastic bags of herbs and roots for various ailments that resembled bags of lawn fertilizer. The smell overwhelmed me; I felt as if I were standing in the middle of a spice rack with all the spice containers open.

I'd never thought about the power of ginseng before. It's used in Korea to help recover from childbirth and chronic illnesses, to boost stamina, and to relieve the lethargy hot summers induce. At home in the U.S., I'd only seen it in bottles of AriZona Iced Tea.

Some of the stores we passed had stuffed heads of deer and other animals hanging from their walls. Others had enormous armoires filled with tiny wooden drawers holding spices, herbs, and medicine. "Can we go see how much it costs to get a small amount?" I asked, thinking of a friend who had asked me to bring him home some ginseng.

"It is very expensive," Apa told me. A very small bottle could cost hundreds of dollars. I wanted to be the ambassador of things Korean, returning home with gifts aplenty, but ginseng wasn't destined to be one of them.

We left the market for Dalseong Park, another site on Apa's must-see list. There, people were selling balloons and noisemakers for children out in front of the large metal gate. Senior citizens strolled through the gates and leisurely walked along the paved, wide walkways, which created the feel of a botanical garden.

Yuri held her mother's hand as we walked as a family. Apa, at around six feet tall, towered over his wife, Yuri, and me. At first glance we may have appeared a biologically related family; we were all Korean in appearance, but I was conscious of how much I was not one of them with my American posture and mannerisms.

Though they'd gone out of their way to welcome me, I felt like a foreign exchange student: I didn't fit. I couldn't speak Korean, and I could barely stomach the food. I didn't feel like a good Korean daughter. Feelings of not wanting any part of this culture began to surface; if it could reject me, I could reject it right back. These people were not really my family.

I felt out of place as I watched Yuri run over to a large emu housed in a tall cage. It was one of four birds in separate cages that were trying to move as far away from passersby as possible. The animals looked well cared for; their feathers were intact, and I couldn't detect any bruises or cuts, but I wondered why they were separated from one another. I felt a kinship with them; their isolation seemed similar to the way I had been separated from my Korean heritage at such an early age. *It's not my fault,* I thought. I had no choice in the matter.

I stood back and watched as people banged on the cages to coax the animals over for photos. I stared at the frantic birds, sensing their frustration. Feelings of shame and abandonment overwhelmed me as I watched the animals pacing back and forth. I knew these feelings were misdirected. I looked over at my host family, who were unfazed by the spectacle that was causing me so much anguish.

They'd moved on to a new row of cages, each about five paces long with concrete walls so the animals housed inside couldn't see each other. In the first cage was a Korean dog, a jindo, with short fluffy fur, pointy ears, and an upturned tail. It remained motionless, sitting on its hind legs and staring straight at me as I approached the cage. Its face was full of resolve.

According to the plaque next to the cage, this breed of dog was designated National Treasure #53 by the Korean government. Valued for its intelligence, courage, and loyalty, it was the most popular dog in Korea. Jindos make extraordinary guard dogs and are known to protect home and family to the death, possessing some of the loyalty I'd known Korean people to have. They also have excellent homing instincts and are reputed to find their way home when lost. They are extremely fast, powerful, and determined.

Why was a national treasure in a cage at a zoo? I wondered. I looked into its eyes to pass on my apologies, but it didn't want to forge any sort of connection with me. *How perfect,* I thought. *I can't even make a connection with a Korean dog.*

Tears formed in the corners of my eyes as I thought about these animals in captivity. I pictured myself locked in a cage, observed by countless spectators: "She looks Korean; why doesn't she speak it?" The pressure of being Korean and yet wholly American was beginning to take its toll. In Kimhae, the university town I was staying in, I'd become famous because people were new to the concept of an American Korean like me. I was a spectacle in my own right. I confused the locals and made them question their notion of what made a *"hanguk saram,"* or Korean person.

"Sae Bom," Apa called out. Oblivious, I'd forgotten that I told him to use my Korean name. "Sae Bom," he called again. When I finally realized he was referring to me, I wondered if maybe I wasn't a "Sae Bom" after all.

I turned to follow my family out of the park. It was getting late, and we needed to head back.

As I walked away from the park, I contemplated the fact that I was here, in the city of my birth. I'd done it. I'd seen the place where I came into the world. Daegu—a city known for beautiful women and hailed as the final line of resistance against the communist regime during the Korean War. I wanted Korea to shine in my mind. I wanted to leave with a positive impression. The fact that my memories of Daegu would be composed of going on a trip to Pizza Hut, feeling out of place with a family that did nothing other than try to make me feel welcome, and witnessing the torturous conditions of the animals at the park left me with an overwhelming feeling of emptiness.

My heart was not in Daegu. This city was not mine. Daegu made me feel even less Korean than I already did. I wondered if I'd ever be able to embrace the Korean side of myself, especially since this experience had been such that it made me never want to go back.

In the years since my visit to Korea, I've come to realize that home is more than a place of birth or an ethnic connection. Home for me has become about putting down roots, feeling part of a community, and being close to friends and family. I found "home" in the last place I expected: the Boston area where I grew up, where I live now with my husband, down the street from my brother and close to my parents. By returning to my homeland, I was able to set myself free, and find the place I truly feel is home.

Urban Nomads

JOSHUNDA SANDERS

In June 2006, I sat in the Centex mortgage company office in Austin, Texas, sleep-deprived and nearly delirious. My three-bedroom, thousand-square-foot house in East Austin was finished being built, and all I had to do was stop my hand from shaking so I could sign away my youth. The loan officer handed me a pen. The pile of papers all looked the same: phrases printed in tiny letters attached to the biggest loan I'd ever applied for.

It was the happiest and most terrifying day of my life.

As I stumbled out to the parking lot, smiling and a little shocked, I made a mental list of how I would move my washer and dryer, my bookcases, and my futon. I settled on the idea that small, multiple trips would help me transition better from my old life to my new one. For the next four weeks, each time I put tape on a box, loaded or unloaded my truck, or drove from my Austin apartment to my new house, I began to understand why I was so terrified.

I had lived with my mother for the first twenty years of my life, and everything in our life regularly collapsed like a house of cards, one thing always knocking down another. We spent the 1980s and 1990s moving to and from a half-dozen homeless shelters, welfare hotels, and subsidized apartments in New York City. She was fine with the fact that we never stayed in one place for too long. If home is meant to be a safe, secure, and familiar place, I did not have a real home until I made my own.

Texas was the last place I thought I'd end up loving. I'd lived here for a brief time during a journalism fellowship I won after graduating from college, and school and work drew me back in 2005. I got a job at the *Austin American-Statesman*—Austin's first-rate newspaper, and I was happy to get back to Texas.

As I started packing, I thought about all the events that had led me here. I stared at the picture of my mother that I kept in the kitchen. She wore a polyester dress and a freshly styled wig, looking fierce and showing off the long brown legs I'd inherited from her. It made me sad to think that she'd be the last person to know I bought a house, that I was unable to share my latest joy with her.

I was the baby girl in my family, born in Philadelphia in 1978, two years after my twelve-year-old brother Jose was killed by a bus. My young life was full of instability, because after Jose's death, Mom could not keep a home or her temper under control. My older siblings went to stay with relatives because of her violent outbursts. My biological father was one of her flings. She spent money wildly and bought wigs and shoes instead of paying rent or buying groceries.

Talking about the trauma of losing a child could have added a necessary order to our lives, but back then, black people didn't talk about going to therapy. And because her own mother had died in a mental institution when Mom was thirteen, she wanted nothing to do with the "system" and instead relied on Catholicism as her therapy; she went to Mass nearly every day.

But more often than not, I witnessed what I referred to as Mom's ungodly moments. When I was four, she burned my arm with a straightening comb and I was sent to foster care for six months. She was often erratically violent or extremely happy. When she regained custody of me, we left Philadelphia briefly for New Mexico, only to return and find our house near foreclosure. That was when Mom decided that we should move to New York City since we had relatives there.

New York was an Emerald City of towering buildings and dazzling lights in comparison to Philadelphia's dark, flat, suburban plains. Skyscrapers lined up like glow-in-the-dark LEGOs from the twenty-first floor of the Harlem senior-living apartment building that my grandaunt Claie lived in. Since I was six and my mom was in her forties, we weren't allowed to stay there. Auntie Claie gave Mom a mink coat and a roll of quarters. She gave me her old red wool gloves and sent us to a shelter in the Bronx that winter. As we crossed the Harlem River Bridge, a man put a gun to my head and ran off with Mom's coat and her quarters.

It was not the last bad experience we'd have in New York. I had no language to describe why we were always leaving one place for another, why bad things always seemed to happen to us for no reason.

The only time I felt settled anywhere before moving out on my own was when I lived with Mom in an apartment in the Bronx, at the corner of 183rd Street and Daly Avenue. Mom and I moved there when I was twelve and lived there for four years—the longest we'd stayed anywhere. It was enough for me to consider the Bronx home.

Because I was so tired of moving, I even loved the ugly things the Bronx had to offer: its tall, bulky train trestles and big, gray box buildings. Our apartment, on the top floor of a five-story tenement building near the Bronx Zoo, had no elevator. Every window had its own guard, a gate to protect project apartments from clear views of the horizon, three bars that limited any illusions of freedom.

I remember being unable to see most of the sky from inside our apartment and sleeping through the wail of ambulances or the thumping bass of neighbors' salsa music. In the Bronx, we settled into a poor nation of old buildings and gutted dreams. I internalized our struggles to mean that I did not deserve anything besides existing.

Before we got to the Bronx, we had slept on white cots in a gym as long as a football field at the Roberto Clemente State Park shelter. We had survived no-frills soap and early-afternoon curfews at family shelters in Manhattan and Queens. Several years later, while living at the Daly Avenue apartment, we washed our clothes in the bathtub and dried them on radiators. All we had for furniture were hand-me-down chairs, a used television set, and a mattress we'd inherited from our neighbors. Bed sheets hung from our windows, and we typically ate canned peaches or rice and beans for dinner.

Early on, I latched on to education as a substitute for home. First, I went to a private Manhattan junior high school, De La Salle Academy, on scholarship. There, I found an escape hatch for the next chapter in my life: Emma Willard School—a boarding school. I was fifteen years old, and Emma Willard was five hours from the Bronx by bus. Just weeks before I started, my mother tried to choke me to death during one of her episodes. I was leaving just in time.

That first move away from my mother was the most exciting one I'd ever made. I was ecstatic that I was escaping, but terrified at what awaited me—the same blissful terror that burned in my gut as I moved the last of my books and files and clothes into my new Austin house. That feeling of not knowing what happens next has been my real home for so long.

I needed that blend of panic and hope to weather my first year at Emma Willard. While there, I slept on the same bed—a bed with a frame!—with a consistency and comfort I hadn't had before then. I ate dinner with heavy silverware. I had a dresser with a mirror. To me, it was decadent.

For my mostly wealthy classmates, for whom vacationing in Milan was an ordinary experience, my awe at such simplicities seemed naive. It was my first exposure to class difference, rubbing elbows with girls who had grown up in homes that had instilled in them a sense of entitlement. My exposure to them changed my expectations for how to live. Like them, I began to believe that I deserved a few meals a day and quiet, pretty surroundings.

My experience at Emma Willard motivated me to apply to Vassar College, where I lived on a polished campus and was surrounded by more wealthy people. My struggles growing up had made me a hard worker, hungry for success and money. I had worked every summer to save money for college. Once enrolled at Vassar, I freelanced for online magazines, submitted poems to anthologies, and braided hair for extra money. I got a part-time job at Pizzeria Uno and worked an on-campus job at the Career Development office while taking a full load of classes and writing for the school paper. But even then, years after living in the Bronx without anything resembling regularity, I refused to let go of it. I hadn't yet reconciled my success with my mother's failures. During my sophomore year, Mom moved across the street from campus after she was evicted from our Bronx apartment. She showed up unannounced at my dorm in the middle of the night. I was just starting to build a "normal" life. Her proximity made it difficult for me to reshape my identity outside of depression and poverty. The only solution, I figured, was to move as far away as possible, even if it meant leaving New York and everything I'd grown to love. I decided I would leave New York as soon as I finished college.

By then I was already fluent in the language of nomads. When I graduated from college in 2000, I won a journalism fellowship that required me to move every six months. I traveled to Houston, Seattle, San Francisco, and Oakland. With all these moves, I felt like a ball of tumbleweed that longed to be an ancient oak tree. Ultimately, when I did settle in Oakland for three years, I felt depressed and homesick for New York. California didn't feel like "home." When I was comfortable there, it was because I felt like an outsider and being an outsider was familiar. I was the only black woman reporter at my job and one of the youngest.

Part of me felt that I could feel settled in anyplace–New York or elsewhere. I was still afraid that the chaos of my childhood would catch up to me no matter where I lived. Then, a couple of years ago, I got a phone call that put my past in perspective. My Mom was diagnosed with bipolar disorder, also known as manic depression. The symptoms include grandiose ideas, spending sprees, deep sadness, and erratic moods. Through this diagnosis, I finally understand my childhood and my mother in a very different way. Being able to name her condition has helped me to see my own battles with depression and low self-esteem. I had always thought of myself as my brother's replacement, a reason for my mother to worry and have episodes. But finding out about her bipolar disorder helped me rethink those beliefs that I'd carried around so long.

Because most black folks don't believe in talking about–let alone treating–mental illness, this news has been ignored by my distant family. Medication might stabilize Mom's moods, but she refuses to take pills. "I tried Valium," she told me recently. "It made me feel funny. Taking that stuff interrupts my relationship with God." Mom has moved at least once a year for much of her adult life. She is now sixty-six, and moving from her fifth Section 8 apartment to another one in New Jersey. I feel like I should help her, but I don't have it in me. She won't take medication and she has made a home for herself in instability.

Despite Mom's best intentions, she could not create a secure life for us. But my success as a young woman is perhaps a testament to the fact she didn't do too badly. She calls me her "professional newspaper career lady" with a pride that makes me giggle, even while her voice reminds me that I still carry the invisible scars of homelessness.

People have often asked me if I ever go "home to visit," and I've had to pause to think of how to answer that common question. How do I explain that I don't feel like I have a home anywhere in a world? How do I convey my reality of having grown up without a home in a society where homelessness—the condition of having events, not places, shape you—is considered shameful?

And yet, there's a part of me that does and always will think of the Bronx as home. No matter where I went, and despite the fact that I only lived there for a few of my formative years, I often felt homesick for the Bronx. As a child, I was trained as a nomad to quietly watch the world and have faith that silence could protect me, even when it didn't. Growing up this way made me the writer I am, but it has also made me prone to deep fear and bouts of sadness. The instability of my young life has its obvious drawbacks. I grew up without a clear idea of what my own peaceful space should feel like. Until I left the Bronx, only survival mattered. Peace, I thought, was a luxury. I've often wondered who I am if not the homeless girl fleeing my mother, her illness, and our life together.

Mom's diagnosis prompted me to go back to the Bronx in 2004, to purge myself of these wounds. I had based my identity on this dually stigmatized world of poverty and depression for as long as I could remember, and I didn't want to live that way anymore. I went back in part to answer some questions for myself and make peace with my history by walking through my old haunts. I expected to fall in love again with the noise and clutter of New York City, but instead my heart ached. The child in me had collected and savored the sights and sounds of New York City, and to see them again through the eyes of an adult was both painful and refreshing. As a young adult moving around in this world and trying to make sense of home, this place had been all there was. Now I knew that other worlds awaited me.

I made my way to the apartment building at 183rd and Daly Avenue. It had been several years since I had last toured Burnside Avenue, Fordham Road, or East Tremont. Water gushed from a corner fire hydrant through a hollow can and fell like summer snowflakes over the heads of kids running in cut-off jean shorts.

As I retraced my steps through the underdog sidewalks of the Bronx, the sky appeared as a blue rectangle boxed in by rooftops overhead. Traveling had introduced me to the wide-open skies of Texas and the cashmere-looking waves of the Pacific Ocean in California. Outside of the Bronx, people enjoyed real space, not just hints of it. That big space had become what I wanted and needed in a home.

But I had taught myself to sing in the musty Bronx air. I learned to cry without making a sound outside those thin windows. This place had taught me how to survive anything and everything, to fall down and get back up stoically, knowing another fall could be just around the corner. This place symbolized my old notion of home: that it should be something portable, a sense carried within instead of a physical placeholder of memories.

The ground beneath my sneakers was the same ground where my clothes had once been bundled in garbage bags alongside empty Heineken bottles. I remember a time when Mom and I were locked out and evicted from this building. We held on to our few possessions, having packed so quickly that we didn't know which bags held our underwear, my schoolbooks, our only framed picture of Jose. Pride prevented us from gathering everything we deemed sacred to carry in our arms on the subway, so we left our stuff right there in the street. Ripping the bags open to try to figure out what to take and what to leave behind would have been like tearing skin from our arms.

Alongside the sad memories were a rush of sweet memories, too: sneaking away to make out with my first love while Mom was at night school, dressing for a block party, the smell of Mom's Primo clinging to our apartment walls. I sat with my memories for a long while before I got up. I touched the side of the building before I walked away. The insecurity homelessness imprinted on my soul did not lift, but my heart soared. I loved the Bronx, but it would always be the past. When I got on a city bus to leave, I didn't look back. There was nothing left there for me to see.

Everywhere I've lived, I have taped a New York City subway map and a Bronx bus map to the wall above the space where I write. I am so nostalgic and fond of the Bronx for the gritty gifts it gave to me. Just looking at those maps reminds me that things can never be as hard as they were before. When I took the maps down from my apartment wall in preparation for my move into my new house, it reminded me of my last trip to New York, the one that empowered me to buy my Austin home. During that trip I realized that the people and places you love will break your heart if you let them. I realized that I could only feel at home when I abandoned my mom, which broke my heart and still does. While I am relieved that I've finally bought a house of my own in Austin, I also have survivor's guilt; I succeeded where my mother has failed.

But I've also learned that there can be healing in heartbreak. There are no curtains in this house of mine, no frame for the bed, no mirror for the dresser I bought from a coworker. Like so many places I've lived, this new place is bare. But I am the happiest I have ever been because this place is my home.

My relationship with my mom is distant at best. She still calls me three times a week and leaves long voice mails about her dreams of moving to South Carolina, where she was born. It is a fantasy that feeds her, but I've heard her talk about it since I was a little girl, and I doubt she will ever actually move there. I listen to her talk about her plans the same way I've quietly listened to her unfulfilled promises to visit me over the years. She asks me when I'll visit again, and I never know what to say. To visit her, in my mind, means becoming a six-year-old again, reliving our traumas and scarcity. No matter how ready I think I am for that, I am never ready enough. I tell myself that staying in Austin is the only way to make sense of our past and our relationship and to make peace with myself.

The catastrophic, far-reaching events of the past five years have helped me put my own personal upheavals in perspective: September 11, because it threatened to destroy the spirit of my hometown, and then Hurricane Katrina, because I could identify with legions of poor and displaced people uprooted by events beyond their control. These events have provided a backdrop for my own struggle to understand what home is, what it means to have one—or not to have had one.

"It is a miracle," a mentor of mine once said to me, "that we survive at all."

After the Hurricane Katrina disaster, a friend from California flew to Houston in October 2005 to volunteer at the Astrodome helping evacuees—America's newest urban nomads. I drove from Austin to help her give out books and comforting embraces. As the world watched Mother Nature evict mostly the poor from one of America's favorite cities, I wept. Being black and homeless in America, be it due to a hurricane, mental illness, bad luck, or the government, is to be pitied and then resented for not living the American Dream, despite the fact that you were never given the tools to become an architect of such a vision.

As I stood in the Houston Astrodome looking at cots lined up across the indoor field like dead soldiers draped in white flannel blankets, I thought of the miracle of resilience. My body remembered the weak temporary beds of my childhood, and I felt a camaraderie with the evacuees. The air was still humid with Mississippi River water and antibacterial gel, despite the fact that a month had already passed since the storm. An old woman in a wheelchair was wrapped in a patchwork comforter, staring with distant eyes at her new neighbors. A few boys tossed a football around between rows of shopping carts and trash bags filled with clothes and toiletries, their brown skin dimly lit by fluorescent lights. Girls braided each other's hair or slept through the morning.

This was nadir of the human experience: no money, no job, no house.

You could see the wounds on the psyches of the evacuees in the vacant sadness of their eyes. All the terror and weight of homelessness burdened their shoulders. I prayed that the youngest among them would not have to experience the constant aimlessness of not having a place in the world, the shadow of shame that follows a person who suddenly doesn't belong where he or she was or the insecurity that works as a spiritual ulcer, eating away at one's dignity. Optimists and those of us not affected by Katrina could say God or chance had given them a new start. I wanted to believe that, but my own experiences led me to believe it would be impossible for this mass of people to recover what they had lost.

One of my college classmates, herself an evacuee, began to shake with anger when we met for drinks months later. By then, evacuees had relocated to Houston, where they have been scapegoats for a rising crime rate, and to suburbs, where they are viewed unsympathetically. Now people speak of Katrina fatigue, as if it tires them to even think of the devastation that other people must live with for the rest of their lives.

My college friend told me how people had tried to comfort her by telling her they understood how she must feel.

"No one can ever know what it's like to have their home taken from them and wake up one day knowing it doesn't exist anymore," she said, her eyes brimming with tears.

I wanted to tell her that some of us *do* know, and that is it a miracle we survive at all. Instead, I offered her temporary solace in my arms, while I prayed for a more permanent peace—for her, for me, for all of us nomads.

The Route Back to Tonga

LOA NIUMEITOLU

In Provo and Orem, Utah, where I grew up from the age of nine, I spent many quiet moments remembering the route I walked home from school every day as a child in Tonga, my homeland in the South Pacific, before my family and I immigrated to the United States. My older sister, Fui, and I would meet at the playground or under the *kasia* (acacia) tree after class and walk home together, short-cutting through the corridors of Teachers College. We bent down and distorted our bodies to fit through the barbed-wire fencing of Old Vaiola Hospital—where my grandfather, a doctor, presided over the births of many children in my generation. I heard the crisp breaking of the neighbors' tall *tanetane* hedges as Fui and I squeezed in between their thin trunks. Sometimes we took the route lined with gargantuan hundred-year-old eucalyptus trees. I loved to rub the bark and sniff its scent on my fingers.

This was the footpath where Lilah, the daughter of an American and Japanese couple, screeched her bicycle to a halt and bragged loudly that she was going to watch the new ABBA movie at the downtown theater. It was 1977, and I had no idea what she was talking about. I spent my time climbing guava trees and rooftops with my cousins instead of following the trends of pop culture. Fui, never missing a beat, shot right back, "I have their new album. I love 'Dancing Queen.'" I stared at Fui with awe. It was on that pathway, returning home from school and watching my older sister talk back to Lilah, a *palangi*,[1] that I believed that we Tongans were important, witty, knowledgeable, and powerful people.

My parents, siblings, and I immigrated to the U.S. in 1981 through an offer that my mother received from the Mormon Church in Tonga. In the mid-'70s, my mother worked as a high school and college math teacher in the Tongan public school system. My father, preoccupied with drinking alcohol, was not an active part of our everyday life at that time. Raising three daughters alone, my mother chose to accept the best teaching wage at Liahona, a Mormon high school in Tonga. As part of her acceptance, we were required to convert to the Church of Jesus Christ of Latter Day Saints. Before we became Mormons, my mother did not raise us as staunch supporters of any one church. My father was a follower of the Wesleyan Church, a religious denomination with roots in Methodism, while my mother grew up in the Church of Tonga, another Methodist sect.

Since 1830, the Mormon Church has sent proselytizing missionaries all over the world to convert families to the Mormon religion. Many new converts, like my own family in Tonga, were lured into joining the religion with opportunities to study at Brigham Young University (BYU) and to immigrate permanently to the United States. Both my parents, like many Tongans in their generation, believed that a university education would teach them, and particularly their children, how to succeed in a rapidly changing world. Tonga did not have any university programs at that time. My parents were willing to take their children to any country that offered us a future in education.

In 1975, when my father was baptized into the Mormon Church, he stopped drinking and returned home to the family. My father got a job as a translator of Mormon scriptures in Tonga and later in Utah. After teaching at Liahona for six years, my mother was offered a scholarship to pursue undergraduate studies at BYU in Laie, Hawai'i. We lived in Laie for three years until my mother was offered another opportunity to pursue a master's degree at another BYU campus in Provo, Utah, in 1981. Taking advantage of this opportunity, our family left Tonga and moved to Wyview Park, a trailer park for BYU students who were married with children.

As a Mormon, my father constantly quoted the words of the Mormon Brethren, using these words to justify his actions. Although he stopped drinking alcohol and became a regular presence at home, he mercilessly beat Fui and me, the eldest siblings, often. We always retaliated and demanded that he not treat us cruelly. In response, he quoted Joseph Smith, the founder of the Mormon Church: "This is a theocracy," he would say, adding, "not a democracy." The Mormon Church dictated the way my father ruled our household. My mother, obeying her role as a Mormon wife, fully supported my father as the head of our home, although he beat her violently too. When I was older, I realized that he was fearful of the new world we had migrated to and he expressed these frustrations by hurting the daughters and wife who cared for him.

In spite of my father's dominance in the household, my mother shared equal ground with him when it came to politics. My parents aligned themselves politically with the Mormon Church. They took the middle ground on every issue, just like the Mormon Church did. As the flux of immigrants of color and non-Mormon religions rapidly grew in the 1990s in Utah, it became apparent to me that the Mormon saints' seemingly apolitical stance was just a cover for the church's Republican neoconservative agenda. I support women's rights, a woman's right to have an abortion, and same-sex marriage, issues that the Mormon Church has staunchly opposed. I also grew increasingly aware that the Mormon Church and its white culture distanced me from my homeland.

As I grew up in the Mormon Church, I was fed their most destructive Mormon belief, which is at the core of Mormon doctrine and culture: that fair-skin Nephites would lead their dark-skinned, misguided brothers, the Lamanites, out of their spiritual wilderness. Living in a state where the Mormon Church owns most properties and dominates politically, I grew up informed by this narrative. That the Mormon Church, as represented by white Nephite missionaries, aspired to "rescue" native Lamanites, families like my own, from the wild South Pacific.

While our parents became indoctrinated into the Mormon Church, Fui and I resisted the rigid borders of Mormon white culture that Utah offered us. We had some very particular ideas and ways of looking at life that we learned growing up in Tonga, Fiji, New Zealand, and during our three formative years in the Pan Pacific communities of Hawai'i. In the Pacific, everyone around us—no matter their religion, color, or class—was a part of our community. I grew up with the Tongan cultural value of sharing resources with anyone who needs them, no matter what they believe. I did not find this in Mormon culture, where I learned that in order to receive, I had to give. As a Mormon teenager, I always accepted the bishop's requests that I be president of the youth groups in my ward, the neighborhood congregation. At first, I read and loved the Book of Mormon. I went on a Mormon proselytizing mission to Arkansas, Mississippi, and Tennessee. My missionary service ended abruptly when a zine I wrote and discreetly distributed called "Consenting Adults" was confiscated by my mission president. The zine included opinions on secular culture, sports, and criticisms of the mission.

In Provo, a town that closed itself to the political world, I grew up thinking that politics only happened outside Utah County. As a young high school student, I spent countless hours in my high school library and the BYU library reading about politics happening around the world: the Anti-Apartheid Movement in South Africa, the antiwar movement against the Vietnam War, and the Civil Rights Movement of the '60s. These were events that empowered me politically and pushed me into a life of activism. As the leaders of the student group, BYU Students Against the War in the Gulf, Fui and I united with other student and community activists to protest the war and assert our dissent against the Mormon Church. By becoming activists, Fui and I have been able to imagine and articulate the kind of life we want to lead as Tongan American women.

When I was older, I wanted to take back the Tongan history that the Mormon Church and my Western education had denied me. In my research, I learned that my Tongan ancestors resisted an all-consuming colonization by Christian missionaries in the 1700s. My mother's name, Litia, is a legacy handed down from the time her family was exiled to Fiji because her family refused to convert to Christianity. When I returned to Tonga in 1995, for the first time since my family's migration to the U.S. in 1981, I joined the Tongan prodemocracy movement that emerged in the 1980s in response to government corruption. Unlike the Catholic and Wesleyan Churches that have been active supporters of this movement since its inception, the Mormon Church leadership does not support it.

When I arrived in Tonga in 1995, I took my childhood route home from Tonga Side School. As I meandered back to my uncle's two-room house that my family lived in when I was a child, I noticed that so much had changed; most of the people I knew had moved away. The old hospital where my grandfather worked was renovated and now housed the Chief Justice from New Zealand's family. Returning to Tonga for the first time after a long absence, I had to relearn my way around, to familiarize myself with what I took for granted as a child. My intention in returning home was to remember my purpose as a Tongan woman and that I had work to do with my people.

I had been told in Utah by Tongan immigrants intent on assimilating into the Mormon Church that my physical homeland of Tonga is not part of me and that I have no right to it. But Tonga is my homeland. Tonga is where my grandmother, Sauliloa, still lives in her wooden house that her mother, Mele, built and maintained. Tonga is where my grandaunt, 'Alavini, lives and continues to care for my uncle Polo, her nephew, who contracted polio fifty-six years ago. In my homeland, all the boys and men in my uncle Pasi's neighborhood of Mataika gather on Saturday nights to watch rugby on Fox World Sports and then spend the rest of the night drinking kava and singing songs to the strumming of guitars. Uncle Pasi's wife, Aunty Taiana, wakes up the next morning and cusses at the urine-stained driveway and the hundreds of cigarette butts piled in coffee cans when she reverses out of the driveway on her way, alone, to church. Tonga is my great-grandfather Peni Tupou's wooden house that he built in 1909, which is shaded by the gigantic *tamaline* tree that serves as a meeting place for lovers under moonlight.

I have learned that by being an activist for Tongan rights in Tonga and in the United States, I create a homeland that I feel liberated and sustained in, one that is different from the patriarchal Mormon household of my Utah upbringing. Tonga is my homeland that I return to in order to learn about my role in the diaspora and what it means to be Tongan. The route back to Tonga is the path I take to creating a community that my ancestors have given me as a legacy.

Coming Out, Coming Home

JENESHA DE RIVERA

In November 2003 I returned to the Philippines, my parents' homeland. Born and raised in New York, I was embarking on my fourth trip home in thirty-two years. The timing was fortuitous: My mother, father, younger sister, and I were all able to take a month out of our schedules for a visit.

When I was two, my father filmed my very first trip with an eight-millimeter camera. In the footage I am dancing in a red and white dress, the skirt flaring around my tiny body like a hula hoop. For me the footage serves only as proof that I was there—without it, I remember nothing. The two trips that followed were prompted by my maternal grandparents' deaths—my grandfather's when I was eight and my grandmother's when I was sixteen. During this fourth visit, much to my relief, no one had died; we were finally going back, as a family, for a real vacation. And this time I was bringing someone with me, my girlfriend, Patty.

My immediate family knows I'm a lesbian. I came out when I was twenty-one. After graduating from college, I got a job as a cosmetic chemist and moved into a converted loft with my then-girlfriend. My mother eventually forgave me for destroying her American dream and rested comfortably in the knowledge that there was still hope—my heterosexual younger sister. I later escaped the windowless laboratories of cosmetic chemistry and moved into the rainbow-filled life of LGBT civil rights work, where I learned that coming out can be a death sentence for many people around the world. Aside from the inevitable encounters with racism, sexism, and homophobia as a lesbian of color, I made it through my turbulent queer twenties relatively unscathed. In November 2003, I was about to embark on a new frontier in my queer experience. Going to the Philippines with my girlfriend meant that I was not only coming home, but also coming out all over again.

I met Patty in a creative writing workshop in New York in February 2003. The two of us were the only lesbians in a fiction-writing workshop called "The Unconventional Voice." I noticed her right away. Not only was she the only identifiable lesbian in the class—short black cropped hair, labret piercing, chunky black boots—but she was also the only other Filipina.

Going to the Philippines with Patty meant taking a brand-new relationship to another level. I was taking a risk. Trouble had been following my romantic life for a while before I met Patty. *What,* I asked myself, *made this situation any different? Wasn't taking a long trip in the first year of a relationship against all dating rules?*

Since my last visit in 1987, the Philippines had become an enigma to me. Everything I knew about being Filipino was tied to my life in America. I lived and breathed in a hyphenated reality. I knew little about what life was like for my Filipino cousins. As kids, language was already a barrier between us, made worse by long-distance connections. In my mind, they lived in a land where static crackled whenever you talked, where living with the lights on wasn't a guarantee, where water always ran cold and was never clean enough to drink from the tap. At the age of thirty-two, it was hard to imagine how much had happened since my last visit. The last time my relatives saw me, I was an awkward, androgynous sixteen-year-old girl. Now I was planning to return as an adult–as a lesbian–with my Filipina American girlfriend. I was consumed with thoughts of what they would think, how they would treat me and Patty, and what it would be like to return after years of creating an identity that was completely separate from my large extended family abroad.

I bought a travel book on the Philippines to prepare. I wanted to own my experience and not be dependent on my family's plans, so I read it from cover to cover. I read it every morning during my commute to work on the 7 train–a line that passes through immigrant neighborhoods–from Flushing, Queens, to Manhattan. Whenever I noticed a Filipino immigrant on the train, I felt the urge to hide my book. Here I was, a Filipina American sitting on a train full of immigrants, reading a book written by a European about *my* country of origin. I snuck glances through the history section and the part about "The People," vigilantly aware that someone might see me and think: *Poor girl, she knows nothing about her homeland.*

Patty and I boarded our plane to Manila on October 31. My parents had flown over a week earlier, and my sister Janelle would join us in a few days.

"Wake me up when we get there," Patty said in a sleepy voice. But I was too excited to fathom sleeping. I nudged Patty, eager to talk about the excursion we planned to the rice terraces in the Northern Cordilleras, but she curled into a ball beside me and closed her eyes.

With no one to talk to, I occupied myself with memories from my childhood. I remembered sweet *longanisa* sausage, fried *bangus* milkfish for breakfast, and hot steamed rice at every meal. I thought about my grandmother's house in Mindanao, the sound of roosters in the morning and the puppies I found in her back yard. I remembered the bus ride to and from my grandfather's funeral, how the bus jumped and skipped along the dusty dirt road, how everyone except my two-year-old baby sister was dressed in black, how on the way to the cemetery hardly anyone spoke, and how on the way back we sang and laughed even though we were all still crying. It had been the first time in ten years that everyone in my mother's family was together.

As Patty and I were about to land in Manila, I could hardly contain myself. I was excited to see my parents' transformation, something I had been aware of as a sixteen-year-old and that I anticipated even more as an adult. My father, a humble and shy man, stood straighter and talked louder when he returned home. My mother, typically the worrywart of the family, looked more relaxed, happier, and less guarded. As a child, I wondered if these mysterious mannerisms were pieces of my parents I'd never know. I wondered which personas were more real: the people I knew in New York or these confident, unfamiliar individuals in the Philippines.

As a child, the Ninoy Aquino International Airport felt like a chaotic, swampy aquarium. Men with thick black hair and dark brown skin pushed walls of boxes past me on rolling luggage carts. Young boys shouted to us for money and held out their hands, expecting *pasalubong*, gifts from abroad. When I asked my mother what they wanted, she said, "Money. The people here are very poor, much poorer than the homeless you see in New York." Some people at the airport handed the young boys five or ten centavos—an offering that amounted to a fraction of our American penny.

Now here I was again. From the window of the plane I could see the blue sky and a line of short palm trees in the distance. Patty and I emerged from the plane and walked down a long corridor with tall windows. "It still smells the same," I told Patty. "Can you smell that?" I took a deep breath. Even though we were indoors, the air smelled salty and metallic, the way my palms smell after gripping a handful of coins for too long. It was weighted with condensation, poor air-conditioning, and body heat. The ninety-degree air was stifling. We walked to the baggage claim and picked up our luggage:

a large black suitcase and one *balikbayan* box each, packed with clothes, shoes, chocolate, and canned food to give as *pasalubong* to relatives.

Patty and I decided to hire a porter to help us with our heavy load. A man with a shock of wavy black hair and a thin mustache carted our luggage through another enclosed corridor. As he pulled our baggage down a descending ramp, he turned to us and smiled.

"Are you two sisters?" he asked.

Patty and I looked at each other and smirked, knowingly. This happened to us all the time in New York, but I expected it to be different here. After all, when Filipinos gather together in the Philippines, no one automatically assumes they are all related.

"Yes, we are." Patty lied with a courteous smile. Even though it wasn't ideal to cloak our relationship with a lie of false sisterhood, we knew intuitively that it was safer to fib.

"I knew it!" he exclaimed, proud of himself.

Pulling off the sister act was an easy routine for us. We share many similarities: we are Filipina women, about five feet tall with short black hair. Among queer people, I assume telling the difference between us is easy: We're a butch-femme presenting couple. Although I don't exactly label myself as "butch," Patty and I never squabble over shared makeup or high-heeled shoes. I wondered if our dynamic would be obvious to Filipinos in the Philippines.

As we made our way through the sliding doors that led us out of the terminal, the porter asked Patty, "Do you have a boyfriend?" The discomfort in our bodies was simultaneous. We eyed each other as if speaking telepathically.

"Yes," she said, "he's picking us up now." Another lie. The two of us had talked before the trip about how we were both going to deal with being queer and "out" in the Philippines. We had focused primarily on our relatives and didn't really have a plan for strangers. Although our families gave us a taste of what Filipino culture held in store for us, including homophobia when we both initially came out, we didn't quite know what to expect. The experience with the porter was the first of many challenges.

The scene outside the airport wasn't as crowded and chaotic as I remembered. There were taxis lined against the curb, skinny porters in flip-flops lifting boxes three times their size. It wasn't long before Tito Tony's green Pathfinder rolled up to the curb where we stood with our luggage and *balikbayan* boxes.

"Hoy!" my father greeted us with the customary Filipino call from the passenger seat. Seeing my father's grin sent a wave of comfort through my body. The sensation made me aware of how out of place I already felt. My father stepped out of the car and hugged us both. I immediately took note of his appearance: the missing bags under his eyes, the absent furrow between his brows, the sound of his voice, and the movement of his body—everything was different. I witnessed him as I did when I was a child, with the curiosity and wonder of seeing someone for the first time, the action of taking in the whole of a man unfettered by worry or hesitation. Just as I remembered, my father was more comfortable and content in his homeland.

"How was your flight?" he asked.

Before I could answer, Tito Tony, my father's older brother, came around the back and greeted us.

I grabbed Patty's hand and introduced her to my uncle. "This is Patty," I said, "my partner." Tito Tony greeted her with a hug and then shook her hand.

"Hi. I'm Tony, Jinky's uncle." The way he said my nickname brought me back to my childhood, the way I was always *Jinky* here—never Jenesha, my formal first name, the one most people call me by in the States. Suddenly, my gut clenched. My thoughts were so focused on my father, on the heat, on how foreign I felt that I didn't have time to notice that I said "my partner." I had months of anxiety over how I was going to introduce Patty to my relatives and this was it: a simple handshake and a smile, or in this case a pleasant hug. A feeling of relief washed over me as I climbed into the air-conditioned car and slid onto the cool vinyl. Although this was a sign of hope, I knew there were more relatives to meet and many more introductions to come.

We drove onto the main road and made our way through midday traffic to a town called Alabang, an upper-class district in the city of Manila. Tito Tony's house was a sprawling Spanish-style home that glowed with lacquered mahogany and Mediterranean tile. I was shocked by its size and luxuriousness. Because my father was the only one in his family to immigrate to the States, I always assumed he was the most successful of his six siblings. On my previous two visits to the Philippines, we were so swept up in the funerals of my mother's parents that I hardly visited my father's side of the family. I had assumed that they had stayed in the Philippines unwillingly, and that coming to America was their ultimate goal, their lifelong dream. But looking around Tito Tony's large house, I realized that their lives in Manila were in fact more lucrative and privileged than I'd ever known in my immigrant upbringing in New York.

A few hours later we drove to Parañaque, where my Tita Leny lived. We took local roads that were just as congested with traffic as the highways from the airport. Jeepneys littered the streets while tricycles and compacts weaved treacherously between cars. Along the side of the road, vendors in stained T-shirts pushed steaming metal carts filled with *lugaw* (rice soup) and *balut* (boiled duck eggs). The air in the city smelled like burning trees and the exhaust of diesel fuel. A series of tiny houses built out of sheet metal and corrugated cardboard stood in the middle of twisting highways.

A tall black iron gate and a cinder block wall surrounded Tita Leny's Spanish-style ranch. When she greeted us, her words came out long and exaggerated. "Hooow aaare you? Weeelcome to Maaanila!" She reached for me with her free hand; the other held a lit Marlboro. Her skin was as cool as if she'd just emerged from a refrigerator as she pressed her cheeks against mine in Filipino custom. Tita Leny was the eldest of seven children and had just celebrated her seventieth birthday a week before our arrival. She visited the States often enough to witness a good portion of our lives in America and was the only one on my father's side of the family who I'd come out to. I assumed that Tita Leny was the reason why all my other relatives, including Tito Tony, had seemed to be in the know about my sexuality. She met my ex-girlfriend six years ago in New York and had hardly batted an eye. The two of them shared cigarettes on the front porch of my parents' house in New York. When I was seven, and she and my mother started making comments about the similarities between Kate Jackson—the tomboy of Charlie's Angels fame—and me; I knew they sensed that I was different. "Come on, Jinky, you'd look so cute with longer hair," my mom would cajole, "look at Sabrina. She has long hair *and* she's the smartest one." I knew I didn't want to look like Jaclyn Smith, so I quietly withstood my family's comments.

Tita Leny led Patty and me into an air-conditioned bedroom. "Make yourselves comfortable," Tita Leny said before walking out to rejoin my father and Tito Tony in the living room. Patty and I stood at the door, staring at the two twin beds. Everything in the room—the bedspread, the walls, and the carpet—was blue. A slight smell of mothballs hovered in the cool air.

"Why did she give us a room with two twin beds?" Patty whispered to me as I closed the door behind us.

"Maybe that's all she has," I said as I sat down, sinking into the mattress. Patty gave me a doubtful look.

For the first time since we'd arrived in the Philippines, I looked closely at Patty. Even though she'd been beside me this entire time, it felt as though I hadn't seen her all day. I moved toward the edge of the bed and sat on the mattress. As Patty stood in front of me I pulled her body into my arms, pressing my cheek against the spot where the skin of her navel poked out between her jeans and T-shirt.

"I love you." I said it to bring her closer to me; the warmth of her flesh touching my face was not enough. She placed the palms of her hands on my back and we sat silently for a few minutes, allowing our bodies to land into the deep cushion of the tiny twin bed, into the deep blue of the thick carpet, allowing the whole of our American lives to settle into the smell and softness of Filipino soil. We laid side by side, enveloped in each other's presence, and fell asleep until someone knocked to say that dinner was ready.

When we woke up, the table was set: a roast duck sat in the middle of the table. *Alimango,* a crab dish, *crispy pata,* a pork dish, and a tall bowl of white rice steamed beside it. By the looks of it we were about to have a feast. Patty eyed the *crispy pata.*

"Wow, Tita, it smells delicious," Patty remarked to Tita Leny, who was sitting at the head of the twelve-person dining table.

"I'm sure you two are hungry. Come on, sit down, and eat!"

We found our places in the middle of the table. The empty chairs around us made me feel small and childlike.

Joining us were my father, Tito Tony, and his three teenage kids, Jono, Missy, and Diego, who he'd gone to pick up from school while Patty and I were sleeping. As we sat down to eat, we talked about my mother, who was in Mindanao visiting her family. My relatives asked about my sister, who would be arriving in a few days, about her boyfriend and whether or not they planned to marry. Lolo Ermis, my late grandmother's youngest brother, sat down to join us. I could hardly believe my eyes as I calculated his age in my head, placing him close to ninety.

"Hello Jinky," Lolo Ermis said. "Do you remember me?"

"Of course I do. How could anyone ever forget you?"

Although no one ever talked about it, we all knew that Lolo Ermis was gay. Whenever Tita Leny came to the States, she brought us handmade embroidered pillowcases and duvet covers that he made for my mother. As a child, I had little appreciation for them, but that changed as I began to understand who Lolo Ermis was. The last time I had seen him I was still very much in denial about my sexuality. This time I was fully aware of him. I knew of no one else in my extended family who was gay. I wondered if he knew about me.

"It's good you two could come here together," Lolo Ermis said. "How were you able to plan this trip together?"

"Well," Patty interjected, "I'm actually here for a conference. My work paid for my plane ticket."

"Really?" Lolo Ermis asked. "What conference?" Everyone at the table looked at Patty with interest.

"Oh," Patty paused and looked at me, as if searching for a cue. I shrugged my shoulders, defaulting to her best judgment, trusting she'd know the right thing to say.

"It's called ILGA, the International Lesbian and Gay Association."

The words careened and crashed into my head, reverberating like bad feedback on a faulty karaoke mic. . . *la-la-la-lezzzbian-an-an, gaaaaay.*

The table fell completely silent. I gulped hard and stared at my plate, concentrating very hard on slicing an already-tiny piece of duck meat. A glass clinked. I heard someone swallow. All these years of being out and suddenly I felt like I was back where I started. Patty was much braver than me, but then I thought: *Of course she is; this isn't her family.* From the corner of my eye, I saw that she was still engaged in conversation, talking more about the conference and her work as an activist. Everyone else looked down into their plates, as if some intricate riddle were in need of immediate resolution.

Finally Lolo Ermis spoke up. "Where do you work, Patty?" he asked.

I looked up, realizing it was time for me to intervene, but before I could open my mouth, Patty spoke.

"Oh, I work for a foundation in New York City," Patty replied. I sighed, relieved that she'd chosen not to name it.

"It's called the Astraea Lesbian Foundation for Justice."

My body stiffened like a spring diving board. I felt ashamed and afraid, like I was twenty again, in the closet, and someone had yanked open the door. My attention quickly turned to my father, whose lips were pursed in a thin tight line. I felt guilty. I thought about how comfortable he looked a few moments ago, and I wondered if I'd humiliated him in front of his family. I wanted to apologize. I tried to think fast, to come up with something to change the subject, and make eye contact again.

"Patty's going to stay at the Bayview hotel." I said.

"Oh, that's a nice hotel!" Lolo Ermis piped in. His eyes widened with enthusiasm. "Its right next to Manila Bay and Intramuros. Jinky, you two should go sightseeing there. It's very romantic."

"Thanks, Lolo." Patty said. She turned to me, her face all aglow, and squeezed my hand. At first I didn't acknowledge it and wanted her to get a clue about the tiny roller-coaster that just transpired beside her. But then it hit me. Lolo Ermis said "romantic."

Here was a moment of recognition, an invitation to come in. In one word Lolo Ermis granted me the permission to come home, to sit with my father at the table and not feel ashamed. Growing up, I had always looked to my parents for acknowledgment, for acceptance, for some sort of sign that could place me in this world. And now, more than a decade since I came out to my father, I felt like hiding in the shadows, not wanting my relatives to reject me because I am a lesbian. I thought about the porter at the airport, how Patty and I were always sisters to those who couldn't see us for who we are, and how just a few minutes ago I wanted to hide the moment Patty made claim to her lesbian identity. Being silent about it rendered me invisible. While the thought of cloaking my identity didn't feel comfortable, I longed to retreat into the safety of my private world, far apart from judgment. But now, with Lolo Ermis's recognition, I could hide no longer. It was safe to come out. Lolo Ermis was part of my family. The shame I felt a moment ago disintegrated, replaced by a connection to my homeland, my culture, and my relatives.

Visiting the Philippines wasn't only about family. It was about coming home to myself, to claiming an identity that I no longer wanted to hide. As I watched my family converse and gossip about other things, I squeezed Patty's hand under the table. I faced her and said, "I don't even think we look like sisters." Lolo Ermis, sitting nearby and listening, replied, "I don't think you do either."

Embrace of the Motherland

CANYON SAM

From the first moment I arrived in Tibet, I could sense something different in the country. Along the spacious main street, only a few leisurely bicyclists rode, unlike the large spectacle of them commonplace in other cities in China. Snow-capped mountains ringed the valley and towered behind soft-sloped brown moraine hills. The bright-white quality of the light, the rich translucent blue of the massive sky, the crisp air so clean it seemed to singe my lungs, struck me. I liked the relaxed atmosphere, the sense of space, and the friendly, open people.

In my room in a backpacker's hotel, I had sworn to myself that I would hibernate, adjust to Lhasa's twelve-thousand-foot elevation, and digest the last few weeks. I was despondent about what I was finding on my solo trip through China. The last four weeks touring southern and southwest China had opened my eyes.

I hadn't liked any place in China well enough to stay longer than a few days. The day before—May 3, 1986—the start of my fifth week in China, I had flown to Lhasa, Tibet, from Chengdu, across ice-blue, snow-draped peaks in a small plane over the rugged Himalayas, the highest mountains in the world, into what seemed like one of the most inaccessible corners of the earth. Soon I was hibernating in my cement hotel room in Tibet, ranting and raving in my journal about the destruction of Chinese culture and the fresh perspective it gave me on Chinese American culture and on being Chinese.

I noticed many things in China that had disturbed me. I saw no caring government in the gaggles of blind people holding each other's shirttails, singing ditties, and shuffling up the streets, begging. I observed no quality healthcare in the sick people I saw in public, like the miserable fellow with a purple ulcer the size of an ice pack growing off the side of his face. In one city in China, I saw flatbed trucks towing men—heads bowed, wrists tied—through town in a honking, flashing, siren-screaming display of government power. Coal-burning smokestacks smack in the middle of crowded cities fouled the air so much that once I couldn't see a lamp standing on the other side of the boulevard. Many people in China did not at all seem welcoming to me, contrary to what I expected from the ardent invitations I'd read to "Overseas Chinese" to "return home to the embrace of the motherland." Instead of a model socialist society, I found Orwell mixed with Dickens in the largest nation on earth.

A few years ago, China had opened up to the outside world for the first time in thirty years. The "Bamboo Curtain" had been drawn over the People's Republic of China my entire life—news blackouts, trade embargoes, severed diplomacy. We had, however, in radical communities in the '70s in San Francisco, studied Mao, practiced criticism/self-criticism, and read glossy magazines from China with glowing progress reports about the success of the new communist system. In the mid-'70s in college, I had adorned my walls with posters from the People's Republic—ruddy-cheeked, smiling workers tilling soil or building tractors in clean modern factories. "Women hold up half the sky," the posters proclaimed. There were images of women on horseback, women driving backhoes, women listening into stethoscopes. My favorite poster showed a woman atop a telephone pole, sheets of rain pelting her determined face as she worked through a fierce storm. I'd never before had a poster with a positive image of an Asian female until I got this one.

Tibet had been cut off for centuries from the outside world in self-imposed isolation, and then for the last forty years by the Chinese government, which had invaded in 1959. But the autumn before my trip, Lhasa suddenly appeared on the list of open cities that could be visited by people holding a Chinese tourist visa. Winter made access over the Himalayas impossible. Now with spring thaw, a small number of independent Western travelers trickled in. I had been the sole foreigner yesterday on the plane of silver-haired Chinese bureaucrats.

In my hotel room in Tibet, I was scribbling furiously in my journal when my bladder called, and on the way back from the bathroom with its resplendent view of the Potala Palace, I noticed an attractive young Asian woman staring at me from the room next to mine. As I peeked through the open door, her megawatt smile beamed like a laser through the knot of Europeans in the room. She looked at me as if we were the dearests of friends. I went inside her room, and she introduced herself as Dekyi, reminding me that she had helped me with my mail the day before. Embarrassed, I realized that Dekyi was the English-speaking front desk clerk in the high-rise hotel on the Chinese end of town where I'd had my mail sent. She'd been in a uniform yesterday; I didn't recognize her in slim-fit blue jeans, a navy parka, and dazzling-white tennis shoes.

We had a long conversation. Freckle-faced with large, lively brown eyes, Dekyi told me that she was born and raised in Lhasa and learned English in India at a Tibetan school that she attended for a year. She told me that when she returned from India a few months earlier, her multilingual skills caught the attention of the Chinese government, which had launched a new tourism campaign in Lhasa. They assigned her to work at the hotel where we'd met, the city's first and only four-star hotel. She lived nearby with her family. Her father was an artist of traditional Tibetan art. The more we talked, the more I was drawn into her energy, an irresistible warmth and joyfulness, which was almost magnetic. When I expressed an interest in seeing her dad's work, we chatted a few minutes more and then she invited me over to her house for tea. I was startled; I had not been asked to a local person's house in all the weeks I'd been traveling in my "motherland." My eyes bugged out in disbelief. She nodded and grinned.

"Yeaaas!" she teased, squeezing the vowel sounds, her eyes dancing with excitement. "Come on!"

I had to reconsider my stout resolution to hibernate. It wasn't a hard choice: Beautiful new friend and Tibetan art? Or solitary angst in my cement cell. Beauty, angst? Friend, cell?

"Let's go!" I piped.

I followed Dekyi home through a narrow space between two shops. We took several quick turns through closely packed buildings until we suddenly arrived at a pair of gigantic medieval wood doors. We crossed over their high threshold, six inches deep, emerging into a sunlit courtyard. I saw a two-story Tibetan building complex, centuries old, with an exterior walkway all along the second floor. Dekyi said the place was former monastery housing, now family residences for her father's work unit.

We climbed a steep, ancient wood staircase, the banister silky smooth from the oil of hands through countless years. Upstairs, at the corner of the balcony, Dekyi pushed open a door. We stepped over another threshold. The door shut behind us, and we were suddenly in what felt like a walk-in cooler.

Ahead, Dekyi pushed aside a heavy cloth door hanging, stepped over another threshold, and we entered a sitting room with low ceilings.

"Please sit," Dekyi said, as she pointed to a daybed, and then left the room.

Dekyi reentered the room with another woman dressed in a traditional long black dress. Each carried an oversize red thermos.

"You like Tibetan tea or milk tea?" Dekyi asked.

I'd read that Tibetan tea was made from rancid yak butter and rock salt churned with black tea; nomads drank up to sixty cups a day in the winter; the fat kept them warm.

"Oh, gee . . . I don't know. I guess I'll try Tibetan tea," I said, eager to try something new.

I sat on a daybed, the middle of three arranged around a gleaming, low, dark table. A plate of carefully arranged butter cookies sat in a pool of light on the table under a hanging lightbulb; they reminded me of my mother's thumbprint jelly cookies. The woman, in her thirties perhaps, poured a frothy, steaming yellowish-brown brew into a cup. As she did this, she bowed. I noticed pink and pale blue tassels had been woven into long thick black braids coiled atop her head. She picked up the saucer and offered it to me with both hands in an extraordinarily careful, gracious manner. I held the warm saucer in my hands.

"Please drink the tea she poured," Dekyi urged.

"A biscuit?" the woman asked, lifting the plate of cookies. I took one of the scallop-edged cookies and took a bite. It was dry and tasteless, not rich and buttery, like my mother's. Dekyi came around the table and sat beside me. The woman knelt and sat quietly, her gaze lowered.

"My father has painted all. . . . " Dekyi said, sweeping her hand at the polished black lacquer table before us decorated in gold leaf paint and then over to a shoulder-high cabinet a few feet away; six panels each displayed a different hand-painted floral bouquet.

"He is teaching himself. From fourteen years old. Schools not teaching." A long row of bronze water bowls sat in front of a Buddha draped in a gauzy white scarf on top of the cabinet. A peacock feather brushed the low ceiling.

"Maybe try milk tea; it is sweet," Dekyi said, noting that I wasn't touching the Tibetan tea after my first sip.

She said something and the woman picked up the other thermos and filled another cup with a steaming brown beverage. She placed it before me with two hands in the same, almost ritual-like manner. The hot sweet tea, the color of coffee with cream, melted down my throat.

"Tibetan people like Tibetan tea. Foreigners like milk tea," Dekyi giggled. The woman beamed now, displaying an impish, laughter-lined face.

"Dekyi, who is this woman?" I asked. She seemed too young to be her mother. Was she a family friend . . . or the cook? I wondered.

"This is my mother," Dekyi said.

"Oh!" I exclaimed.

Her mom acknowledged me with a shy nod and a broad, endearing smile.

"Does she speak Chinese?" I asked.

"No, only Tibetan."

"Tashi delek!" I said, addressing her with the traditional Tibetan greeting. I mimed my thanks.

"What's her name?"

"Amala."

"Is that what I should call her?"

"Yes," Dekyi nodded.

Amala had an ineffable quality about her, something so present, so serenely lovely. It shone through even though I couldn't speak to her. According to Dekyi, Amala did tailoring; she could sew anything. *Chubas,* blouses, suits. The *chuba* was the traditional dress—ankle-length for women and thigh-length and long-sleeved for men. Later I learned that the word *"amala"* means mother in Tibetan. Although it was not her name, Dekyi insisted that I should call her mom "mother" too.

"Canyon Sam, do you speak Chinese?" Dekyi asked.

"My family speaks Cantonese, but I can only speak a bit. And I studied Mandarin before I came but I know only enough to travel." I told her my family had been in California for more than a hundred years. I drew a map of the United States and pointed to San Francisco.

"America is very nice, yes? Very nice things there, yes? Many cah-sits?"

"Many what?"

"Cah-sits."

I drew a blank.

"Like Michael Jackson . . . "

"Oh, cassettes! Music tapes!"

Dekyi nodded and told me how she'd discovered music tapes in India, but nothing was available here. "Now America, on the hand . . . " She gushed at length about America—in her vision, a veritable bonanza of pop music, hip fashion, and fun discotheques. You'd think everyone in America spent their time partying and nightclubbing.

"Would you like to go to America?" I asked her.

"Yes, very much," she swooned.

Gold Mountain, I thought. It was no different from what my forebearers had believed when they dreamed of coming to America: Gold dust glittered in the streets and dollar bills grew on trees.

My maternal great-grandfather first sailed to America from Guangdong, China, in the mid- to late 1800s. His three sons—the eldest being my grandfather, who was born in San Francisco in 1886—ran a restaurant and raised their families together in one big clapboard house on a tree-lined street—fifteen kids, six adults, one bathroom. The sons of these sons were all doctors; the generation after—the one I belonged to—had a predominance of engineers.

Then, there was me.

After my second year of college at the University of California at Berkeley, I dropped out and began doing nontraditional skilled trades to support myself as a writer and an activist. I published pieces reflecting the experiences of Asian American women, a group largely invisible in the mainstream women's movement and the budding gay rights movement at the time. I lived in the Castro District in the mid-'70s and watched the neighborhood transform store by store, week by week, into a gay mecca. By the mid-'80s though, I'd withdrawn from these movements—having been scorched in too many nasty political battles. I kept to myself, worked a civil service job, and did team sports.

One soggy, dark New Year's night I was depressed and miserable. After two years, the nine-to-five routine felt like a grind. *There must be more to life than this,* I thought. I was still in my twenties but I felt like the living dead. I glanced through an old journal and seized on something in a list of life goals I'd penned in my youth: to live and work in China for a year. My family roots were in southern China, Guangzhou, and my beloved maternal grandparents had been the bedrock of our extended family. I'd never been to Asia before. *I'll travel a few months, then settle down somewhere,* I thought, *then work and learn the language.*

I hadn't felt purpose or passion in life for a long time, and the trip promised to restore it. I poured myself into preparations the next year and a half: Rounds of letters to schools and potential employers in China. Haggling with my boss for a leave of absence then taking the leap to quit. Reading history. Researching independent travel. Taking language classes. Undergoing dental work. Buying gear. Separating from friends and family.

My coworkers, immigrants from all over the world, thought I was deranged. According to them, people angle for a way to leave poor Communist countries so they can come to America, get a civil service job, and go to heaven. I was doing the reverse. Was I nuts?

We were still in the sitting room drinking tea as Amala plucked the cork out of the thermos.

"No, please," I begged, covering my cup. She had already topped off my teacup several times. We were in a bit of a cultural conundrum. I kept trying to finish my tea, she kept filling, which kept me drinking, which kept her filling. Tibetans, I learned later, thought it polite to keep a guest's cup full at all times, up to the very brim. If they didn't top off, it meant they didn't prefer you stay.

"La, la, la," she said, egging me to move my hand away as she held the spout of the thermos poised an inch above. I looked at Dekyi for help. She just laughed. Amala mock-frowned.

I shook my head no. Firm, but polite.

Amala nodded even more insistently. We were in a standoff. She grunted encouragingly, nodding yes. I grunted in protest, shaking no. She had such a sense of lightness and fun about her.

I gave up and moved my hand. We all burst out laughing.

By the end of tea, Dekyi and Amala invited me to stay with them, live with the family, right in that very room where we were drinking tea. After clearing the bolster cushions, the daybeds we sat on converted to three single beds at night. One for Dekyi, one for her youngest sister, and one for me. I could scarcely believe my luck.

The next day, I spent the night. In the middle of the night I was awakened by a strange sound, like the sound of an engine humming, but not localized. It never got closer or louder, but neither did it stop. Dekyi and her sister slept through it, so I thought it must not be worrisome. Dekyi later told me that it was the monks praying at the Jokhang Temple. The Jokhang was the holiest temple in all of Tibet. Since the old part of Lhasa had high-walled, circular streets, I didn't realize the Jokhang was so close. Dekyi said the monks started before dawn and prayed for several hours.

In the hushed darkness the following night, I felt secure in the snug, lair-like home. I liked the simplicity of it and the care that its warmth and order revealed. I liked the lush blue carpets we slept on and the sociability and gentility of the family. I felt a sense of impenetrable safety from the three-foot thick mud and straw walls—like being in the womb of the earth. The only light was a red prayer lamp in the corner, on top of the altar, its shade cut with the Sanskrit letter "Om." Glowing from the candle flame within, it spun in circles whispering *Ooom shush shush* with each revolution.

In the middle of the night the deep, sonorous drones woke me again. They reverberated in the darkness, like moans from the earth. I felt a deep, extraordinary peace. Bone deep. Soul deep. I felt at home like I'd never felt anywhere. It had been five weeks since I left the States. Now in this remote land, in this room, with these people, I finally felt I had landed.

I stayed in Central Tibet for seven weeks. I trekked into the outlying countryside and to Everest base camp, to monasteries and caves and rivers, always coming back to Dekyi's house in between. I fell in love with the land, the light, the cloud-canopied sky. I was warmly taken in by the people and was fascinated with their deep palpable faith—though I knew nothing about their Buddhist beliefs.

One night for instance, at the family house, Amala sat at the table polishing dozens of small brass bowls. She left them in stacks on the table overnight. I thought they'd been taken out for a special occasion and tomorrow she'd put them away somewhere, like you take out fine china for a special event. But the next morning she simply placed them back on the altar, from where she had cleared them, lining them neatly in a row along the front edge. Then, tipping a mammoth-size teakettle, Amala filled each one with water up to the brim with the same mindfulness and devotion that had left a deep impression on me when we first met. They were a kind of offering, I realized.

I watched people perform a kind of full-body prayer at the Jokhang Temple. In front of one side of the building, nearly two dozen people performed a sequence of movements—from standing to a full belly-down extension, arms extended, hands in prayer—over and over, up and down, for hours. The slate beneath their feet polished smooth from what I imagined had been centuries of practicing this ritual.

I developed a loving and affectionate relationship with Amala, who was full of pranks and playfulness. However cordial and straight-faced the

Tibetans were in public, in private they loved making light of the woes and calamities of the day, and sharing them with the family at night to howls and shrieks of laughter. A group of Amala's women friends would stop by some afternoons, and I loved to sit among them, hearing the music of their lilting, laughing voices.

Later that summer, Amala suffered a mild heart attack. But a mere few days later, still weak, she insisted on walking the Lingkor, the holy walk around the Potala Palace, to the Jokhang, and to other holy places in Lhasa, setting off slowly with Dekyi and her sister to each side. That day, she declared, was the Buddha's birthday.

In Han China, a few weeks after I had left Tibet, I was floating up the Yangtze River, in the heart of China, on a passenger boat. I'd reluctantly left Tibet to resume my traveling in China. *I am Chinese, I should like China,* I told myself. I had come a great distance and gone to great trouble to be here. I had gotten the last bunk available in a twelve-passenger cabin—the upper bunk by the door. The first morning I discovered why.

A speaker mounted in the hall, one foot from my head, screamed garrulous government directives and martial music at eardrum-splitting volumes at 6:00 AM. This was the same broadcast that railed at people everywhere in China; speakers hung from buildings, telephone poles, in cities, in the countryside—they were even wired into train compartments. The shrill military voice screamed for a solid twenty minutes; plugging my ears or covering my head with a pillow couldn't block it out. We were all forced to rise.

From the traveler's co-op in Lhasa, I had borrowed a book titled *In Exile from the Land of Snows,* by John Avedon, an award-winning volume about the modern political history of Tibet since the Chinese takeover in the '50s. For the first time I learned of the brutal destruction of the culture and people. Thousands of monasteries had been cannonballed to ruins. Millions of Tibetans were killed—by hanging, vivisection, execution, torture, starvation, and more hideous and unimaginable means. The religious art and literature was looted or burned. The Dalai Lama fled on horseback over the Himalayas to India. Over the next twenty-five years, the Chinese attempted to brainwash these devout people, to break them and strike Buddhism out of their hearts, to replace it with Maoism.

At 6:00 AM every morning and several times throughout the day, the public-address system blasted the state harangue, screaming directives and propaganda. I couldn't understand the content, but the tone of belligerence, aggression, and sheer volume made the objective unmistakable: to subjugate, intimidate, and control.

I was fascinated yet saddened by Avedon's book. I recalled the many times in Tibet when I had seen evidence of the Chinese subjugation of the Tibetans and their culture. When I'd accompanied Amala to the hospital that summer for an EKG test after her heart attack, I saw how the Chinese staff had treated her. They looked down on her, ignored her, made her wait an hour while they filed their nails, spoke to her in an imperious tone when I insisted she be helped. It slowly dawned on me that her dress, hairstyle, and language pegged her as Tibetan, and that this made her a second-class citizen in their eyes. She, who treated people with such care and consideration, was not even given basic courtesy and respect in her own country.

Every morning, rising with my nerves rattled and temper boiling, I cursed the public-address system for assaulting the delicate passage between my dreaming and waking. I went out and studied the speaker in the hall. The power source, a small gray cable, lay exposed. Low voltage, I thought. No danger of shock. But I didn't act.

Avedon's dog-eared text offered vivid profiles of about a half a dozen individuals, each utterly fascinating, each with a uniquely different background:

a psychic channeler or oracle, a resistance fighter, an imprisoned monk, a traditional medical doctor. As much as I was totally absorbed, at the end of the 380-page text I realized that none of these engrossing portraits was of a woman. It was as if women didn't exist. Or they didn't matter. Yet my richest experiences of Tibet had often been with women. What were women's lives like during this tumultuous period? Why weren't they included?

The withering heat and humidity during the day drained me to the point that all I could do was try not to move. One afternoon after reading in my bunk for hours, after the sun set and the temperature finally cooled, I got down from my bunk. It took me a moment to gain a sense of balance in the moving ship after lying prone so long. Suddenly I felt something come over me, an inner heat rising through my body, flushing through my entire being like a wave. Something resounded as clearly as the tone of a bell: This is not right. I must not let this situation rest. It was like hot lava when it finally reached the earth's surface—unstoppable—a force larger than my life, my own experience, or my personal will. I felt fierce resolve and a powerful determination, like a fever, to act to help Tibet.

The next day while trimming my nails, I suddenly saw my nail clippers in a new light: the width of the opening was large enough, the cutting surface sharp enough. Over the next two days I monitored the foot traffic in the hall. People loitered about everywhere, day and night. Always, there were people in China—everywhere. Million upon millions. One could not escape them.

At ten minutes before midnight one night, the ship fell quiet. My cabin mates dozed in bed. The other cabins along our corridor were silent. I made my move. I slipped out the door. The hall was clear in both directions. I took my nail clippers from my pocket, reached behind the speaker, and squeezed.

This essay is adapted from the author's memoir-in-progress titled Embrace of the Motherland: A Chinese American Journey in Search of the Wisdom and History of Tibetan Women.

Sowing for Lineage

CLAUDIA VIRGINIA NARVÁEZ-MEZA

For as long as I can remember, my name, *Claudia Virginia Narváez-Meza,* like the dark copper of young braids, held its history in the struggle of fabled women. I have always believed that although men in my family held their place of status among us, no other set of hands sprang harmonies of cilantro and clove in the noonday sun like those of the women in my family. The rough palms of soft-fleshed women bent over the potbelly hearth of their families infuse this remembrance. My mother and her peoples' customs nourished and sustained me: their food, their laughter, their stories that healed me, their songs that hummed over the fevered heads of their children.

I listened before my chin could reach my mother's table; I imagined my mother and grandmother's lives in Nicaragua before I created my own survival in Brooklyn projects with children who raced bullets and knife wounds instead of kites. I have been raised to know my female elders by honoring the resilience that made their lives. Somewhere between the sadness of lost husbands and dead children caused by malnutrition, family violence, and war, I grew to understand how my mother's and grandmother's experiences helped shape my survival in the United States.

Since I was six, my parents, siblings, and I have visited Nicaragua, a country my mother longed for both spiritually and culturally. An unseen thread constantly pulled her to its mysterious shores, where we would land, sleepy and disoriented by the surge of family running to greet us at the airport gates.

During these trips, I remember being handed strange but calming sweet teas made out of ground corn, cacao, and powdered milk. For as long as I can remember—surrounded by the adobe walls, earthen floors, and clay griddles that fed and sheltered me—my love for the women in my family grew at the first drop of their stories. Their narratives were often told by the light of votives, which illuminated the tender face of the mother of all mothers—the Virgin Mary—who instilled in me quiet waters.

Living to tell the truth was what compelled them to speak, and it has persuaded me to write these women into existence. They survived the drunken hands of brutes, the despair of poverty, the violence of a government that did not protect them, the silence that did not unite them. I grew to believe that my matrilineal strengths were forged before my name was chosen by my grandmother, who was there at my beginning, on the rosy hip of Nicaragua.

My brother and I were born in Managua, Nicaragua, before the 1972 earthquake that leveled most of the country, killing more than twenty-thousand people. Under the reign of Somoza—a wealthy dictator schooled at West Point and a fierce ally to the Americans—Nicaragua's political climate had gone from neoliberalist to conservative. Poverty and corruption ran like torrents in the midst of a bipartisan economy that favored Managua's elite.

The Somoza regime had been in power for four decades. After Anastasio Somoza García's assassination in 1956, his son Luís succeeded him but died eleven years later, leaving his youngest and most ruthless brother, Anastasio Somoza Debayle, in power until the Sandinistas marched victorious into Managua during the Revolution of 1979. The armed revolt of the Sandinista National Liberation Front (FSLN), named after the nation's first revolutionary guerrilla, Augusto César Sandino, began in 1961.

My parents described a climate of absolute terror under the reign of the National Guard before the dictatorship was overthrown by the Sandinistas. There were disappearances; people were tortured and thrown live into the mouths of active volcanoes or in shark-infested waters; boys as young as eight were drafted into the military. In 1983, the cruelty of the Somoza reign finally ended as Anastasio Somoza Debayle was tracked down in Paraguay and blown up when his limousine pulled in to a driveway.

As the dictatorship was dismantled, the country was beginning to heal through various initiatives—literacy campaigns, farm cooperatives, and land distribution—and many organizations were working to raise awareness of violence against women and children. But my grandmother and her family did not benefit under this new government. People, especially the poor, were still traumatized by the dictatorship. Many feared that the Somoza bloodline could reclaim the country and wreak havoc for Sandinista sympathizers. Somoza had left behind enough of his seed to warrant a small army. Much of this came to me as I listened to adult conversations in the hushed quarters of my mother's kitchen or at gatherings with other Nicaraguan families. Despite the hopeful ideals presented by this new government, my grandmother refused to respect a leadership that came into power through the spilling of Nicaraguan blood.

In the fall of 1972, almost two years after my father had left for New York on a student visa, I was thirteen months old when my mother sold everything she owned in Nicaragua to pay for plane tickets to the United States. Although she abhorred the very notion of living in America, she felt she had no choice if she planned to stay married and raise us well, far away from the threat of the Somoza regime in Nicaragua.

Living in the States meant reaching for anything that resembled my mother's beautiful but tragic country. I listened carefully as she would read to me from her collection of Nicaraguan newspapers and books. I loved the impassioned folk songs and revolutionary epitaphs of fallen poets of war. Without knowing it then, the connection to my birthplace soon began in the first stirrings of pride and belonging to a people who triumphed over their oppressors. Like many mothers in Brooklyn projects who struggled with poor wages and the absence of fathers, the women of Nicaragua were at the helm of their children's survival.

At the time of my little sister's birth in 1973, both of my parents were working in factories: My father was a forklift operator, while my mother manned the pressers and the needles. We lived near the factories in Williamsburg, Brooklyn, sharing a tiny apartment in a dilapidated tenement with the typical nightmare conditions of urban squalor.

I remember sitting by my mother in our Bushwick apartment as she pushed her daily quota of denim under the needle of her Singer. With its motor humming, my mother would let me push the cool pedal at my knee and jump-start the workhorse. I was captivated at how swiftly it plunged its tiny beak down between her fingers like a seagull to its prey. I always felt as if I were born between two banners: my mother's childhood in Nicaragua and my father's allegiance to the United States, a new country void of love or tolerance for our kind. It is difficult to pen here where his gypsy footfalls had begun to undo the delicate threading of my mother's many passages: from daughter to mother, from a celebrated seamstress and dressmaker to factory worker, from an indentured project dweller to a battered mother of three with no nation to claim.

My father concentrated his energies between the time clock and the pool hall, pacing the apartment with a slow-climbing desperation that seemed to swallow us whole. Shortly after a rat had crawled into my little sister's crib and had bitten her hand, we were approved for a three-bedroom apartment in the new housing projects of North Brooklyn. But the situation at home didn't improve. My parents were making around $3 dollars an hour and trying to raise my siblings and me with help of other immigrant families in the housing projects.

I never understood what came first, the casual unmasking of my father in this country two years before we joined him or his alcohol-induced distance after we arrived. I learned that my father suffered many losses as a boy in Nicaragua, such as a stable home and education, but what lacerated him most was being abandoned by his birth mother, unclaimed by his birth father, and left in the care of two aunts.

My memory encases my father, the stoic, yellow-eyed giant clad in a midnight blue uniform, his bastard name sewn on the right pocket of his chest. I remember the worm's eye view, trying to stay tip-toed so I could see how much whiskey he had consumed. My chin perched against the dining table covered with crippled beer cans, studying him while Elvis's love songs spun in the undulating dark—a darkness I recall for its hostile, crouching violence. As a child, the darkness metamorphosed into a monster capable of destroying what I loved. It was a shape-shifter ready to spring at the throat of a child who is trying to scream for help, a soundless chasm gaping wide open to reveal its velvet wound.

Very early on, I became aware that my father had the power to take my mother away from me through violence, so the darkness manifested a terror so surreal, not even a child's prayer could disperse it. I poured into that abysmal wound all of my anguish and rage for every blow he ever dealt to my mother's head, her arms that held the three of us close and safe, her bruised legs that walked me to school every morning, her shattered jawbone that sang my name when bullies roamed, the purple vein clotting her morning eyes—eyes that loved and searched our faces for proof of his violence from the night before. And I remember the silver-plated tooth she almost left embedded in his forearm when he locked her breath with his own calloused hands while the three of us screamed from under our beds.

It was the landscape of my mother's body, voice, and hands that provided a constant presence in the spaces that surrounded us and kept our bodies *safe*. Pulling us tight against her softness, she nursed us into fragile beauty. We painted, drew, wrote, and sang past the sadness of witnessing destruction at the hands of our father, who was supposed to protect us. We were so far from Nicaragua, with very little to reap from an urban pavement.

Prejudice can ripple past a person's coping ability and leave its quiet scar. I remember our lives in the States: embarrassing cheese lines, bitter-tongued case workers, scowling teachers, racial slurs in the spit of dark-skinned children, the Jewish factory owner who fired my mother for being sick, the bus operators who barked at us for sitting, standing, looking, asking. Racism becomes a covert venom that seeps into one's skin and stays there for a long time; it's hard to reckon with and even harder to talk about. I can still remember those cold Brooklyn mornings: my mother hurrying me into my thin coat, late for school, pigtails in the wind as I rushed into the church schoolyard, calico-spun bodies of brown children standing silently in straight lines. Under the gaze of nuns folded like autumn crows, I trembled in my chafed Buster Browns.

I knew I would never belong.

In the solace of my pain, I discovered reverence for the Virgin Mary. Everything she came to embody for me conflicted with the nuns' angry God. God never did answer my prayers, especially at a time when my mother's life was being peddled nightly by a drunken maniac. I soon inherited my mother's creed, La Virgen, with her woeful eyes, upturned palms, and the small ivory face watching over me, as vigilant as an August moon. I prayed to her with small white candles at her feet. Beads held between forefinger and thumb helped me to bridge this country to the imagined homeland, a place where mothers survived and their daughters blossomed. Perhaps the saints and goddesses could not keep the darkness from entering our home and our lives, but watching my mother evolve into self-awareness and a deep love for her children compelled me to continue looking for La Virgen to guide and protect me. If we rose the next morning and found fragments of the violence, the point is that *we rose.*

My maternal grandmother, Adelaida Meza, was also a survivor. She was the youngest of three born to a single mother who sold tortillas for a living in the era of a new liberalism that was taking place in the major cities of Nicaragua in 1895. Chinandega, León, and Granada—built among the ruins of an indigenous land—were cities built by pirates, British colonists, Miskitu-Rama loggers, Chinese merchants, African slaves, and Spanish conquistadors. Like so many countries before and after Columbus's footprint, Nicaragua—with its Mayan roots deep in volcanic earth and rich mineral beds—had become a mere spike on the treasure map of brutal wayfarers.

My grandmother was an orphan: Her father walked out on her when she was a baby, and she lost her siblings and mother ten years later when they died from malaria and malnutrition. Completely alone, illiterate, poor, and female, my grandmother was eventually taken in by *madrinas* (godmothers). Her child status in a country and society that kept women and girls oppressed and silenced left her prey to random violence, homelessness, and exploitation. My mother remembered the *cuentos* told under the midnight arms of a willow, stories of how her mother survived by lighting white votives for strength, drinking rice water and witchgrass to kill parasitic worms, balming her feet with cactus oil after traveling from pueblo to city in search of work.

In 1935, my grandmother gave birth to my mother, a baby barely born alive, asphyxiating on the umbilical cord that would later be buried under the roots of a Ceiba. It was a tradition my grandmother believed would help ward off the tragedy and circumstance of being born a female in *la tierra de Dios* (the land of God). My mother remembers how the family wandered for some time before they would settle down. As if a perpetual reel is caught in the spool of her memory, she described how her mother would lace palm leaves together and sheath a roof into place.

In our old Brooklyn apartment, my mother—now a seventy-year-old scribe—sits picking beans from an old dented pot. She speaks with tender courage, bringing her family, Poneloya (the beach of her youth), the rattlesnake that haunted her, barefoot orphans selling salted mangoes, and the ruby-throated hummingbird out of the shadows and onto my pages. Through her I could see the literacy campaign workers, glue-sniffing children, young cedar trees after rainfall, bustling streets—before the earthquake, before revolution, before Reagan's contras—come to life. With tempered agility, she climbs the stairs to the attic in her mind and sets loose the crows that flutter and squawk with ancient song. There is much pain in the telling. She squints in the evening light, mincing onion. Her mortar and pestle holds a splayed rainbow. My mind whirls as I watch her hands. How often they balmed my chest open as I wheezed in the dark. My mother's palms are flattening out small balls of dough for our dinner, *"Remember to husk the corn and keep the seeds in your mouth."*

The ritual of surviving what has been beyond our reach and knowing that others, like Nicaragua's poor, are tending similar wounds, have given us the determination to live. From the journeys to my mother's homeland, I learn to weave the testimonies of the women in my family to the women of my birthplace, always feeling their collective strengths plait the hours I've spent learning their history, which I've claimed as my own. By telling their stories, I honor the lineage that hums in my blood, the name I was given when all else felt impossible. I was born to a tribe of women once imagined, but now flesh-real: in sandals, in aprons, their long thick braids coming undone in the purple twilight of my own story.

Voyage, War, and Exile

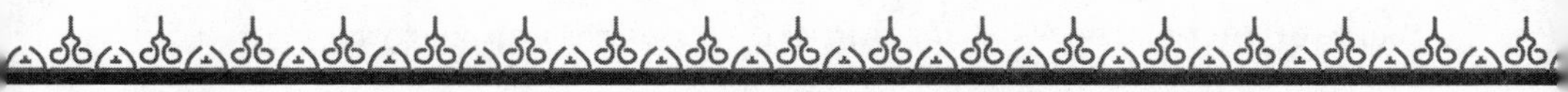

ETEL ADNAN

I come from a part of the world where war has been made and unmade since the beginning of the twentieth century. I am the only child of a family exiled as a consequence of war. My memory, as well as my daily life, is woven with war. My Syrian father was a high-ranking officer of the Ottoman Empire, and my Greek mother was the daughter of a wood-carver from Smyrna. My parents met and married during World War I. In 1922, Smyrna burned in a cataclysmic fire, the war was lost, and the Ottoman Empire was dismantled. They came to Lebanon and settled in Beirut, a garden city with a view of the most beautiful Mediterranean harbor.

They exiled themselves into charm and beauty. Geographically, it was a bearable exile for my father since he was on Arab land and close to Damascus, his birthplace. But he was living another terrible exile: The empire that he knew and served had disappeared. In Beirut he was living on enemy territory, a country under French occupation. Since my childhood, this knowledge has remained inscribed in me: that geographical exile is a frame for a particular type of exile that goes much deeper and renders one helpless.

My mother thought of Smyrna day and night and suffered from its absence. Many times I saw her questioning the Beirut horizon, wondering where Smyrna would have been—behind which cloud and on which side north of the setting sun. Her education had been reduced to hazard and to the meanderings of her life, and she resided in a twilight zone where most people orient themselves according to their desires and sorrows.

After I turned twenty, I left for Paris to study philosophy. I was impatient and yearning to go. My father had died, and I left behind my mother, who lived with a pain whose scope I realized only much later. The amplitude of her sorrow took years to reach me. I was a bird who flew out of her cage, eager to venture farther away, everywhere and nowhere. Going to the café in those years was already a voyage.

After Paris, I went to California. I landed in Berkeley, far, very far, from every point of view, from Beirut, and from everything I knew.

This radical break was not an exile—it was an adventure. After a few years of study, I taught at a small college near San Francisco, giving up my preparations for a PhD. In 1958, I found a roof, a salary, a reason to be, and some kind of new identity. The '60s and the worldwide cultural revolution followed. I became intensely American and intensely an Arab. Most of all, I felt an exhilarating belonging to the world. I was not living in exile but had found a freedom on my own and at my own risks.

Like the Earth, with its formidable plates constantly moving in contradictory directions, I was creating, within my soul, opposite currents equally ominous: I was espousing the Arabs' dramatic dreams of freedom, dignity, and unity, all symbolized then by the president of Egypt, Gamal Abdel Nasser. At the same time, I plunged wholeheartedly into America—its history, people, art, and literature—yet I was aware and practically hypnotized by its frightful capacity for mass destruction and by its incredible conquests of the moon and in space. I was living in the absolute present, merging my own mythical time with America's.

Following the *Apollo* missions and its rockets, I was extraterritorial and tuned in to the universe.

But the foreseeable earthquake did manifest itself—war broke out in 1967, involving Egypt, Syria, and Jordan. America decisively participated in the destruction of Arab dreams and lands. I experienced terror that others around me did not share, and began losing ground, feeling wounded, isolated, and detached although still attached—a conflict that would later make me ill. Not knowing what the future would be, I felt the urge to break away and return to Beirut without looking behind me. I had come full circle. In the summer of 1972, I returned to Beirut literally on a stretcher. I had left as a voyager, and I was coming back an exile.

I had no family left in Beirut. My half sisters and brother on my father's side were living in Damascus. Because of the Smyrna fire, my mother's brothers and sister had evacuated to different places, such as Cyprus, Alexandria, Saloniki, and Genova. But Beirut was home, and I thought that I was returning "for good." I found a tiny apartment with a view, five stories of steep stairs to climb, and no telephone. I could barely walk then. I had to rebuild myself physically and morally while looking for a job. I reconnected with childhood friends.

A new French-language paper hired me as the editor of its cultural daily pages. There was excitement in the air. The personnel, mostly young women and men whose enthusiasm was contagious, had the impression that they were participating in the creation of a better world, one where Arabs would recover their rights and cease to be excluded from decisions that affected them.

I shared the feelings of this new generation while simultaneously expecting the worst. Beirut was a laboratory and a stirring volcano. After Black September of 1970 and after Nasser's death, I wrote a long poem, the "Beirut Hell Express," announcing Beirut's total destruction. Of course, I did not follow my own visionary knowledge of the catastrophes that I had predicted in my own writings, but instead gave in to my most obscure wishes and desires.

Civil war did break out again, in April 1975. It was as if a galaxy of fire and death had been born and had churned with no end in sight, feeding on its own energy till its bitter end.

The Lebanese started to leave. A real exodus: first a trickle, and then a gradual and constant flow. The buildings were disappearing too, and so were the neighborhoods, and the streets. With every wall falling and every man dying, a collective life and memory was obliterated.

I was discovering–and living–exile's profound meaning. What is exile if not the violent and involuntary loss of all the living symbols of one's identity? At this point, instead of me leaving, Beirut was leaving me. This was an exile that was total, absolute: I was in Beirut witnessing that she was never going to remain the core of what she once was. I was seeing (without any exaggeration) the meaning of "Paradise Lost."

Exile is a dispossession with no recourse. It is always accompanied by a feeling of humiliation: it is the "other," somebody or something, who takes possession of what you give up and leave behind. It makes you feel pushed aside, as if you were a displaced material object.

My awareness of exiled peoples' conditions, and that of whole nations, grew as I witnessed the different forms of exile created by the Lebanese civil war. Exiles are not only people displaced from their native lands, but those who live under diverse forms of oppression from foreign occupation and from their own governments.

I had seen, over and over again, with my own eyes and on television, these faces–Palestinian faces. They were forced to abandon their country, were shuffled into camps, or lived as foreigners in their own territory. They were denied the power to run their own affairs. They have been exiled from their own selfhood. (And this is true today of Muslim Bosnians, and Indians of the Americas and the United States, where among other indignities, they are forbidden to study their own languages and cultures in their own schools and practice their own religious rites.) To be exiled in one's homeland and from one's culture is the most desperate form of exile. It is living hell.

From the days when I was a restless child, I have been on the move. I loved to be on the go. Even with chronic back pain and after numerous operations, I moved around from one country to another with little financial means. I chose to travel to Paris, America, Mexico, Greece, and the Arab countries. For a period in my life, I didn't think of exile.

As a resident, then as an American citizen, I did not perceive my life in California as an exile but as an open-ended provisional situation. I spent some of the best years of my life in California, and it is also linked to some of my real personal tragedies.

But then the destruction of Beirut acted on me (and on so many others) as a revelatory factor. After spending the first three or four years of the war in that city (with occasional excursions abroad), I decided to return to California to resettle, so to speak. The break was never complete. But this time I felt obliged to go. Through this, I felt exiled. Beirut's destruction forced me to move and shed a sharp light on my whole life.

I started to look back. I thought about my parents' life, and what their exile meant to them. I became engulfed in the desire to understand them. I started counting their years, realizing things that never previously occurred to me. What year was my father born? The family papers and the old photographs had disappeared because of the war and little was left. I remembered that it was 1880, which meant that he was only thirty-eight years old at the end of World War I. He was a defeated man, his military career a thing of the past, and he never adapted to the jobs he found. My mother was only twenty years old, married already four years, when my father—the man who had been the Commander of Smyrna—became poor, his best years already behind him. A few years later they left Smyrna for good, never to return. The end of the Ottoman Empire was also the end of the best, but shortest, part of their lives.

Once things go wrong, all that follows goes wrong too. For a man like my father, who fought the French and the Allies in World War I, it was impossible to find a decent job in French-occupied Lebanon (or Syria, for that matter). The French gave power to the Maronites. My father was marginalized like so many Arab nationalists living under French or British rule.

One exile calls to the mind another kind of exile, which it intensifies, defines. Thus I find that I am more and more violently angry at colonialism and its consequences because I see it as the root of my family's predicament.

By the time I was born, my parents already understood that their new lives were very limited. I had a happy childhood and was impervious to their difficulties. It would only be much later—when I experienced my own exile—that I'd understand.

At the end of World War I and following the occupation of Syria and Lebanon, the French administration installed an educational system dominated by the French language and French curricula in Christian schools. The teachers were French missionaries at the service of both the Church and colonialism. My generation of the early 1930s received an exclusively French education. We were punished for speaking Arabic, even at recreation time. All the textbooks were imported from France, and all our references, our mental tools, were becoming French. This famous Francophone—so praised in the former French colonies—continues to be a political tool for colonization and alienation. We, like others in Algeria and in Black Africa, were separated from our cultural past, exiled from our essential language, and by way of consequence, from the history of our parents and ancestors. We became alienated from our environment. We didn't have to leave our country; we were forced to leave it in its most meaningful dimensions.

Our teachers made us believe that we were being civilized because we were learning French and that there was nothing in Arabic worthy of knowing. Young and impressionable, we felt superior to those who did not share our education. In this kind of an exile, the prisoner of the new system loves his or her guardian, and the victim loves its conqueror.

I gradually became alienated from my parents as a result of French colonization: Everything I knew, they didn't, and everything they represented was becoming strange and remote. We were raised by the schools to be cultural bastards, to yearn for France, and to go there.

The tragedy of Lebanese education was not learning French, but that we were meant to consider it superior to native Arabic. This was one of many things that created political attitudes that contributed to the confusion preceding the Lebanese civil war. My visits to Lebanon have not been encouraging on that score. Public school buildings were destroyed during the civil war. The French schools are taking over, and the balance is being lost once again. A "grateful" citizenry is rushing to enroll its children into schools that minimize, openly and arrogantly, the place of Arabic in their midst. This profound alienation, recreated in the aftermath of the Lebanese disaster, leaves the public indifferent, or rather, unaware. Unfortunately, when people are tired of controversy, they accept whatever seems to be a good deal.

War, a cataclysmic event that shakes the psyche, stirs emotions once believed resolved or forgotten. Memory gets heightened, overheated, thrown into a state of urgency. Life is forcefully questioned, and new light is shed on old beliefs.

In the beginning of 1975, before the civil war, I was living in moral and intellectual comfort. I was at peace with America and at peace with the Arab world. I had a sense that problems were going to be solved, slowly but surely, both personal and national. Lebanon was a happy place to be in.

I was aware that people living in Lebanon had private tragedies. The country was full of refugees, officially recognized exiles, refugee camps, and nearly four hundred thousand Palestinians who were (and still are) forbidden to go back to their original towns and villages. There were also the numerous political refugees from all over the Arab world who came to Beirut to breathe an air of freedom and shelter their dreams. It was a land made up of exiles: the Armenian refugees and Russian refugees from World War I; Greek refugees from Smyrna; Egyptian refugees from the nationalizations of the Nasser era; all the political exiles from Syria, Iraq, and Libya; the Palestinians of 1948, and those of 1967.

Despite an overwhelming presence of exiled people, there was an excitement in Beirut, a confidence in the future, and an enormous amount of political activity. We were caught in the romanticism of revolution—not in its harsh realities. Not even the most ardent Palestinian sympathizer really knew what it meant to be a Palestinian refugee in Lebanon (or elsewhere). We, the Lebanese, were citizens in our own country, and they were guests at best, enemies at worst; we had passports and could travel, and they were paperless. Palestinians were prisoners of their condition, no-people in the eyes of the world, and this predicament lasted not for one or two years, but for ten, twenty, thirty years. Some were born, raised, and had grown old without ever leaving their camp, without knowing if they had a future. We didn't know what it meant for them to listen to the radio every hour for ten, fifteen, or thirty years without hearing one good piece of news, one possibility of ever returning home. We didn't know that kind of exile even though we were living one mile away from it, next door to it. We had to read some of Mahmoud Darwish's poems just to get a glimpse of it. And yet there was a denial of these anguishing situations until the whole thing, as we saw it, blew up and surprised the whole world.

The war in Lebanon instilled in me (and in many, of course) great bitterness. I found it useless from the start—cruel in its very premises. It killed a beautiful country and an extraordinary city. Such catastrophe, and for what?

Bitterness takes you back, creates distance between you and the other, between you and history. It therefore gives rise to a deep sense of exile, an almost metaphysical sense of exile. But exile does not kill passion; on the contrary, it enhances it but makes it utterly desperate.

Somewhere, from the middle of these long fifteen years of unending war, I entered a zone of frightful clarity. Beirut and Lebanon were at the center of my apocalyptic vision of the Arab world, one that I expressed later in a book-length poem entitled "The Arab Apocalypse."

Western powers decided to destroy the Arabs at the beginning of this century with various treatises after World War I. From the betrayal of Faysal by the British and the French, on to the partitions, colonizations, political assassinations, we entered a destiny of doom mapped for us outside our will. Exile became the existential and metaphysical condition for every Arab, in our own countries and elsewhere. It reminded me of historical mythology: Hajer and Ismail, the first wife and son of Abraham, the mythical founder of the Arabian tribes. His son is disinherited, and his wife is forced into wandering and exile. Following this real and mythical past, this tragic origin, Arabs today live as if pushed aside and removed from the center of decision-making for his or her own future. Arabs in the present world are cut off from themselves. Look closely at the devastating destruction of the Arab world—Palestine, Lebanon, Algeria, Iraq (which has been eradicated physically and totally), Sudan (in havoc), and Egypt (threatened from the inside). When we look at all the humiliations that Western media and politicians feel free to heap on Arabs, it must be understood that Arabs are operating from the existential statement: "I am not, therefore I am." Exile is the awareness of this marginalization and irreparable loss—loss of one's identity that is tied to history and geography. Arabs have been profoundly wounded in both.

Exile is a complex experience. Sometimes people fall in love with the country where they have been forced to live. Quite often the heart and mind follow unpredictable courses. Mahmoud Darwish passionately expressed his love for Beirut. The city had become his second home, his private legend, and again he had to leave, a second-time refugee, a tree twice uprooted. People in his situation are denied ordinary happiness. They can find exaltation in their work, but they will never have the casual taste for living that ordinary people can enjoy in continuity, in familiarity with their land.

Exiled people usually function on multiple tracks: They could adapt to their new surroundings and live a life of memories, hidden landscapes, and double and triple allegiances. All of these predicaments are honest but excruciatingly painful when conflicts arise between the country of adoption and the old motherland. Sometimes tensions become unbearable and people sink into depression or commit suicide. I can think of so many individuals, or whole communities, who seem to lead "normal" lives but who inhabit a private, imagined paradise, forbidden and closed, where they roam like ghosts of another age. Some are successful while others are not. Some are treated as outcasts, terrorists, or unwanted foreigners waiting for some final solution to their predicament, a solution that most of the time means deterioration or death.

I have observed a special phenomenon in exiles, a syndrome: Exiled people (contrary to immigrants, for example) carry a sense of failure that rules their actions. That deep-seated feeling, so often unconscious, is a hindrance, a factor for further defeat. Exiles tend to hide, stay as anonymous as possible, as if marked by a dark star, and when they have no support group or larger community that gives them sustenance, they seem to accept their condition as a fate that they cannot prevail over.

For a while I thought that I had resolved my conflicts in my writings. I believe that my books are the houses I inhabit. It's true. And it looks simple. And it is not. Even here the harbor is not safe from trouble.

In their condition, expatriate and exiled writers find a new perspective on their original countries and on themselves that they might not have found if they had stayed "home." The examples in contemporary literature alone are numerous: Rilke, Hemingway, Gertrude Stein, and Joyce. Writing and art seem to be the only meaningful activities when one is uprooted: They give form and substance to what otherwise would be devouring chaos.

While the expatriate can function within the literary tradition and historical continuity of his or her own country, the exiled writer usually adopts the language of the country where they live in exile. They acquire its whole context. I write in two languages, English and French, neither of them being what should have been my original language–Arabic. Then the crucial questions follow: What do I write, and for whom? These are painful problems that writers in exile have to face. There aren't many ways out of marginality. I am an American writer who is an Arab. I am an Arab writer who is an American. I am at home in California. I feel close to some of the American poets I know and whose works I read; I belong to their world too. Some of them, such as Lyn Hejinian and Barbara Guest, enchant my mind the same way that poets, such as Baudelaire and Rimbaud, did when I was living in Beirut and anxious to leave everything behind for a new adventure in France. Back then I was impatient to read them. I often sat on the edge of a sidewalk with their books in my hand. But in me, and in writers like me, who function in societies they were not born in, there has always been an undercurrent of uncertainty, and again a certain distance. For whom do I write? I have always thought and believed that poetry is essentially tribal. It relates to archetypes, collective memory, and communal language and interests. Even one of the most formal French poets who had the greatest influence on Western poetics wrote a famous verse: *donner un sens plus pur aux mots de la tribu* (to give a purer meaning to the tribe's words). For my American readers, my references come too often from Arab culture and history, and for my Arab readers, my poetic environment is the American landscape and experience. Who, then, follows me through my work?

One thing is certain: I cannot go back "home"—the initial home. In other times emigrants couldn't go back because travels were costly and uncommon. Today this is not the problem. Beirut represents a unique case: The Beirut I once knew does not exist anymore and will not exist. It has been destroyed and will not be rebuilt according to its old patterns. So when I go there to look for the street where I was born and the places I used to go to, I know too well that I will never find them. It's as if when I am there, I am not there, and some people could lose their minds for less.

What am I to say? That our illusions of the Arab world have been destroyed? Yes. I often wonder how the human body's fragile system can bear upheavals as chronic as the ones that the Arab East has known and is still experiencing. We as Arabs have dreamed of Arab unity. But today we have a hard time imagining that any one of our countries will hold together. We believed, against all evidence, that America somehow would become a positive factor and help the world out of its degradation, but its policies have been a recipe for more chaos and devastation.

I have come to think that our predicament is not only our own. Amid ecological disaster, economic predatory tactics, and political bankruptcy, a human being appears to be a fallen angel exiled from the old Paradise as well as from the future. Exile is not the sad privilege of only a few individuals: It has become synonymous with the human condition. Some of us are eaten by this illness in evident and definitive ways, while others are not yet conscious of their suffering. As contemporaries of this day and age, we are all very close to each other, but very few of us share this knowledge.

Off the Edge of the World: An Ethiopian Story in Metaphors

MAAZA MENGISTE

The heat was heavy in our Lagos, Nigeria, apartment. Sticky and thick on my skin. The sound of street traffic three flights below was loud and chaotic. And inside, a ceiling fan, white and brilliantly new, whirled in smooth circles like a headless bird.

I sat on the carpet and stared at the fan, following its rotations with my eyes, making myself dizzy. My mother slid the balcony door open to get a better breeze as she cooked in the kitchen. The weighty scent of spicy red pepper and garlic butter rushed through the apartment and mingled with the exhaust fumes outside. My little brother tottered on unsteady legs toward her, his arms outstretched. She held him for a quick hug then set him down next to me.

"Watch Teddy," she told me. "Don't let him play on the balcony."

It was 1975 and I was four years old, the older sister to a nearly two-year-old boy who was more stubborn than me. Stout, with rolls of baby fat layering his arms and legs, Teddy was built like a miniature wrestler with a temper to match. I was thin, small, and wiry. I was the quiet one in my family, the one who wouldn't fight back when my brother hit me, no matter how hard. Perhaps even back then, I didn't think it was right to strike someone younger and smaller.

Though I wouldn't physically retaliate when he struck me, I knew how to coax him into made-up games that could have easily sent him to the hospital. My instructions were simple enough for him to follow and challenging enough to goad his competitive streak: Go to the beehive in the back garden and catch bees; sneak into our parents' car on a hot day and sit inside with the windows rolled up until I tell you to come out; keep your finger on the cigarette lighter in the car for as long as you can. He did everything I told him to, willingly, with complete trust.

There was no way to stop my brother if he wanted to play on the balcony. So when he tumbled forward toward the glass door and stood at the threshold between the living room and outside, I didn't do much.

"Teddy, don't go out there," I warned. But it was halfhearted and he knew it.

He stretched his legs as wide and as fast as they could go, pushed them tight against the cinched elastic of his diapers, and ran to our narrow balcony. He shoved his face between the white iron slats of the railing as if to squeeze through them. He stepped onto the first of two horizontal rails that were part of the railing's design and climbed the first rung. He was suddenly taller than me, his head reaching almost to the top of the slender white rail. That was when I realized that the rail was much shorter than it looked. If he took one more step up to the next rung, his head would be above the rail, the top of the arrowed tip reaching his belly.

He climbed the next rung like he was scaling a ladder to the sun. For a brief moment, I was exhilarated. He was so high, so tall, bent at the waist, tipping over the edge, leaning beyond the balcony like a bird in flight. As he placed one chubby foot on top of the rail, I held my breath. I heard the ceiling fan swirling behind me, rattling. Then he jumped. My brother flew, wingless and unafraid. I watched him disappear into the sky while I stood in a corner, my heart caught in my throat, my voice gone.

I've tried to invent new memories about my brother's descent and the car antenna that broke his fall and saved his life. I've tried to imagine scenes where I draw him away from the rails, where I run fast enough to get my mother before he dips into nothingness, where I'm the one who unhooks his diaper from the car antenna. But my dreams betray the truth, and they hold up another image, as true as a metaphor can be. In one dream, I find myself on a barren, sun-bleached balcony, my hand out toward a sweltering emptiness that's thick with echoes of my mother's voice.

"Watch Teddy," she tells me. "Don't let him fall."

And I awaken, skin sticky with sweat, my arms outstretched, reaching into a space where once, long ago, my own voice should have been.

In my brother's story, I've seen parts of my own. It's a story of a girl in flight who lands among foreigners, who cannot speak, but whose tongue must grow accustomed to a new, flat landscape. It's about a girl who writes to create a world where she belongs, where it's possible to fly back home, wingless, and without fear.

My family left Ethiopia the same way my brother fell from the balcony, with deliberate steps that flung us into the unknown. There were thousands of other Ethiopians fleeing the Communist revolution and the bloody reprisals against "counterrevolutionaries." Ethiopia's new dictator, Mengistu Haile Mariam, called this two-year period of intense violence that killed untold thousands—mainly high school and university students—the Red Terror. I've wondered if the constant references to red when I was a child made it my favorite color today.

As an employee of Ethiopian Airlines, my father was transferred from our native Ethiopia to Nigeria in 1975. He accepted the transfer to get us out of Addis Ababa. The dictator Mengistu was blanketing Ethiopia with shrill, threatening rhetoric that was leading to mass arrests and random killings. My father wanted to shield my brother and me from images of bullets whizzing through silent streets and broken bodies dumped on roadsides.

But these are my earliest memories: bullets pushing through the air like fiery ribbons, soldiers planted on every street corner, and my aunt disappearing in the back of a military jeep, her cries muted by fear. I knew the smell of a discharged gun. I grew accustomed to the nightly rounds of gunfire outside our door. I learned not to answer when soldiers came to our house at night and asked me about one of my uncles, assuming a three-year-old girl held no secrets. I lived with the heavy weight of dread, and it pulled me toward the safety of solitude and silence. I cringed at sudden noises: My mother's quick laugh made me cry; a dropped plate sent me running to my grandmother. And then one night, I told my mother I wanted to leave my country. "Never bring me back here again," I said.

That night was Ethiopian New Year's, September 11, 1975, and I was four. I carried a sparkling firecracker in my hand, bright as a drop of sunlight in the dark. A group of neighbors, each carrying a firecracker, had gathered around a tall tree in my grandfather's yard. In the night, the slender, lit sticks seemed to float on their own like a buzzing cluster of dragonflies. The singing and celebratory stomping of feet began, and I remember looking up into the face of a man next to me, who sang without reservation, who jumped with energetic joy. Behind me, women punctuated the men's stomps with trilling ululations, their voices rising high. I imagined birds resting on the waves of their song. I heard sound and didn't cry; I felt the impact of sharp laughter and didn't cringe. I was outside of my silence, beyond the reaches of dread. The moment was pure, washing away every other moment that came before it. People all around me threw their firecrackers into the air, up into the lone tree, and we all cheered as the sparks flew into the sky. *A lost star is going home,* I thought.

The first shot merely thumped against the din of our singing. The second pierced the growing murmurs of the nervous crowd. The third clipped the sudden hush in half, and my ears burned from its terrifying closeness. I still held my firecracker, my throw stopped short by the first gunshot, and at the third bullet's release, I shook so badly I dropped it. The firecracker burned a star-shaped scar into my foot, and before the stinging of the wound had subsided, I ran to my mother inside the house. That's when I demanded to be taken away from Ethiopia, not realizing my wish would come true and would eventually take me across the ocean to a new home in America.

My mother tells me that New Year's 1975 is a day she'd hoped I'd forget. But I still carry the star-shaped scar—it is with me every step—and any time I see it, I recall the third shot, its sound sharp as a razor, drilling through the quiet. Until now, the memory has stayed silent; I have not put it down on paper, in English. I have not given it the chance to come out and breathe into my American life.

I came to America when I was seven years old, a skinny girl with no front teeth, holding my mother's hand tightly as I stepped off the plane and into a cold Colorado winter. It was 1978. My father had been ordered back to Ethiopia from Kenya, where we had moved after he was transferred again from Nigeria. He received notice that he was to report to the Ethiopian military and work for a government that had killed my mother's two brothers and stripped my maternal grandparents of nearly everything.

My parents were afraid to go back, and they were trying to find ways to disobey the orders, to run from Kenya and escape the Ethiopian government's grasp. And yet, they could not expose my grandparents in Addis

Ababa to the consequences if my father refused to follow orders. In the midst of this, a family friend told them of an American sponsor family in Colorado who was taking in Ethiopian refugees and that there was room for one more. My parents made the agonizing decision to send me to America. My mother would take me, then fly back alone. I could begin school immediately, in safety, and my brother would follow me in a few years. A door had opened as quickly as another slammed on the life I knew.

I have yet to find ways to describe those first days, months, years of confusion and loneliness. I do not have the words to fill the deep hollowness of a mouth that can no longer find refuge in its native language. I have lost count of the number of times I've dreamed of the road that would lead me home to my grandparents' house in Addis Ababa. Instead, I write fictional stories of courage and defiance, of people who plant their feet firmly in native soil and refuse to be moved. I search for a language to express the roads my family has traveled, a scarred girl in tow. I want to make my way to the center of my myths, unmask the metaphors, strip the pain naked, and stare. But the only words that come to me line up in orderly fashion, neat soldiers at attention, ready for duty, prepared to do battle with carefully structured storylines and adjectives. And they are not enough.

Once upon a time, there was a seven-year-old girl who made a single-stringed guitar from a shoebox and a rubber band. She raised her voice to sing "Tizita" ("memory"), a favorite Ethiopian song, and realized English words had crammed their way into her mouth. She picked up the phone to speak to her grandmother in Addis Ababa and discovered her tongue was more comfortable in the flat, open sounds of her adopted language. She tried to force herself to dream of home, to carve faces and streets into memory, but her mother's voice wove its way into her thoughts:

What would you do
if I held you off the edge of the world
and dropped you?

And so this girl pretended she could fly. She told herself that the cacophony of sounds in her new American life was old Amharic lullabies transposed to fit her new American tongue. She made believe a house full of strangers was really her mother and father dressed in costume. She promised herself that the next time she stepped off the yellow school bus to go to her new house, she'd veer left instead of right and walk until she found her way back to her aluminum-roofed home in Addis Ababa. This girl found herself staring for hours at a small dark speck in her eye, remembering a handful of flung mud that had hit her in that same spot years ago, relieved that she'd somehow managed to keep a piece of Ethiopia with her, in her, permanently.

Every story holds another, tucked just out of view, like a speck of dirt in a tearing eye.

We have secrets in my family. We do not talk about my mother's brothers who were killed in the Red Terror. Memories of them are still heavy with the weight of grief and helpless anger. We speak in hushed tones of an aunt's ex-husband, an officer in Mengistu's Marxist regime who ordered his "counter-revolutionary" brother shot and killed. One cousin cannot return to Ethiopia because he's fled the present government after being jailed on undisclosed charges. He doesn't talk of those days in jail or how he managed to get out. These stories are not unusual. They do not set my family history apart from others in Ethiopia, or in Africa. They are part of the larger thread of African life, part of the bigger story of hope and the undying hunger for a home where secrets and whispered truths are not necessary.

For many, the stories of African refugees are muted tales, meant to be enjoyed in brief bursts. They are meant to be pitied, then pocketed into memory, pulled out for a moment when other atrocities of the world are discussed. No one talks about the cold and the vomit of a fateful boat ride ferrying frightened Africans toward Spain, the stink of unclean bodies crammed in a space meant for dying fish. No one will talk about a mother who secretly rejoices in the news that her son is being tortured, who finds damning solace in his suffering, who prays that he can hold back death with each new day.

I made a journey home to Ethiopia in July 2003. I was thirty-two years old, a grown woman preparing myself to say goodbye to my dying grandfather for the last time. My grandmother had died years earlier, slipping away from us too quickly for me to make the long trip from America. A static-filled phone call between us was our only farewell. The weight of that call still hung around the edges of my memories when I returned in 2003, tingeing all thoughts of her with guilt and regret. In her was my strongest sense of home, safety, and silent solitude. I made the trip to fulfill what was once her last wish, and what had become my grandfather's—to see me one more time before he died. I went to Ethiopia to keep the promise I'd made to her, a promise that I hadn't been able to keep because time and distance made it impossible for me to reach her quickly enough. That final farewell to my grandfather, standing outside the gate of his house on a hot July afternoon, was meant for both of them.

The Ethiopia I returned to was very different from the one I left when I was a child, and it was different from the one I used to visit as a teenager when Mengistu was still in power. Internet cafés lined busy sidewalks, statues of proud warriors had replaced the stony stares of Marx and Lenin, billboards advertising the latest technology jutted above shantytowns, and glossy high-rise buildings—funded by a growing number of Chinese businesses—shouldered their way between older concrete structures. Addis

Ababa was bustling, free of curfews and military oppression. It had been more than ten years since a young guerrilla fighter named Meles Zenawi, spouting promises of equality and freedom for all Ethiopians, had forced dictator Mengistu to flee in 1991. In 2003, Prime Minister Meles Zenawi was still hailed by the West as the architect of African democracy.

By 2003, my grandfather had lived through the Italian occupation during World War II, Emperor Haile Selassie's subsequent exile in Europe and his return to power in 1941, the Communist revolution of the 1970s, and the rise to power of Meles Zenawi in 1991. But he had experienced much more: the death of his sons, the disappearances of his neighbors and friends, the nationalization of all his land, and the eventual departure from Ethiopia of every single one of his living children, including my mother. My grandfather took the details of these memories with him when he died. He left only an old photograph of him in his judge's gown that sits in my New York apartment near my desk today. But photographs and metaphors cannot bridge the silence left by his death.

In 2006, I went back to Ethiopia in the midst of large, sweeping events, a lost daughter who had made her way home again. I found a country hushed of stories, silenced and fatigued by years under a succession of tyrannical governments. I met people too afraid to speak in anything but whispers about Meles Zenawi's latest battles with a growing opposition. Ethiopia was once again in the throes of government oppression. Rumors of mass graves, disappearances, and tortures were slowly being confirmed by human rights groups. Addis Ababa was rocked with a series of bombings, no one claiming responsibility, the government pointing fingers.

Federal police in blue camouflage paced on street corners with rifles, their uniforms the color of a dirty sky. Poverty was a thick, physical presence. And I saw truckloads of boys—bruised, beaten, and handcuffed—being driven to jails every day to join the rumored hundred thousnd other youths imprisoned by the government for undisclosed charges.[1] One young boy, no more than fifteen years old, stared back at me as I watched the truck pass a busy intersection in the center of Addis Ababa, his gaze unflinching and uncompromising.

I traced my steps back to my grandparents' old house on a dirt road near the stately and imposing stone fence of the French Embassy, comforted by the familiarity of each bend in the road. I went alone. My mother was still too grieved by the deaths of her parents years ago to make the trip to the house with me. I stood in the bedroom where I once slept, the sky-blue walls reminding me of my brother's long-ago leap into a bright Nigerian sky. I visited the cemetery where my grandfather and grandmother were buried and kissed the grounds, promising to return again. And one morning, at my parent's home near an Ethiopian Orthodox church, I woke to the soaring chants of a monk sending prayers into the sky. I listened while looking up, following the path of the wailing voice as it climbed toward the rising sun, thinking of another voice I once heard in a dream.

What would you do
if I held you off the edge of the world
and dropped you?

I would find my way home.

Notes

INTRODUCTION

1. Suketu Mehta, *Maximum City: Bombay Lost and Found* (New York: Vintage Books, 2004), 31.2.
2. Andrea A. Lunsford, "Toward a Mestiza Rhetoric: Gloria Anzaldúa on Composition and Postcoloniality," *JAC: A Journal of Composition Theory* 18, no. 1 (1998): 1–27.

IN SEARCH OF THE NEXT HARVEST

1. *Paisano* means compatriot: a person from one's same town, state, or country.
2. *Tostadas* (fried, flat tortillas used as a base or dish for wonderful toppings) and *churritos* (thin corn chips served with red hot sauce and lime) are both made out of corn and are well-known food items throughout the U.S. Southwest and elsewhere.
3. Gas prices in 2002–2004 in southern New Mexico ranged from $2.67 to $2.89, which is costly considering the state's rural layout.

DIFFERENT BLOOD: A JOURNEY TO MYANMAR

1. The Kayin (or Karen) are one of the many ethnic groups in Burma. They have historically been persecuted for their desire to maintain themselves as an independent nation as well as for their strong belief in Christianity, which was brought to them by white missionaries. While the term "Karen" is more popularly used, "Kayin" is the preference of my boyfriend's family.

DAKOTA HOMECOMING

1. Dakota is the dialect spoken by the Santee or Eastern Dakotas, a Siouan language of the Great Plains that is now endangered because so few fluent speakers remain, another consequence of colonization.
2. Historical grief is the collective emotional and psychological injury that spans generations as a result of genocide.

LEAVING BATTAMBANG, THE CITY OF ANSWERS

1. Thai/Cambodia Border Refugee Camps 1975–1999 Information and Documentation Website, www.websitesrcg.com/border/index.html.

HEARTBROKEN FOR LEBANON

1. Second Intifada or Al-Aqsa Intifada, the wave of violence that began in September 2000 between Palestinian Arabs and Israelis. Source: Wikipedia.

NEVER GONE BACK

1. Palm sugar.
2. In the 1980s in Sri Lanka, during the height of the civil war and tensions between Sinhalese and Tamil people, the government introduced national ID cards that stated one's ethnicity. Like pass cards used in South Africa during apartheid, they were a tool of terror, making Tamil and Muslim people vulnerable to police and military harassment. In a country where

many people have culturally mixed heritages, they also erased the complexities of people's identities and lives.

HOME, ADOPTED

1. Kimchi is a fermented cabbage, a national dish that is served at every meal.

THE ROUTE BACK TO TONGA

1. The term *palangi* translates to "white people from the West," and it also refers to skin color, being light-skinned.

OFF THE EDGE OF THE WORLD: AN ETHIOPIAN STORY IN METAPHORS

1. Amnesty International released a report in June 2006 that states, "Many thousands of people are still believed to be detained incommunicado in camps, despite the release of 8,000 people without charge in November 2005. Arrests have continued into 2006." Western reporters estimate the number of detainees, many of them schoolchildren, college students, and teachers, at 40,000. The exact numbers of those who have been killed or taken into police custody is unknown, but the figures are steadily increasing.

Acknowledgments

Tremendous thanks to the women whose stories make this anthology come to life. Without your courage in telling the truth as you see it, and your unwavering trust in us, this anthology could not have evolved.

We thank many people and institutions that have been crucial in making this anthology possible: Seal Press and Avalon Publishing Group for believing in the project; Brooke Warner for her insight, guidance, and editing assistance; Marisa Solís for her fine copyediting skills; the *Literature of the Arab Diaspora* class at Mills College (Fall 2005) for inspiring us to come up with the idea for the anthology; Edwidge Danticat, Elmaz Abinader, and Cristina García; Maiana Minahal and Leilani Nisperos for helping us see the light; Diana Ip, Tanya Pluth, Angela Jane Fountas, and Daisy Hernández for their support and advice; Gary Lemons, Patricia's mentor and professor at Eugene Lang College, for inspiring her to write personal and political essays; our VONA-Voices writers of color family (www.vona-voices.org) for giving us tools of empowerment; the Mills College MFA Creative Writing program (and community) for giving us a foundation; Kreatibo for queer

Pinay *pamilya;* Margaret Benson-Thompson for her encouragement and support; Patricia's parents, Teresita and Renato Tumang, and Jenesha's parents, Elenita and Eduardo de Rivera, and sister, Janelle Dolorico, for cheering us on; and Diva and Stonewall for their unconditional love and affection. *Maraming salamat!*

Finally, this anthology emerged and was nurtured by the partnership we share. We are deeply grateful for each other's gifts, talents, and big hearts.

About the Contributors

LEILA ABU-SABA lives in Oakland, California, with her husband and children. She has published essays, fiction, and poetry in the *Olive Tree Review, Tikkun Magazine, The Womanist, Crux*, and in a forthcoming anthology of Anglophone Arab writers. Currently at work on a novel, she is completing her MFA in Creative Writing at Mills College and is a proud member of the Radius of Arab Writers, Inc.

ETEL ADNAN, a Lebanese American poet, painter, and essayist, lives in Paris, Beirut, and the San Francisco Bay Area. Adnan was born in 1925 in Beirut, Lebanon, to a Muslim Syrian father and a Christian Greek mother. Adnan has published more than ten books of poetry and fiction, including *Paris When It's Naked, Of Cities and Women,* and *Sitt Marie Rose,* which has been translated into more than ten languages and is considered a classic of Middle Eastern literature.

NANCY AGABIAN is the author of *Princess Freak,* a collection of autobiographical poems and performance art texts. Her writing has appeared in numerous anthologies and journals, most recently in *Women's Studies Quarterly* and *Ararat*. "Seeing Istanos" is a chapter from *Me as Her Again*, a memoir about her Armenian American family that explores generational reverberations of genocide, particularly on sexuality and the shape of women's lives. She is currently living in Yerevan, Armenia, on a Fulbright grant to teach nonfiction and to research her next book.

C. L. CARLTON lives and writes in middle Tennessee and is currently at work on a novel. She gets out of the house occasionally to garden and hike, usually taking her camera along to record some flower, butterfly, or vista she finds beautiful.

ELLEN CASSEDY was a founder of 9to5, a national organization of working women, and is a winner of national awards for fiction and drama. Her writings on Yiddish themes have appeared in *Bridges*, *Utne Reader*, *The Forward*, and other publications. Her translations of Yiddish fiction appear in *Beautiful as the Moon, Radiant as the Stars*. She is at work on a book about how Lithuanians are engaging with their nation's Jewish heritage. She lives near Washington, D.C.

ANANDA ESTEVA was born in Chile and raised in the San Francisco Bay Area. Her first solo book of poetry and short fiction is called *Pisco Sours*. Ananda is a coauthor of both a book of poems called *Explosive New Writing* featuring the Molotov Mouths Poetry Troupe and *June Jordan's Poetry for the People: A Revolutionary Blueprint*. Ananda is currently working on a memoir detailing her first trip back to Chile in 1987 during Pinochet's dictatorship.

KIM FOOTE is currently writing a memoir and a novel based on her experiences in Ghana. Her work has appeared in the MoAD Stories Project, *Black Arts Quarterly*, and *WarPland* and was selected for the Guild Complex's nonfiction reading series. She has an MFA in Creative Writing from Chicago State University and received a 2006 Walker Foundation Scholarship from the Fine Arts Work Center in Provincetown.

MEETA KAUR is a creative writer living in Oakland, California, with her husband, Banjot Chanana. She is a graduate of the Mills College MFA Creative Writing Program and was awarded a 2006 Hedgebrook writing residency. She is currently working on short stories and a novella that depict self-saving heroines who develop the emotional endurance, resilience, and intelligence it takes to triumph in their life journeys. Meeta can be reached at meeta@thechananas.com.

LISA SUHAIR MAJAJ publishes creative and scholarly work on Arab American, Palestinian, feminist, and other topics. She is coeditor of the anthologies *Going Global: The Transnational Reception of Third World Women Writers, Etel Adnan: Critical Essays on the Arab-American Writer and Artist,* and *Intersections: Gender, Nation and Community in Arab Women's Novels.* Her poetry chapbooks *These Words* and *What She Said* are available from http://Palestineonlinestore.com. She lives in Nicosia, Cyprus, and may be reached at lmajaj@cytanet.com.cy.

ERIKA MARTÍNEZ, an MFA candidate in Creative Writing at Mills College, began writing for the stage when she was an ensemble member of Teatro Luna. She performed her work with Teatro Luna in Chicago at Gallery 37's Storefront Theater and in New York at INTAR Hispanic Arts Center, as well as PSNBC's Here Theater. She has written for *ColorLines* magazine. Currently, she is developing her first full-length play and working on her memoir.

SARAH MCCORMIC grew up on an island in the Pacific Northwest. She lives in Seattle, where she works as an editor at the University of Washington. Her writing has appeared in *Seattle Weekly, Bitch* magazine, and Outside Online.

MAAZA MENGISTE received her BA in English from the University of Michigan, where she was a recipient of the Avery Hopwood Literary Award. She earned an MFA in Creative Writing from New York University, where she also taught and served as the international editor for *Washington Square Review*. Her work has appeared in *42opus*, *Ninth Letter*, and *Dragonfire*. She's completing a novel that takes place during the Communist Revolution in Ethiopia and writing a collection of short stories based on musicians. She lives in Brooklyn, New York.

CLAUDIA VIRGINIA NARVÁEZ-MEZA is a Nicaraguan-born teaching artist and poet raised in Brooklyn, New York. She has worked as a domestic violence crisis counselor for New York's LGBT and Latino communities. She remains committed to social justice and community outreach and renewal by working or volunteering with nonprofit organizations dedicated to ending violence and bringing the arts into the lives of women and children. She completed an MFA in Poetry at Brooklyn College and is currently pursuing a master's in social work at New York University.

APHRODITE DESIREE NAVAB is an Iranian Greek American artist and writer. She received her BA in Visual and Environmental Studies at Harvard University and an EdD in Art and Art Education at Teachers College, Columbia University. Her poetic series, *Tales Left Untold*, is published in the anthology *Let Me Tell You Where I've Been: New Writing by Women of the Iranian Diaspora*. Navab's visual art has been featured in more than sixty exhibitions around the world and is included in a number of permanent collections.

AGATE NESAULE was born in Latvia, experienced war and the camps in Germany, and came to the United States at the age of twelve. Her memoir, *A Woman in Amber: Healing the Trauma of War and Exile,* received the Before Columbus American Book Award in 1996 and has been translated into six languages. She has recently completed a novel, *In Love with Jerzy Kosinski,* and is at work on *Coming Home,* a memoir about various returns home.

LOA NIUMEITOLU was born and raised in Tonga, a country in the South Pacific. She also spent some of her childhood in Fiji, New Zealand, and Hawai'i. She moved to Provo, Utah, when she was twelve years old. Niumeitolu writes for ProTongan.org, a news and information website concerning Tongan politics and identity. She earned an MA in English from Simmons College. She lives with her eight-year-old son, Nikolasi, in Worcester, Massachusetts, where she's a graduate student in Clark's International Development and Social Change program.

GUILLERMINA GINA NÚÑEZ is a former migrant education student who traveled with her parents and four siblings to work in the lettuce harvest throughout the U.S. Southwest. She and all four of her siblings have earned graduate degrees and are now working as educators. Dr. Núñez is an assistant professor and an applied anthropologist in the Department of Sociology and Anthropology at the University of Texas, El Paso, where she teaches courses in Cultural, Urban, Applied, and Environmental Anthropology.

PAULINE PARK is the chair of the New York Association for Gender Rights Advocacy, the first statewide transgender advocacy organization in New York. She has written and spoken widely on issues of race, nationality, and gender. She is also the subject of a documentary by Larry Tung about her life and work.

LEAH LAKSHMI PIEPZNA-SAMARASINHA is a queer Sri Lankan writer, spoken word artist, and teacher. The author of *Consensual Genocide,* she has performed her work widely throughout North America. Her work is anthologized in numerous books. She produces the Browngirlworld queer/trans of-color spoken word series and is one of the cocreators of Toronto's Asian Arts Freedom School. She is currently working on a memoir, *Dirty River,* and collaborating on *Blood Memory: A Sri Lankan Storytelling Project.* Her website is www.brownstargirl.com.

CANYON SAM is a San Francisco–based writer, acclaimed performance artist, and activist. Her work, including memoir, short stories, plays, and nonfiction, has been published in *Shambhala Sun, Seattle Review,* and numerous feminist and Buddhist anthologies. Her one-woman shows explore Buddhist themes in contemporary situations. Her first book, a memoir, from which her essay is excerpted, is forthcoming. You can visit her at www.canyonsam.com.

JOSHUNDA SANDERS is a writer and reporter for the *Austin American-Statesman.* Her essays have appeared in *Secrets and Confidences: The Complicated Truth about Women's Friendships* and *My Soul to His Spirit: Soulful Expressions from Black Daughters to Their Fathers.* She has written for *Bitch* magazine, *Vibe, Suede, Pop Matters,* and several newspapers.

PHOENIX SOLEIL is a poet, playwright, filmmaker, and performer from East Flatbush in Brooklyn, New York. She describes her writing as emotional realism: putting feelings at the center and letting reality drip around them. Her best compliment was from her seven-year-old cousin Axelle, who asked, "Are you a kid or an adult?" She makes her living as a computer and multimedia professional focused on bridging the left- and right-brain cultural divide. When she performs, she fills the room with her heart.

JILL KIM SOOHOO is currently making history by being part of the only Asian women's lion and dragon dance troupe in North America, Gund Kwok. She lives in Boston, Massachusetts, where she is editor in chief of *The ASPIRE Connection*, a magazine for a career-development organization for Asian American women. She has an MA in Creative Nonfiction from Emerson College.

SOKUNTHARY SVAY was born in a Khmer refugee camp in Thailand and raised in the Bronx, New York. She is an MFA Candidate in Creative Writing at the City College of New York (CUNY) in Harlem and is currently working on a book of poetry about her family's life before the Khmer Rouge regime.

WENDY MARIE THOMPSON is a PhD candidate in the American Studies program at the University of Maryland. She is currently working on a book that looks at racial hybridity, cultural landscapes, and creative arts as they relate to the different ways Chinese people and Chinese communities negotiate diaspora identities throughout North America. Born in Oakland, California, she is an Aquarius who doesn't believe in credit cards.

DIANE WILSON is a creative-nonfiction writer whose essays and memoir use personal experience to illustrate broader social and historical contexts. Her first book, *Spirit Car: Journey to a Dakota Past,* is a historical memoir about cultural identity and heritage. Her work has been published in *The American Indian Quarterly, The Reader, The View from the Loft, Wolf Head Quarterly,* and many other local publications. She currently works as a freelance writer and editor from her home in Shafer, Minnesota.

© DANIEL CHAPMAN

About the Editors

PATRICIA JUSTINE TUMANG (also known as Patty) was born and raised in California. In 2001, she received a BA in Cultural Studies with a path in Race, Ethnicity, and Postcolonialism from Eugene Lang College in New York City. In 2006, she earned an MFA in English and Creative Writing from Mills College in Oakland, California. Her commitment to social justice, reproductive rights, and antiracist feminism from a Queer Filipina American perspective permeates her life, writing, and activism. Her writing has appeared in the Seal Press anthologies *Abortion Under Attack: Women on the Challenges Facing Choice, Waking Up American: Growing Up Biculturally,* and *Colonize This! Young Women of Color on Today's Feminism*, as well as *The Womanist* and *Hyphen Magazine*. She serves on the Editorial Board of Exhale's *Our Truths/Nuestras Verdades,* a grassroots, bilingual (Spanish/English) magazine focused on women's experiences with abortion. She has received multiple honors for her writing and activist work, including a Third Wave Foundation grant from its Scholarship Program for Young Women and Transgender Activists and a Zora Neale Hurston Award for writers of color. She is a freelance writer and editor who lives in Oakland, California. Visit Patty online at www.patriciatumang.com.

JENESHA ("JINKY") DE RIVERA is a first-generation Filipina American writer, performer, and activist. She was born and raised in New York City. In 2004, she moved to Oakland, California, to pursue an MFA in English and Creative Writing at Mills College. Her essay "A Lesson in Posture" was published in the Seal Press anthology *Waking Up American: Growing Up Biculturally*. She is an active member of LGBT and people of color activist communities in both New York City and the Bay Area, serves on the Board of Directors of the International Lesbian and Gay Human Rights Commission, and works as a nonprofit financial consultant. Her long commitment to social justice informs her craft. Her short story "Bayan Ko" was featured in *Colorlines* magazine's first fiction issue (November 2006). She plans to publish a collection of short stories soon. Visit Jinky online at www.jenesha-derivera.com.

For more information on *Homelands: Women's Journeys Across Race, Place, and Time* and to contact the editors, please visit www.homelandsanthology.com.

Credits

"The Reciters," by Agate Nesaule, originally appeared in *Northwest Review,* Vol. 32, No. 1, and is reprinted with the permission of the editor.

"Voyage, War, and Exile," by Etel Adnan, originally appeared in *Al-Arabiya* © 1995.

"Dakota Homecoming," by Diane Wilson, is excerpted from her memoir *Spirit Car: Journey to a Dakota Past* and is reprinted by permission of Borealis Books © 2006.

"Journeys to Jerusalem," by Lisa Suhair Majaj, was originally published in *South Atlantic Quarterly* 102:4 (Fall 2003): 729–745, and is reprinted by permission of the author © 2003.

Selected Titles from Seal Press